MEMPHIS

MARGARET LITTMAN

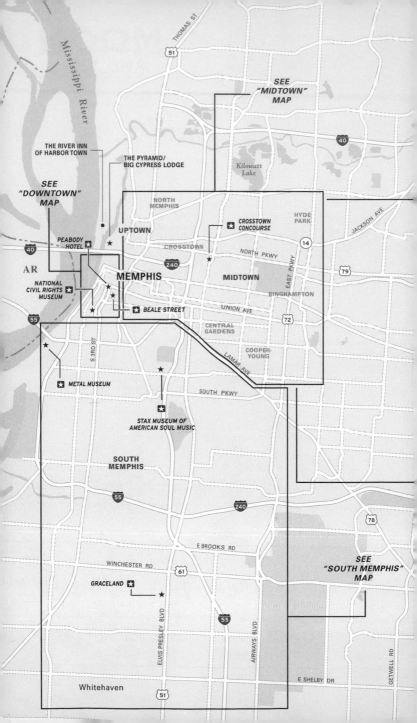

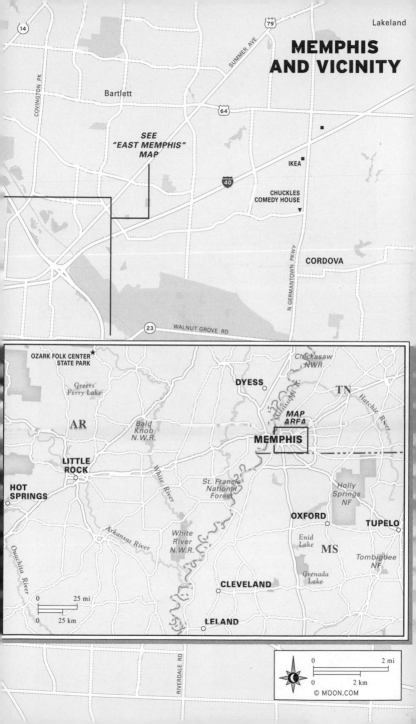

MEMPHIS AND VICINITY

Lakeland

Bartlett

SEE "EAST MEMPHIS" MAP

IKEA

CHUCKLES COMEDY HOUSE

CORDOVA

COVINGTON PK

SUMMER AVE

N GERMANTOWN PKWY

WALNUT GROVE RD

OZARK FOLK CENTER STATE PARK

Chickasaw NWR

DYESS

TN

Greers Ferry Lake

AR

Bald Knob N.W.R.

Mississippi River

Hatchie River

MAP AREA

MEMPHIS

LITTLE ROCK

White River

St. Francis National Forest

Holly Springs NF

HOT SPRINGS

Ouachita River

Arkansas River

White River N.W.R.

OXFORD

TUPELO

Enid Lake

MS

Tombigbee NF

CLEVELAND

Grenada Lake

LELAND

0   25 mi
0   25 km

RIVERDALE RD

0   2 mi
0   2 km

© MOON.COM

CONTENTS

1 Blues Hall of Fame

2 mural on South Main Street

3 Hot Springs National Park

4 Elvis Presley's costumes

5 monument to the Little Rock Nine

6 Memphis streetcar

DISCOVER
MEMPHIS

Take away music and Memphis would lose its soul. The Bluff City may owe its physical existence to the mighty Mississippi, but it is music that has defined it. The spirituals and work songs of the poor Mississippi Delta cotton farmers who migrated here formed the basis for a new sound known as the Memphis blues. The blues then spawned its own offspring: soul, R&B, country, and, of course, rock 'n' roll, as performed by a former truck driver from Tupelo, Mississippi, named Elvis Presley.

On any given night, you can find joints where the music flows as freely as the booze. Sitting still is not an option. On Beale Street, music wafts from lively bars and out onto the street, inviting you to come inside for a spell. And on Sundays, the sounds of old-fashioned spirituals and new gospel music can be heard at churches throughout the city.

While you're here, you can sustain yourself on the city's world-famous barbecue or its fried chicken and catfish, not to mention modern twists on Southern classics. Eating may not be why you come, but it might be why you stay.

Memphians are gregarious and proud of their city, so they will want to show you its beauty, from rich visual arts masterpieces to scenic vistas. You may even be invited over for some barbecue spaghetti.

8 TOP
EXPERIENCES

1 **Listen to Live Music:** Musical roots run deep here. Yes, the focus is on the blues, reflecting the city's connection to the Mississippi Delta, but soul, gospel, and rock are played nightly, too. It isn't a night out in Memphis until someone takes out a guitar (page 20).

2 **Embrace the Legend of Elvis:** He was born in Tupelo (page 128), but Memphis claims Elvis Presley as its own. Listen and learn about how he became the King, make a pilgrimage to Graceland (page 56), and learn which burger he loved best.

3 **Honor Civil Rights Legacies:** The fight for equality shaped the South physically and psychically. The National Civil Rights Museum in Memphis (page 40) is a good place to start understanding the movement. Dive deeper with a side trip to Little Rock Central High School National Historic Site (page 143). >>>

4 **Do the 'Cue:** Barbecue, that is (page 17). Plan on plenty of helpings of the local specialty, including barbecue spaghetti. That said, the restaurant scene doesn't end there. This is a foodie city with many ways to feast.

5 **Taste Craft Brews:** Toast to good times (page 72).

>>>

6 **Explore Local Art:** Thanks to a long fine arts tradition, Memphis is home to fascinating galleries and a thriving maker culture (page 25).

<<<

7 **Follow the Missippippi Blues Trail:** This multisensory road trip traces the roots of American music (page 121).

>>>

8 **Soak in the Hot Springs:** Naturally occurring mountain springs have made Hot Springs National Park in Arkansas a resort destination for generations (page 160).

PLANNING YOUR TRIP

WHERE TO GO

MEMPHIS

The blues were born in Memphis, and they still call the city home in nightclubs on **Beale Street.** But the Bluff City isn't just the blues. It's gospel, Elvis Presley, Rev. Al Green, Isaac Hayes, **Soulsville, Stax Records,** and **Sun Studio.** And it's more than music. Memphis is an urban center with **fine dining,** parks, significant historic sites, and the state's best **visual arts scene.** Unwind by watching the ducks get the red-carpet treatment at The Peabody Hotel Memphis or fuel up with a plate of **barbecue.**

EXCURSIONS

Memphis's location nestled on the bluffs of the Mississippi River make it an ideal launching pad for excursions that will entertain you, whether you seek music, food, history, or the great outdoors. Jump in the car and wind through the towns of the Delta on the **Mississippi Blues Trail.** In **Tupelo** and **Oxford,** you can feast on Southern cooking, explore Civil War history, and see the former homes of two native icons: Elvis Presley and William Faulkner. In Arkansas, you can visit a presidential library and sample the world's best cheese dip in **Little Rock,** then enjoy jaw-dropping scenery in **Hot Springs National Park.**

KNOW BEFORE YOU GO

WHEN TO GO

Summer is certainly the popular season for visiting—**Elvis Week** in **August** sees the most visitors—but the hot, humid Memphis summer is not for the faint of heart. If you like the energy of crowds, the best time to visit Memphis is **May,** when summer is still fresh and mild and the city puts on its annual Memphis in May celebration. Memphis in May includes the World Championship Barbecue Cooking Contest, the Beale Street Music Festival, and the Memphis International Festival. The Memphis Music and Heritage Festival held over

Labor Day weekend is a great reason to come to Memphis, and probably the best choice for fans of traditional Memphis music.

Memphis is a city with four seasons. The average temperature in January is 50°F (10°C), and in July it hits 92°F (33°C). During **spring,** the weather is mild, flora is in bloom, and you can enjoy springtime festivals. During the **fall,** the trees change color and temperatures drop. Even in the South, where people are used to hot and humid, the **summer** humidity can be oppressive. Visitors in **winter** may encounter cold weather

downtown yellow trolley

and rare snowstorms, but the cooler months can also be a nice time to tour because you'll have many attractions to yourself. If you can't come when the weather is temperate, don't fret. Memphis attractions are open year-round, and the city continues to rock, day in and day out.

TRANSPORTATION

Memphis has an **international airport.** Visitors making a getaway to Memphis may be able to subsist on bicycles, public transportation, ride-hailing companies, and taxis. To explore beyond the city, **a car is essential.** If it's practical, bring your own car. If you're flying in, arrange a rental car ahead of time. A good road map or GPS is helpful to have before you set out.

WHAT TO PACK

A **cell phone** with a good roaming plan, GPS, and Wi-Fi should cover your basic needs. Prepare with **maps and apps,** particularly if you are likely to get off the interstate and out of the range of cell phone signals on excursions. Download a **playlist's** worth of Memphis-appropriate tunes to get you in the mood: classic country, bluegrass, blues, or Elvis albums. Cowboy boots and an Elvis-style embroidered jacket aren't required, but they're certainly always appropriate. Grab some stylin' sunglasses for all the photos you'll take.

EXPLORE
MEMPHIS

THE BEST OF MEMPHIS

Follow in the footsteps of the King (that would be Elvis). Learn from the city's civil rights struggles. Admire the Mississippi, eat tangy barbecue, and listen to the music that came up from the Delta. There's no limit to how long you can spend getting to know the Bluff City's charms, but this itinerary will give you a satisfying taste.

DAY 1

Arrive in Memphis and check into a centrally located downtown hotel, such as the historic **Peabody Hotel Memphis** or the modern **Hu. Hotel.** Grab barbecue ribs from **Rendezvous** for dinner, then stroll down to **Beale Street** in the evening.

Barhop to get your bearings, and then settle in somewhere to listen to live music. You can hear them play the blues at **Blues City Café,** jazz at **King's Palace Café,** or rock at **Alfred's**... or just take it all in from the street, where you'll be surrounded by many new friends.

cityscape over Beale Street

CHOOSE THE BEST BARBECUE FOR YOU

If there's one thing you gotta eat when you come to Memphis, it's barbecue. What makes this tangy treat different from what's served in Nashville? Or Texas? Or Virginia?

Memphis barbecue is all about the pig. If you don't eat pork, you may not be able to partake. We're talking pulled pork or a rack of ribs. Sauces are thin, both vinegary and sweet, made with tomato and molasses. Some believe that Memphis's status as a port city (hello, mighty Mississippi) allowed it access to more ingredients, enabling a sauce with lots of different tastes.

Memphis barbecue is also often served on top of other dishes, particularly spaghetti, pizza, and nachos. A simple bun just won't do. Depending on your personality, here are the best barbecue experiences in the city:

Memphis barbecue

- **If you don't like to make decisions:** Let the fine folks at **Tastin' 'Round Town** (page 91) give you a tour of the city's barbecue highlights.

- **If you want to eat as much as possible:** Downtown's **Cozy Corner** (page 92) has ribs, barbecue spaghetti, barbecued Cornish hens… you name it, they barbecue it!

- **If you're all about those ribs:** They might not technically be barbecue, but in Memphis they count! People have been heading to **Rendezvous** (page 96) for ribs since 1948.

- **If you think being a purist is overrated:** Try the barbecue pizza at **Coletta's** (page 104).

- **If you want to eat like a local:** Order the barbecue spaghetti at the **Bar-B-Q Shop** (page 98) in midtown.

- **If you want it for dessert:** Get some Memphis Mix popcorn (which includes a barbecue flavor) at **Sweet Noshings** (page 102).

- **If you're a completist:** Try it all at the **World Championship Barbecue Cooking Contest** (page 80) in Tom Lee Park in mid-May.

DAY 2

Wake up with a cup of joe at **Front Street Deli.** Then take the Beale Street Walking Tour in the morning. Stop at the **W. C. Handy Home and Museum,** take your picture with the Elvis statue, and go treasure hunting at **A. Schwab.**

Eat lunch, delivered by the kindest servers in town, at **The Little Tea Shop,** then head over to the **Cotton Museum** for the afternoon to learn what made this city thrive. Afterward, stroll along the banks of the Mississippi River at **Tom Lee Park.**

Eat poutine for dinner at **Dirty Crow Inn.** Stick around for low-key live music on the back porch or head to midtown to see a show at **Minglewood Hall** or **B-SIDE.**

DAY 3

This is Significant Sights Day: Go to the **National Civil Rights Museum** in the morning for an understanding of the fight for equality and the aftershocks that Martin Luther King Jr.'s assassination had on the city. Process your experience as you eat lunch at **Evelyn & Olive** in the South Main Arts District.

Head to the **Stax Museum of American Soul Music** and the **Blues Hall of Fame** for the afternoon, where you'll learn about the music that makes the city sing.

Wash up and head to midtown for dinner at **The Beauty Shop.**

Elvis Presley, the king of rock 'n' roll

Cap off the night with live music at **Hi-Tone.**

DAY 4

Make it Elvis Day: Start early at **Graceland** to avoid the crowds for a leisurely visit to the mansion, where you can see his airplanes, cars, and museum. Lunch at **Coletta's** allows you to feast on Elvis's favorite pizza. Then make

Stax Museum of American Soul Music

an afternoon visit to **Sun Studio,** where Elvis recorded his first hit.

Return to downtown to Beale Street for dinner at **Dyer's,** where you can eat a burger in memory of the King. End the evening with a great jukebox and even better people-watching at **Earnestine and Hazel's.**

DAY 5

Head to midtown for a visit to **Elmwood Cemetery.** Take the audio tour to hear the stories of the city's elite, and then keep the historical vibe going with lunch at **The Four Way,** a place both Elvis and Martin Luther King Jr. dined. The nearby **Memphis Brooks Museum of Art** gives you an excuse to frolic in **Overton Park.** Stick around midtown and stroll the cute retail boutiques, followed by dinner at **Alchemy.** Wrap it all up with a drink and a low-key live music experience at **Bar DKDC.**

WITH MORE TIME

If you have more time to spend, there are several enticing Southern side trips within two hours' drive of Memphis.

The Mississippi Blues Trail

With two days, you have enough time for a 170-mile blues-themed road trip into the heart of the Mississippi Delta.

Head south from Memphis to Tunica, Mississippi, where you'll find the **Gateway to the Blues Museum.** Next, make your way to Clarksdale, where you'll get a more in-depth overview at the **Delta Blues Museum.** Listen to music and eat and drink at **Ground Zero Blues Club.**

The Mississippi Blues Trail starts in Memphis.

Keep heading south to Cleveland, where you want to devote time to the **Grammy Museum Mississippi.** Spend the night at the **Cotton House** and listen to more live music while you dine at **Airport Grocery.**

In Leland, you'll get more blues education at the **Highway 61 Blues Museum,** and fine Southern hospitality at **The Thompson House,** plus some American history that isn't specifically related to the genre when you stop at the **Jim Henson Boyhood Home Museum.**

Tupelo

A two-hour drive from Memphis, Tupelo makes a worthwhile side trip. Start your day in Tupelo at **Connie's Fried Chicken,**

blueberry doughnuts at Connie's Fried Chicken

MEMPHIS MUSIC

Sun Studio

Memphis has a beat to its soul…it is hard to find a place in the city *without* some kind of music. Take your pick depending on your interests. Or treat your ears and pick 'em all.

BLUES

Beale Street is the birthplace of the blues. Visit the **W. C. Handy Home and Museum** to see where the father of the blues lived while he was in Memphis, then head over to the **Blues Hall of Fame.**

After dark, hear live blues and jazz at the **King's Palace Café** and **Rum Boogie Café.** Memphis's juke joints get kicking late on Friday and Saturday nights. **Earnestine and Hazel's** in the South Main Arts District is a perennial favorite.

SOUL

The best musical museum in Memphis is the **Stax Museum of American Soul Music.** You will learn not only about the remarkable story of Stax, but also soul's musical roots in gospel and country music. Lace up your dancin' shoes; this is a museum where you'll boogie as you read. To keep moving, end your evening at **Paula & Raiford's Disco,** a time-honored Memphis tradition that plays soul along with disco (and everything else).

ROCK

No place in Memphis is more important to music history than **Graceland,** home of Elvis Presley. Here the King lived with his parents, wife, extended family, and his buddies, whom he called the Memphis Mafia. See his remarkable taste in decor and pay your respects at his grave.

Sun Studio is where early blues records were made, where Elvis, Jerry Lee Lewis, and Johnny Cash laid down tracks. This hallowed ground is still a working studio, so you can record here if you are a pro; the rest of us can take the tour.

To hear local rock music, check out the lineup at midtown's **B-SIDE.**

At **Goner Records,** you can find music to take home with you.

where everyone in town goes for a chicken biscuit and a blueberry doughnut. Head next to **Brices Cross Roads National Battlefield,** which commemorates a bloody encounter in the U.S. Civil War. Lunch should be at **Johnnie's Drive-In,** because that's where Elvis liked to eat. The rest of the day is focused on the King: The **Elvis Presley Birthplace** gives insight into his humble beginnings. **Tupelo Hardware Company,** right downtown, is where he got his first guitar. Finish the day with live music and good beer and food at **Blue Canoe.**

Oxford

Built on land that once belonged to the Chickasaw Nation, the city of Oxford was founded to be a university town like its namesake in England. Mission accomplished: Oxford is home to **University of Mississippi,** affectionately called Ole Miss. Assuming you are not in town for an SEC football game, start with breakfast and coffee at **Bottletree Bakery** before heading to campus for a tour. Follow the **Bailey's Woods Trail** to reach **Rowan Oak,** the home of celebrated author William Faulkner. Pay your respects at **Saint Peter's Cemetery,** where he is buried. For dinner, enjoy a sustainable feast at **Oxford Canteen.** End the evening with an author reading at **Off Square Books** or a live music performance, such as the **Thacker Mountain Radio Hour.**

Little Rock

Your first stop must be **Little Rock Central High School National Historic Site,** with a moving tour that tells the story of the desegregation of public schools and the bravery of the Little Rock Nine who made it happen. Eat lunch at **The Root Café,** which sources most of its ingredients locally from within the state of Arkansas. Spend the afternoon strolling in SoMa, a charming neighborhood with restaurants, shops, and the **ESSE Purse Museum,** which documents women's history through the contents of their handbags. Next head to the **William J. Clinton Presidential Library and Museum,** repository of the archives of the city's favorite son. Treat yourself to a fine dinner at **One Eleven at The Capital,** where you can take in the beauty of the **Capital Hotel,** even if you are not staying the night.

Hot Springs

Nicknamed "America's First Resort," Hot Springs still makes for a relaxing getaway, just three hours from Memphis. Soak in 143°F waters at **Quapaw Baths and Spa** on historic Bathhouse Row, which is part of **Hot Springs National Park.** Visit the museum and visitors center inside **Fordyce Bathhouse Row.** After walking and soaking, you can eat lunch and drink beer made with the thermal waters at **Superior Bathhouse Brewery.** Grab your empty water bottles and fill them with natural spring water from the taps all along Central Avenue. Grab a sweet from **Fat Bottomed Girls Cupcakes**— they've been featured on the Food Network's *Cupcake Wars*— for your drive back to Memphis.

Bathhouse Row in Hot Springs National Park

WALKING BEALE STREET

Beale Street runs from the Mississippi River to Manassas Street in mid-town Memphis, but it is the three blocks between 2nd and 4th Streets that really matter. In its heyday, the Beale Street commercial and entertainment district extended farther east and west, but it has since been condensed into a half-dozen blocks.

This walking tour begins at the intersection of Beale and Main Streets and heads eastward. While this is an area of nearly 24-hour activity, it is best to follow this walking tour in the later morning or early afternoon, should you want to stop, see the sights, and reflect. Come back at night for the live music and lively crowds. For more insight into Beale Street's history, call the **Withers Collection Museum and Gallery** (333 Beale St., 901/523-2344, www.thewitherscollection.com) for a guided tour ($12).

1 Near the corner of Beale and Main Streets is the **Orpheum Theatre** (203 S. Main St., 901/525-3000, www.orpheum-memphis.com). This site has been used for entertainment since 1890, when the Grand Opera House opened there with a production of Les Huguenots. Later, the opera house presented vaudeville shows and theater. Fire destroyed it in 1923, but in 1928 it reopened as the Orpheum, a movie theater and performing arts venue for the likes of Duke Ellington, Cab Calloway, Bob Hope, and Mae West. The Orpheum remains one of the city's premier venues for the performing arts, with Broadway productions, mainstream musical artists, and movies.

Welcome to Beale Street.

2 A block east of the Orpheum is **Elvis Presley Plaza,** home to a statue of Memphis's most famous native son, Elvis Presley. Depicting the King during his early career, the statue is a popular photo op.

3 **A. Schwab** (163 Beale St., 901/523-9782, www.a-schwab.com) has served Memphis residents for more than 140 years, although it focuses now on odd, out-of-date, and hard-to-find items rather than traditional general store necessities. Some say this is the oldest store in the mid-South. Stop in for a souvenir or to visit the A. Schwab "museum," a collection of old-fashioned household tools and implements

4 Make a quick stop at **Rum Boogie Café** (182 Beale St.) for a peek at the more than 200 guitars on display.

5 A few doors down from A. Schwab you can see what remains of one of Beale Street's most magnificent old buildings. The facade of what was once the **Gallina Exchange Building** (183 Beale St.) is held up by six steel girders. From the 1860s until 1914, this facade kept watch on the business empire of Squire Charles Gallina, who operated a saloon, restaurant, and 20-room hotel, as well as a gambling room. Today, it's the home of Irish pub Silky O'Sullivan's.

6 For fuel to sustain you during your tour, stop at **Dyer's** (205 Beale St.) and grab one of the city's best burgers.

7 Beyond 3rd Street is **Handy Park,** named for famous blues composer and musician W. C. Handy. Beale Street's Market House was

23

torn down in 1930 to build the park. Since it opened, Handy Park has been a popular place for street musicians, peddlers, concerts, and community events, all of which are presided over by a life-size statue of W. C. Handy.

8 About midway up the southern side of the next block of Beale Street is the **Daisy Theater** (329 Beale St.), built in 1902 as a movie house. Much of the original interior remains. The theater is closed to the public but may be rented for private events.

9 The stately **First Baptist Beale Street Church** (379 Beale St.) was built between 1868 and 1885 and is home to one of the oldest African American congregations in Memphis. In the 1860s, the congregation met under brush arbors at the present location, and the first temporary structure was erected in 1865. The cornerstone was laid for the present building in 1871. The First Baptist Beale Street Church was an important force in 6 Memphis's African American history. It was here that black Memphians published their first newspapers, the *Memphis Watchman* and the *Memphis Free Speech and Headlight*.

10 Hard-core music fans may want to make a stop at the **Memphis Rock 'n' Soul Museum** (191 Beale St.), which tells the story of local music from B. B. King to Elvis to *Shaft*—and beyond. You could spend hours (or days) here, so plan accordingly.

11 Today, **Church Park** (4th St. at MLK Ave.) is a humble city park. But in 1899, when Robert Church built Church Park and Auditorium at the eastern end of the Beale Street commercial district, the park was something truly special. Church is said to have been the first black millionaire in the South. He was troubled that there were no public parks expressly for Memphis's African American residents, so in 1899 he opened Church Park and Auditorium on 6 acres (2.4 hectares) of land along Beale Street. The park was beautifully landscaped and manicured, with bright flowers, tropical trees, and peacocks. The auditorium was a venue for black performers and speakers. Church Park remains a venue for community events, particularly the annual Africa in April event every spring.

12 Head back to the Gallina Exchange Building and Irish pub **Silky O'Sullivan's** (183 Beale St.), where you can toast to Memphis and maybe even imbibe with a beer-drinking goat. Looking out at the number of cafes, bars, and clubs on Beale Street, you can begin planning your evening's entertainment.

The Dixon Gallery and Gardens

ART AND CULTURE WEEKEND

Memphis's rich arts tradition can be explored throughout the city, from its indoor galleries to its outdoor murals.

DAY 1

MORNING

Grab some breakfast—with coffee, it'll be a jam-packed day—at **Edge Alley** in the South Main Arts District, and then start exploring the creative energy of this neighborhood. Make your way to **Robinson Gallery** to see the works of former *Vogue* photographer Jack Robinson Jr.

AFTERNOON

Head to **Art Village Gallery** next. Owners Ephraim and Sheila Urévbu have designed a space that is inclusive and thought-provoking. Make an advance appointment at **Marshall Arts,** where you'll tour 15 different artists' studios. Sweets and shopping at **Primas Bakery and Boutique** and **Shop Mucho** or **Stock and Belle** are your last stop in South Main.

EVENING

Stroll through the shops and galleries in the Broad Avenue Arts District, browsing for artful gifts at **T. Clifton Art Galleries** or **Five in One Social Club.** Enjoy a flavorful Cuban dinner at **The Liquor Store.** End the night with a cocktail in Crosstown Concourse's **Art Bar.**

DAY 2

MORNING

Caffeinate at **Bluff City Coffee** in South Main before heading east. Peruse a permanent collection of more than 2,000 paintings, not to mention a magnificent botanical garden, at **The Dixon Gallery and Gardens.** The on-site **Park & Cherry** is a good stop for lunch or a quick snack.

AFTERNOON

Head to South Memphis to explore the works of African American artists. Start at **CLTV at the CPLX** and **The Orange Mound Art Council,** adjacent facilities on Lamar Avenue. Then see what's on display at the **Memphis Black Arts Alliance** before heading back downtown.

EVENING

Experience culinary artistry during early dinner at **Catherine & Mary's** in the Hotel Chisca. End the day with a walk across the **Big River Crossing** bridge to see the city's lights reflected in the Mississippi River—perhaps Memphis's most stunning work of art.

CIVIL RIGHTS LEGACY

No event had a more profound effect on Memphis than the 1968 assassination of Dr. Martin Luther King Jr. His work, of course, lived on after his death—and will continue over lifetimes and generations. A visit to Memphis offers a way to focus on his mission and his legacy. To explore further, consider the **Memphis Heritage Trail** (901/250-2700, www.memphisheritagetrail.com), a list of sites developed by the city to honor the contributions of African Americans.

Memphis Heritage Trail

DAY 1

The **National Civil Rights Museum,** built on the site of the Lorraine Motel—where King was killed—ought to be the first stop, given its historical significance and the way it puts events in a greater context. Take a break for lunch at nearby **Central** **BBQ,** which will sate your appetite for the classic dish.

A nice companion to the museum is the **Withers Collection Museum and Gallery,** which houses an archive of more than 1.8 million photographs, including many documenting the civil rights movement. Finish at the powerful **I Am**

National Civil Rights Museum in Memphis

a **Man Plaza** memorial next to the historic **Clayborn Temple,** where you can learn about the 1968 Sanitation Workers' Strike and the organizing work that went on here to fight for better rights for workers.

Downtown, **Sage Memphis** is the perfect place to cap your evening, offering a menu of Asian and soul food fusion.

DAY 2

The Underground Railroad helped thousands of slaves escape to freedom. The guided tours of the **Slave Haven Underground Railroad Museum** help tell their stories. Plan to spend the bulk of the day here. Have lunch at Southern eating institution **The Four Way,** where many civil rights leaders have dined. Then head to **Mason Temple Church of God in Christ,** where Martin Luther King Jr. gave his "I've Been to the Mountaintop" speech the night

before his death. End the evening sitting outside at **Carolina Watershed** in midtown, reflecting on your day over dinner.

DAY 3

Much of Memphis's civil rights progress came through music. The father of the blues once lived in Memphis. See his home and learn about his legacy at the **W. C. Handy Home and Museum.** Follow it with a traditional Southern lunch at **Alcenia's.** Next, explore the connection between gospel and soul and their roles in Memphis's development at **Stax Museum of American Soul Music.** End the day with dinner and live music at **Onix.**

WITH MORE TIME

EXCURSION TO LITTLE ROCK

To dive further into the country's difficult story of segregation, make a day trip to the **Little Rock Central High School National Historic Site,** roughly a two-hour drive from Memphis. The tour explains the battle the Little Rock Nine fought to be able to attend public school. Also stop by the **Arkansas State Capitol,** where the sculpture *Testaments* tells more of their story. Eat lunch at **South on Main,** where you can learn more about how residents are revitalizing their neighborhoods for a more inclusive future.

EXCURSION TO HENNING

Take an hour's drive from Memphis to Henning, Tennessee, the location of the **Alex Haley Museum and Interpretive Center.** The work of this major African American author, best known for his novel *Roots*, changed the national conversation about race. Most local tours from Memphis last about three hours, including travel time and a stop at **Fort Pillow State Historic Park.** It's a day well spent.

MEMPHIS

Memphis is a city of the South. As

such, it is a melting pot of cultural, musical, culinary, and economic influences from the entire Mississippi River delta.

It is a city that has been shaped by the river that runs alongside it; by its music, its food, its artists, and, of course, by Elvis. But Memphis is also shaped by the protests and violence that made it come to grips with its racist past. The assassination of Martin Luther King Jr. more than 50 years ago changed the city forever. Memphis has a legacy as rich and complicated as its history.

HIGHLIGHTS

✪ **MOST ICONIC STREET: Beale Street** gave birth to the Memphis blues and celebrates its legacy every night of the week (page 35).

✪ **MOST POWERFUL REMEMBRANCE OF MEMPHIS'S LEGACY:** For years the Lorraine Motel merely represented the tragic assassination of Martin Luther King Jr. Today, it also tells the story of the continuing struggle for equality at the **National Civil Rights Museum** (page 40).

✪ **PLACE WHERE FOWL WALK THE RED CARPET:** Even the ducks in the fountain get the red-carpet treatment at the landmark **Peabody Hotel**—a must-visit, even if you aren't staying the night (page 42).

✪ **MOST CREATIVE WAREHOUSE OVERHAUL:** Art galleries, restaurants, bars, mobile DJs, and more make the **Crosstown Concourse,** a creative hub in midtown (page 52).

✪ **PLACE TO LEARN AND MOVE AT THE SAME TIME:** Irresistible soul music is what made Stax famous in the 1960s—and it is what makes the **Stax Museum of American Soul Music** sweet today (page 54).

✪ **PLACE TO HONOR THE KING:** The Elvis legend is alive at **Graceland** mansion, as much a testament to Presley's fans as it is to his music (page 56).

✪ **BEST PLACE TO PICNIC:** The park-like **Elmwood Cemetery** is the final resting place of dozens of local characters: madams, blues singers, mayors, and pioneers of all types (page 58).

✪ **BEST PLACE TO LEARN AND APPRECIATE A CRAFT:** Explore the craft of metalworking in a museum, workshop, or park-like setting at the world-class **Metal Museum** (page 60).

✪ **THE ULTIMATE MUST-EAT TREAT:** Tangy, juicy, and just a little sweet, Memphis **barbecue** is the stuff of Tennessee dreams (pages 92, 98, 104, and 105).

Still, this is a city that lives in the present. Today, this more integrated city is festive, an ongoing celebration of food, music, and visual art. It is the headquarters of major corporations including FedEx and AutoZone. An NBA franchise (the Grizzlies) arrived, the National Civil Rights Museum opened on the grounds of the historic Lorraine Motel, a fantastic AAA baseball field opened downtown, and Memphis made its mark with films such as *Hustle & Flow, Forty Shades of Blue,* and *Black Snake Moan.* In 2019, Memphis celebrated its bicentennial, both honoring its past and planning for a vibrant future.

To really love Memphis, study its past and embrace its future. Do so with an open mind and enough time to explore. And of course, slow down for some signature barbecue.

PLANNING YOUR TIME

You can knock out Memphis's main attractions in a weekend, but it takes a bit longer to soak up the city's special mojo: the music, food, and laid-back attitude. In fact, if you want more than just a taste of Memphis's famous blues, its legendary barbecue, or its rich history, plan to stay at least a week.

If you want to be in the center of the tourist action, choose downtown Memphis as your home base. The city center is home to the bars, restaurants, sports venues, live music clubs, and, of course, Beale Street. If you prefer a neighborhood feel, you can't go wrong in midtown, which has bars, restaurants, boutiques, art, and theater, but fewer hotels.

While a lot of Memphis's attractions are downtown, others are located in the eastern and southern stretches of the city. A free shuttle is available to Graceland and Sun Studio from downtown, but for other attractions like the Stax Museum of American Soul Music and the Memphis Brooks Museum of Art, you will need a car or taxi. Take note that two of the city's best barbecue joints (a Memphis must), as well as its most famous juke joints, are not within walking distance of downtown.

A word about safety: In some circles, Memphis has a reputation as being "dangerous." Official statistics confirm that it has its share of crime (less than Baltimore and Detroit in 2018, for example, but slightly more than Chicago). Police and community groups have made some strides to change this. It should not deter you from visiting a gem of a city.

However, it can't hurt to remind yourself of best practices for personal safety. Memphians say "stow it, don't show it": Don't leave valuables in your parked car. Be aware of your surroundings when you are out and about. Don't walk with headphones or your attention focused on your phone. Don't carry valuables you don't need. Don't drink to the point of losing your inhibitions. At night, stick to well-populated areas. Most restaurants, bars, live music venues, and hotels have security teams. If you feel uncomfortable, ask someone to escort you to your car or wait for your ride-hailing driver. Certain areas, including around Graceland and the area around the airport, are not ideal for strolling at night.

ORIENTATION

Memphis is perched atop a low bluff overlooking the majestic Mississippi River (hence one of its official nicknames, Bluff City). The center city district lies, roughly speaking, along the river. Main Street, a pedestrian-only mall (except for the trolleys), runs north-south, while Union, Madison, and Poplar Avenues are the main east-west thoroughfares.

While not compact, central Memphis is entirely walkable for people willing to sacrifice a little shoe leather. The Main Street Trolley makes it easy to see downtown and uptown attractions without a car.

DOWNTOWN

In this guide, locations south of Union Avenue are considered downtown. One of downtown's main attractions is Beale Street. Also contained within the downtown district is the area known as South Main Arts District, a several-block strip along and near Main Street that is home to small boutiques, art galleries, restaurants, condos, and repurposed historical

Greater Memphis

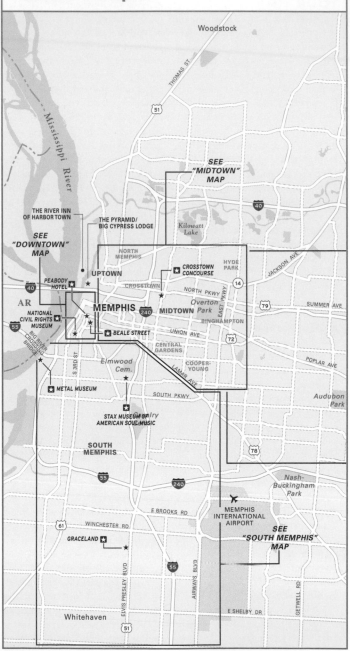

Woodstock

THOMAS ST

51

SEE "MIDTOWN" MAP

40

Kilowatt Lake

THE RIVER INN OF HARBOR TOWN

THE PYRAMID/ BIG CYPRESS LODGE

SEE "DOWNTOWN" MAP

NORTH MEMPHIS

UPTOWN

CROSSTOWN CONCOURSE

HYDE PARK

JACKSON AVE

PEABODY HOTEL

40

CROSSTOWN

NORTH PKWY

14

79

SUMMER AVE

AR

MEMPHIS

240

MIDTOWN

Overton Park

EAST PKWY

NATIONAL CIVIL RIGHTS MUSEUM

55

BEALE STREET

UNION AVE

BINGHAMPTON

72

BIG RIVER CROSSING BRIDGE

CENTRAL GARDENS

POPLAR AVE

S 3RD ST

Elmwood Cem.

COOPER-YOUNG

LAMAR AVE

Audubon Park

METAL MUSEUM

SOUTH PKWY

STAX MUSEUM OF AMERICAN SOUL MUSIC

SOUTH MEMPHIS

55

240

Nash-Buckingham Park

78

E BROOKS RD

MEMPHIS INTERNATIONAL AIRPORT

61

WINCHESTER RD

SEE "SOUTH MEMPHIS" MAP

GRACELAND

ELVIS PRESLEY BLVD

55

AIRWAYS BLVD

GETWELL RD

Whitehaven

51

E SHELBY DR

Mississippi River

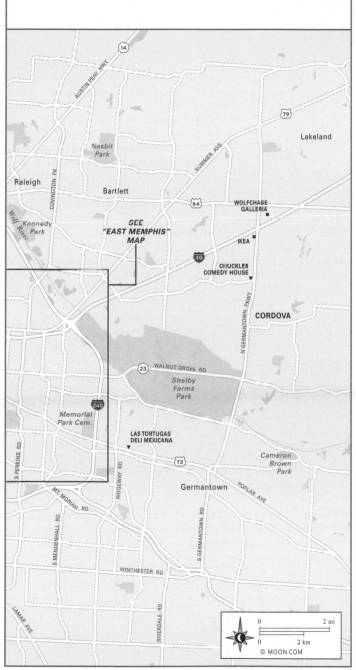

architecture. South Main is about a 15-minute walk or a 5-minute trolley ride from Beale Street.

UPTOWN

Locations north of Union in the city center are uptown. Originally settled by German immigrants, the uptown Pinch District is now a hub of restaurants and nightlife. It is also the gateway to gentrifying residential neighborhoods farther north. Restaurants in the Pinch have been categorized as uptown in this guide. You can walk to the Pinch from downtown, but the best way to get there is to ride the Main Street Trolley. Also part of the uptown area is Harbor Town, a planned riverside community with green space, views of the Mississippi, homes, retail, and a hotel.

MIDTOWN

Memphis sprawls south, east, and north from the river. Head east from downtown, and you are in midtown, a district of revitalized neighborhoods and the city's best park and art museum. Poplar Avenue is the main artery of midtown, and it's a good point of reference when exploring by car. The city's original suburb, midtown now seems positively urban compared to the sprawling burbs that creep farther eastward every year.

Located within midtown is Cooper-Young, a redeveloping residential and commercial neighborhood that lies around the intersection of Cooper Street and Young Avenue, as well as the Broad Avenue Arts District. Since the 1970s, residents of this neighborhood have fought the tide of urban decay by encouraging investment, good schools, and amenities like parks, art galleries, and independent restaurants, and generally fostering a sense of pride in the area. The result is a neighborhood where you'll find lots of restaurants, breweries, a great used-book store, record shops, and other attractions that draw the city's young and young at heart. Crosstown, named for the Crosstown Concourse mecca of restaurants, apartments, shops, and galleries in an old Sears warehouse, is also in midtown. This area is also referred to as the Medical District.

EAST MEMPHIS

East Memphis is where you will find large shopping malls with restaurants and movie theaters, major hospitals, the University of Memphis, and a few traffic jams. There are also a few attractions out here, the Dixon Gallery and Gardens and the Memphis Botanic Gardens among them.

SOUTH MEMPHIS

During the day, visitors beat a path to South Memphis to see attractions like Graceland and the Stax Museum of American Soul Music. Built on land of a former plantation, Orange Mound was the first neighborhood in the city to be built by African Americans for African Americans. After years of economic hardship, it is now seeing signs of revitalization. However, along with North Memphis, this remains one of the most economically depressed areas of the city. Visitors should avoid this neighborhood at night, unless accompanied by a local who knows the way around.

Sights

DOWNTOWN

Downtown refers to the area south of Union Avenue in the city center. It is the heart of Memphis's tourist district.

✪ BEALE STREET

If you want to delve into the history and character of Memphis music, your starting point should be **Beale Street,** home of the blues. For a step-by-step walking tour, see page 22.

A combination of forces led Beale Street to its place in musical history and popular culture. Named after a war hero, Beale Street was originally part of South Memphis, a separate city that rivaled Memphis during the 1840s.

Beginning in the 1850s and continuing in greater numbers during and after the Civil War, African Americans began to settle along the western part of Beale Street. By the 1880s and 1890s, a middle class of black professionals began to emerge, and Beale Street became the center of commerce, entertainment, and life for many of them. Together with black-owned businesses on Beale Street were laundries, bars, restaurants, pawn shops, and more operated by immigrants from eastern Europe, Ireland, China, Greece, and Germany.

From the 1880s until the 1960s, Beale Street was the epicenter of African American life, not just in Memphis but also for the entire mid-South region. It was here that blacks felt free from many of society's restrictions.

Beale Street

Downtown

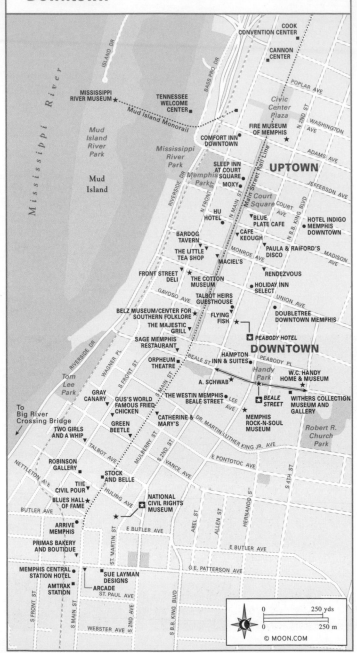

Mississippi River

COOK CONVENTION CENTER

CANNON CENTER

ISLAND DR

BASS PRO DR

POPLAR AVE

Civic Center Plaza

MISSISSIPPI RIVER MUSEUM ★

TENNESSEE WELCOME CENTER ■

Mud Island Monorail

WASHINGTON AVE

S 2ND ST

FIRE MUSEUM OF MEMPHIS ★

Mud Island River Park

Mississippi River Park

COMFORT INN DOWNTOWN ■

ADAMS AVE

Memphis Park

RIVERSIDE DR

N FRONT ST

N MAIN ST

Main Street Rail Line

SLEEP INN AT COURT SQUARE ■

MOXY ■

Court Square

COURT AVE

JEFFERSON AVE

UPTOWN

Mud Island

HU HOTEL ■

BLUE PLATE CAFE ■

CAFE KEOUGH ■

N B.B KING BLVD

HOTEL INDIGO MEMPHIS DOWNTOWN ■

BARDOG TAVERN ▼

MADISON AVE

THE LITTLE TEA SHOP ▼

MONROE AVE

PAULA & RAIFORD'S DISCO ▼

MACIEL'S ▼

FRONT STREET DELI ▼

THE COTTON MUSEUM ★

RENDEZVOUS ▼

TALBOT HEIRS GUESTHOUSE ■

HOLIDAY INN SELECT ■

GAYOSO AVE

BELZ MUSEUM/CENTER FOR SOUTHERN FOLKLORE ★

UNION AVE

FLYING FISH ★

THE MAJESTIC GRILL ▼

DOUBLETREE DOWNTOWN MEMPHIS ■

SAGE MEMPHIS RESTAURANT ▼

PEABODY HOTEL ✚

RIVERSIDE DR

WAGNER PL

S FRONT ST

S MAIN ST

ORPHEUM THEATRE ■

HAMPTON INN & SUITES ■

DOWNTOWN

PEABODY PL

Beale St

Handy Park

W.C. HANDY HOME & MUSEUM ■

A. SCHWAB ★

Tom Lee Park

GRAY CANARY ▼

GUS'S WORLD FAMOUS FRIED CHICKEN ▼

THE WESTIN MEMPHIS BEALE STREET ■

LEE AVE

BEALE STREET ✚

WITHERS COLLECTION MUSEUM AND GALLERY ■

To Big River Crossing Bridge

GREEN BEETLE ▼

CATHERINE & MARY'S ▼

E & DR. MARTIN LUTHER KING JR. AVE

MEMPHIS ROCK-N-SOUL MUSEUM ■

Robert R. Church Park

S 4TH ST

TWO GIRLS AND A WHIP ▼

NETTLETON AVE

ROBINSON GALLERY ■

S 2ND ST

E PONTOTOC AVE

TALBOT AVE

MULBERRY ST

VANCE AVE

THE CIVIL POUR ▼

STOCK AND BELLE ▼

BLUES HALL OF FAME ★

NATIONAL CIVIL RIGHTS MUSEUM ✚

ABEL ST

ALLEN ST

HERNANDO S

BUTLER AVE

ARRIVE MEMPHIS ■

HULING AVE

E BUTLER AVE

PRIMAS BAKERY AND BOUTIQUE ▼

ST. MARTIN ST

E BUTLER AVE

MEMPHIS CENTRAL STATION HOTEL ■

SUE LAYMAN DESIGNS ■

G.E. PATTERSON AVE

AMTRAK STATION ■

ARCADE ▼

ST. PAUL AVE

S FRONT ST

S MAIN ST

S 2ND AVE

WEBSTER AVE

S B.B. KING BLVD

0   250 yds

0   250 m

© MOON.COM

W. C. HANDY: FATHER OF THE BLUES

W. C. Handy was born in a log cabin in Florence, Alabama, in 1873. The son and grandson of African Methodist Episcopal ministers, Handy was exposed to music as a child in his father's church. Handy was also drawn to the music of the black laborers of the area, and when he moved to Memphis in the early 20th century, he recognized the wealth of the blues music he heard in bars, on street corners, and in back alleys around Beale Street.

Handy was a trained musician, so he was able to set down on paper the music that had, up until then, been passed from one musician to another.

In 1909, Handy composed Memphis mayor Ed Crump's campaign song, "Mr. Crump," which he later published as the "Memphis Blues." But he is most famous for his composition "St. Louis Blues," published in 1914. Handy also created the "Yellow Dog Blues," "Joe Turner Blues," and "Beale Street Blues." Known as the Father of the Blues, Handy passed away in 1958.

Beale Street's decline began in the mid-20th century, and by the 1970s it was a shadow of its former self. Investment during the 1980s and 1990s led to the street's rebirth as a destination for tourists and a source of pride for residents, who could now show off the street that gave birth to the blues.

Today, Beale Street has two distinct personalities. During the day it is a laid-back place for families or adults to stroll, buy souvenirs, and eat. You can also stop at one of several museums and attractions located on the street. At night, Beale Street is a strip of nightclubs and restaurants, a great place to people-watch, and the best place in the state, if not the country, to catch live blues seven nights a week.

W. C. HANDY HOME AND MUSEUM

The story of Beale Street cannot be told without mentioning William Christopher Handy, whose Memphis home sits at the corner of Beale Street and 4th Street. The building was originally located at 659 Jeanette Street, but it was moved to Beale Street in 1985. Now the **W. C. Handy Home and Museum** (352 Beale St., 901/527-3427, www.wchandymemphis.org,

10am-5pm Tues.-Sat. summer, 11am-4pm Tues.-Sat. winter, adults $6, children $4) is dedicated to telling the story of Handy's life. It was Handy who famously wrote, in his "Beale Street Blues": "If Beale Street could talk, married men would have to take their beds and walk, except one or two who never drink booze, and the blind man on the corner singing 'Beale Street Blues.' I'd rather be there than anyplace I know."

The Handy museum, which is on the Memphis Heritage Trail, houses photographs of Handy's family, one of his band uniforms, and memorabilia of the recording company that he founded. You can also hear samples of Handy's music.

A. SCHWAB

During Beale Street's dark days of the 1970s and 1980s, when the clubs and restaurants closed and the pawn shops opened, one mainstay remained: **A. Schwab** (163 Beale St., 901/523-9782, www.a-schwab.com, noon-5pm Mon.-Wed., noon-7pm Thurs., 10am-9pm Fri.-Sat., noon-6pm Sun., summer open until 8pm Mon.-Wed.). This landmark general store opened in 1876 and was owned and operated by the same family until 2011. Some say this is the oldest store in the mid-South. Originally the source for household necessities for thousands of Delta residents, A. Schwab remains a treasure trove of goods. Here you will find practical items like underwear, hats, umbrellas, cookware, and tools, as well as novelties like old-fashioned candy, incense, and actual cans of Tennessee whoop-ass. Upstairs is the A. Schwab museum, a hodgepodge of old-time tools, clothes, and memorabilia of the store's history.

The new owners, who purchased the store from the Schwab family, added a turn-of-the-20th-century-style soda fountain and a private event space, and spruced up this landmark for the next century.

ORPHEUM THEATRE

Near the corner of Beale and Main Streets is the **Orpheum Theatre** (203 S. Main St., 901/525-3000, www.orpheum-memphis.com). This site has been used for entertainment since 1890, when the Grand Opera House opened there with a production of *Les Huguenots*. Later, the opera house presented vaudeville shows and theater. Fire destroyed it in 1923, but in 1928 it reopened as the Orpheum, a movie theater and performing arts venue for the likes of Duke Ellington, Cab Calloway, Bob Hope, and Mae West. The Orpheum remains one of the city's premier venues for the performing arts, with Broadway productions, mainstream musical artists, and movies.

FIRST BAPTIST BEALE STREET CHURCH

The stately **First Baptist Beale Street Church** (379 Beale St.) was built between 1868 and 1885 and is home to one of the oldest African American congregations in Memphis. In the

Orpheum Theatre

1860s, the congregation started to meet under brush arbors at the present location, and the first temporary structure was erected in 1865. The cornerstone was laid for the present building in 1871. The First Baptist Beale Street Church was an important force in Memphis's African American history. It was here that black Memphians published their first newspapers, the *Memphis Watchman* and the *Memphis Free Speech and Headlight*.

CHURCH PARK

Today, **Church Park** (4th St. and MLK Ave., 901/636-6507, 6am-8pm daily mid-Mar.-Oct., 6am-6pm daily Nov.-mid-Mar.) is a humble city park. But in 1899, when Robert Church built Church Park and Auditorium at the eastern end of the Beale Street commercial district, the park was something truly special. Church is said to have been the first black millionaire in the South. He was troubled that there were no public parks expressly for Memphis's African American residents, so in 1899 he opened Church Park and Auditorium on six acres of land along Beale Street. The park was beautifully landscaped and manicured, with bright flowers, tropical trees, and peacocks. The auditorium was a venue for black performers and speakers. Church Park remains a venue for community events, particularly the annual Africa in April (africainapril.com) event every spring.

GALLINA BUILDING

The facade of what was once the **Gallina Building** is held up by six steel girders. From the 1860s until 1914, this facade kept watch on the business empire of Squire Charles Gallina, who operated a saloon, restaurant, and 20-room hotel, as well as

a gambling room. Housed within the building today is the Irish pub **Silky O'Sullivan's** (183 Beale St., 901/522-9596, www.silkyosullivans.com, 4pm-midnight Mon., 11am-midnight Tues. and Sun., 11am-1am Wed.-Thurs., 11am-3am Fri.-Sat.).

MEMPHIS ROCK 'N' SOUL MUSEUM

Music fans should plan to spend several hours at the **Memphis Rock 'n' Soul Museum** (191 Beale St., 901/205-2533, www.memphisrocknsoul.org, 9:30am-7pm daily, adults $13, children 5-17 $10, children 4 and under free), right next to FedEx Forum, off Beale Street. An affiliate of the Smithsonian Institution, this museum tells the story of Memphis music from the Delta blues to *Shaft*. Start with a short video documentary, and then follow the exhibits with your personal audio guide, which includes recordings of dozens of Memphis-influenced artists, from B. B. King to Elvis. Exhibits are dedicated to Memphis radio stations; the influence of the Victrola, Sam Phillips, and Sun Studio; and, of course, all things Elvis, among others. It takes several hours to study all the exhibits in detail and to listen to all (or even most) of the music, so plan accordingly.

A free shuttle runs between the Rock 'n' Soul Museum, Graceland, and Sun Studio, making it easy to tour the trifecta. At the museum, it picks up every hour on the half hour starting at 10:30am, with final pickup at 5:30pm and final drop-off at 6:30pm. At Graceland, it picks up every hour at the top of the hour, starting at 10am until 6pm from Graceland Plaza. At Sun Studio, the shuttle drops off every hour at 15 minutes after the hour, with service from 10:15am through 6:15pm.

Look for the black van with the Sun label's distinctive yellow sun on the side.

❂ NATIONAL CIVIL RIGHTS MUSEUM

If you do nothing else while you are in Memphis, or, frankly, the state of Tennessee, visit the **National Civil Rights Museum** (450 Mulberry St., 901/521-9699, www.civilrights-museum.org, 9am-5pm Wed.-Mon., until 6pm June-August, adults $16, students and seniors $14, children 5-17 $13, children 4 and under free, active U.S. military free). Built on the Lorraine Motel site, where Dr. Martin Luther King Jr. was assassinated on April 4, 1968, the museum makes a thorough examination of the American civil rights movement, from slavery to the present day. Exhibits display original letters, audio recordings, photos, and newspaper clippings from events including the Montgomery bus boycott, *Brown v. Board of Education,* Freedom Summer, and the march from Selma to Montgomery. Original and replicated artifacts, such as the bus where Rosa Parks made her stand in 1955 and the cell where Dr. King wrote his famous *Letter from a Birmingham Jail,* help to illustrate the story of civil rights.

When Dr. King visited Memphis in March and then again in April 1968, the Lorraine Motel was one of a handful of downtown hotels that welcomed African Americans. The room (and balcony and parking lot) where he spent his final hours has been carefully re-created, and a narration by those who were with King tells the shocking story of his death. Across Mulberry Street, in the building that was once the boardinghouse from where James Earl Ray is believed to have fired his sniper shot, exhibits probe various theories about the assassination, as well as the worldwide legacy of the civil rights movement.

Visitors to the museum can pay an extra $2 for an audio guide—a worthwhile investment. This is a large museum, and it is overflowing with information, so visitors who want to give the displays their due attention should plan on spending 3-4 hours here. A good way to visit is to tour the Lorraine Motel exhibits first, take a break for lunch, and then go across the street for the second half of the museum when you are refreshed.

Spending half a day here is a powerful experience, and one that raises many thoughts about civil rights. Expect interesting conversations with your travel companions after coming here. The gift shop offers books and videos for more information on the topic.

Admission is free on Monday after 3pm to Tennessee residents. In June, July, and August the museum stays open until 6pm.

The Lorraine Motel is now the site of the National Civil Rights Museum.

WLOK RADIO STATION

Another site on the Memphis Heritage Trail, **WLOK Radio Station** (363 S. Second St., www.wlok.com) played an important role in the city's civil rights movement. Founded in 1956, it was only the second station to direct its programs entirely to a black audience, even though its ownership was white. After the 1968 assassination of Dr. King, racial tensions increased. By 1970, on-air staff walked out in protest of low wages and poor working conditions. It took a 10-day strike and months of negotiation to come to terms. In 1977, WLOK became the first black-owned radio station in Memphis. Today, it continues to thrive. While it's not open for public tours, you can stop by and read the about its history—or listen at 105 FM/1340 AM.

BELZ MUSEUM OF ASIAN AND JUDAIC ART

Tucked away without fanfare is the **Belz Museum of Asian and Judaic Art** (119 S. Main St., 901/523-2787, www.belzmuseum.org, 10am-5:30pm Tues.-Fri., noon-5pm Sat.-Sun., adults $6, seniors $5, students $4, children under 5 free); you'll likely walk by this basement museum without realizing you've found it. Once called Peabody Place Museum, this unassuming facility houses one of the largest collections of artwork from the Qing dynasty. Forged from the private collection of Memphis developers Jack and Marilyn Belz, owners of the Peabody Hotel and the now shuttered Peabody Place mall, the museum features some 1,000 objects, including an array of jade, tapestries, paintings, furniture, carvings, and other artifacts. The museum, located on the basement level, is also home to the largest U.S. collection of work by Israeli artist Daniel Kafri.

The Belz Museum's Holocaust Memorial Gallery includes portraits and testimonials from Jewish survivors of the Holocaust in the *Living On* exhibit. Special exhibits also change semiannually. There's a small gift shop as well.

BLUES HALL OF FAME

The **Blues Hall of Fame** (421 Main St., 901/527-2583, www.blues.org, 10am-5pm Mon.-Sat., 1pm-5pm Sun., adults $10, students $8, U.S. military $8, children under 12 free) has existed as an entity—a project of the **Blues Foundation**—since 1980. But the physical building that you can tour didn't open until 2015. The $2.9 million building is across the street from the National Civil Rights Museum at the Lorraine Hotel and is listed in the Memphis Heritage Trail. It celebrates the music for which Memphis is famous and honors the musicians who make it.

More than 350 people have been inducted into the Blues Hall of Fame; of the 130 performers, 120 of them are African American. At the museum, you can learn about all of the inductees and listen to their contributions to the genre. The mission of the Blues Foundation is to both preserve and support the continuation of this essential American art form.

CLAYBORN TEMPLE AND I AM A MAN PLAZA

Built in 1887, **Clayborn Temple** (294 Hernando St., www.claybornreborn. org) is a building of both architectural and historical significance. Once the Second Presbyterian Church, this Romanesque Revival-style building, with its commanding presence

The Blues Hall of Fame

and stained glass windows, was sold to the African Methodist Episcopal Church (AME) in 1949 and was renamed Clayborn Temple (signage with both remains on the building today). Efforts to restore the historic building are underway.

In February 1968, the church became a key gathering place and a safe haven for civil rights leaders. Protestors met here during the sanitation workers' strike to discuss strategy. It wasn't unusual for Dr. Martin Luther King Jr. to stop here when in town. The iconic "I Am a Man" signs that were part of this movement were distributed here. In 2018—the 50th anniversary of King's death—the I Am a Man Plaza was dedicated next to Clayborn Temple. The plaza is a place of powerful remembrance, bearing the names of all the striking sanitation workers.

Clayborn Temple and the I Am a Man Plaza are stops on the U.S. Civil Rights Trail and the Memphis Heritage Trail. Nearby street parking is usually available.

UPTOWN

Uptown refers to locations along Union Avenue and points north in the center city district. Here tall office buildings rise above the city blocks.

✪ THE PEABODY HOTEL MEMPHIS

The Peabody Hotel Memphis (149 Union Ave., 901/529-4000, www.peabodymemphis.com) is the city's most famous hotel. Founded in 1869, the Peabody was one of the first grand hotels of the South, a place as well known for its elegant balls and big-band concerts as for the colorful characters who sipped cocktails at its famous lounge. Named in meory of the philanthropist George Peabody, the original hotel was located at the corner of Main and Monroe. It closed in 1923, and a new Peabody opened two years later in its present location on Union Avenue. It remained the place to see and be seen for generations of Delta residents. It was historian and journalist David Cohn who famously wrote in 1935 that "the Mississippi Delta begins in the lobby of the Peabody Hotel." The Peabody is also home to **Lansky Bros.** (901/529-9070, www.lanskybros.com, 9am-6pm Sun.-Wed., 9am-9pm Thurs.-Sat.), a men's clothing store known as the "Clothier to the King" because it dressed Elvis Presley.

Even if you don't stay here, you must stop by the elegant hotel lobby to see the twice-daily march of the **Peabody ducks** (a trip to Memphis is incomplete without this experience). The ducks live on the roof of the hotel and make the journey—by elevator— to the lobby fountain every morning at 11am. At 5pm they march out of the fountain, back onto the elevator, and up to their accommodations on the roof.

The hotel employs a duck master who takes care of the ducks and supervises their daily trip downstairs. Watching the ducks is free, frenzied, and undeniably fun. It is also one of the most popular activities among visitors to Memphis, so be sure to get there early and secure a good vantage point along the red carpet to watch the ducks march.

THE COTTON MUSEUM

The **Cotton Museum** (65 Union Ave., 901/531-7826, www.memphiscottonmuseum.org, 10am-5pm Mon.-Sat., noon-5pm Sun., adults $10, seniors and students $9, military $8, children 6-12 $8, children under 6 free) is located in the broad rectangular room that once was the nerve center of the mid-South's cotton trade. The Cotton Exchange was established in 1873, and it was here that buyers and sellers of the South's most important cash crop met, and where fortunes were made

Ducks walk the grand lobby at The Peabody Hotel.

43

and lost. Located just steps from the Mississippi River, the Exchange was the trading floor of Cotton Row, the area of town that was defined by the cotton industry.

The Cotton Museum is home to information-dense exhibits about cotton's history, its uses, and the culture that its cultivation gave rise to in Memphis and the Mississippi Delta. There are several videos you can watch, as well as a live Internet feed of today's cotton exchange, now conducted entirely electronically. It's quite a change from the days when the worldwide prices of cotton were hand-written in chalk—you can see still see that chalkboard on display here. There is also a replica of the Western Union office, where buyers and sellers sent telegrams using an intricate system of abbreviations known only to the cotton trade. You can stand in a booth and make a trade, touch a giant bale, and take kids through hands-on exhibits and an educational wing. There's a small gift shop as well. The museum is on the Memphis Heritage Trail.

MUD ISLAND

A trip to **Mud Island River Park** will remind you that wherever you are in Memphis, you're just steps away from the Mississippi River. Mud Island rose from the Mississippi River as a result of two seemingly small events. In 1876, the river shifted slightly about 20 miles south of Memphis, causing the currents that flowed past the city to alter course. And then, in 1910, a U.S. Navy gunboat, the USS *Amphitrite*, anchored at the mouth of the Wolf River for almost two years, causing a further change in silt patterns. When the ship left in 1912, the sandbar continued to grow, and Mud Island was

born. Today, it's a lovely place for a stroll along the river. An outdoor amphitheater hosts big-name concerts and has a snack bar, outdoor tables, and restrooms.

This narrow band of land is also home to the seasonal **Mississippi River Museum** (125 N. Front St., 901/576-7241, www.memphisriver-parks.org/mud-island, 10am-5pm Tues.-Sun. May-Oct., adults $10, seniors and children 5-11 $8, children 4 and under free), which has exhibits about early uses of the river, steam- and paddleboats, floods, and much more. Begin with a refresher course on European exploration of this region—de Soto, La Salle, and Marquette and Joliet—followed by information about early settlement. The highlight is a replica of an 1870s steamboat. In the Riverfolk Gallery, there are wax depictions of Mark Twain, riverboat gambler George Devol, and steamship entertainers. Admission to the museum includes a five-block scale model of the entire Mississippi River—from Minnesota to the Gulf of Mexico.

It's worth walking across the pedestrian bridge to take advantage of the great photo opportunity. A monorail runs to the park from a station at Front Street at Adams Avenue, but it's currently closed awaiting repairs.

SLAVE HAVEN UNDERGROUND RAILROAD MUSEUM

The legend of the Burkle Estate, a modest white clapboard house on North 2nd Street, has given rise to the **Slave Haven Underground Railroad Museum** (826 N. 2nd St., 901/527-3427, slavehavenmemphis. com, 10am-5pm Mon.-Sat. summer, 10am-4pm Mon.-Sat. winter, adults $12, seniors $11, students 4-17 $11,

THE BIRTH OF MUD ISLAND

Mud Island rose from the Mississippi River as a result of two seemingly small events. In 1876, the river shifted slightly about 20 miles south of Memphis, causing the currents that flowed past the city to alter course. And then, in 1910, a U.S. Navy gunboat, the USS *Amphitrite*, anchored at the mouth of the Wolf River for almost two years, causing a further change in silt patterns. When the ship left in 1912, the sandbar continued to grow, and Mud Island was born.

Residents initially disliked the island, since it was ugly and proved to be a danger to river navigation. Beginning in the 1930s, poor Memphians squatted on Mud Island in ramshackle homes built of scrap metal and wood. Between 200 and 500 people lived on the island during this time.

In 1959, a downtown airport was built on the island, but the airport was closed in 1970 when the DeSoto Bridge was built. In 1974, plans were developed for what is the present-day Mud Island River Park, which includes a full-scale replica of a riverboat, a monorail to the island, and the signature 2,000-foot flowing replica of the Mississippi River.

---

college students $11). The museum tells the story of slavery and the legendary Underground Railroad, which helped thousands of slaves escape to freedom in the North (and, after the 1850 Fugitive Slave Act, to Canada). Jacob Burkle, a German immigrant and owner of the Memphis stockyard, is said to have built the Burkle Estate around 1850. Escaping slaves would have hidden in a root cellar beneath the house before making the 1,500-foot (455-meter) trip to the banks of the Mississippi, where they continued their journey north.

Skeptics say that there is no evidence to support this story and even point to documents that show that Burkle may not have purchased the property until 1871, well after the end of slavery. Advocates for the Underground Railroad story say that it was the nature of the railroad to be secret, so there is nothing unusual about a lack of concrete evidence.

Visitors today need not be too concerned with the details of the debate; the Slave Haven museum does a good job of highlighting the brutality of the slave trade and slavery and the ingenuity and bravery it took for slaves to escape. Perhaps the most interesting part of the exhibit is the quilts that demonstrate the way that slaves used quilting patterns to send messages to one another. Other displays show advertisements for Memphis slave auctions and images from the early 20th century that depict damaging racial stereotypes.

The museum is operated by Heritage Tours of Memphis, and staff is available to conduct guided tours of the property.

FIRE MUSEUM OF MEMPHIS

The **Fire Museum of Memphis** (118 Adams Ave., 901/320-5650, www.fire-museum.com, 9am-4:30pm Mon.-Sat., adults $10, seniors $8, children 3-12 $8, children 2 and under free, firefighters and military $8, family pack for four $30) is a good place to take children. There is a huge display of fire-engine toys, lots of firefighting paraphernalia, and a "fire room" that presents important lessons on fire safety. You can also see old-fashioned fire engines, and youngsters will enjoy playing in the kid-friendly fire truck. The museum is located in the old Fire Station No. 1 in downtown Memphis.

ST. JUDE CHILDREN'S RESEARCH HOSPITAL

The sprawling complex of **St. Jude Children's Research Hospital** on uptown's northern fringe has been saving lives and bringing hope to children and their families since 1962. St. Jude was founded by entertainer Danny Thomas in fulfillment of his promise to God to give back to those in need.

Over the years and thanks to the success of its fundraising arm—the American Lebanese Syrian Associated Charities—St. Jude has expanded many times over and now leads the world in research and treatment of catastrophic childhood diseases, especially pediatric cancers. Many major country music stars have followed Thomas's lead, from Brad Paisley to the Avett Brothers to Cam, and choose St. Jude's for their charitable outreach, meaning concerts to benefit the hospital are frequent. The hospital never turns anyone away due to inability to pay, and it never makes families without insurance pay for their treatment.

Take a self-guided tour of the small museum about Danny Thomas and St. Jude in the **Danny Thomas ALSAC Pavilion** (332 N. Lauderdale St., 901-595-4414, www.stjude.org, 8am-4pm daily except when there are special events, free), located inside a golden dome on the hospital grounds. Just outside are the graves of Danny Thomas and his wife, Rose Marie. Hospital tours are available to the public if scheduled at least one week ahead of time by phone or email (800/877-5833, hospitaltours@stjude.org; include preferred tour date and time and number of guests).

THE PYRAMID

The Memphis **Pyramid** is the most physically dominating feature of the northern city skyline. Memphis's affiliation with all things Egypt began when it was named after the ancient city. It continued in 1897, when a large-scale replica of a pyramid was built to represent Memphis at the Tennessee Centennial Exhibition in Nashville. Pyramids have been popular symbols on Memphis paraphernalia for many years.

The first serious proposal for a life-size pyramid to be built in Memphis was written in the 1970s, but the idea did not take off until the 1980s, when the city and county governments agreed to fund it. Denver developer Sidney Shlenker promoted the plan and promised restaurants, tourist attractions, and lots of revenue for the city. The 321-foot (98-meter) pyramid was built and opened in 1991, minus the moneymaking engines that Shlenker promised.

For years the $63 million "Great American Pyramid" sat empty. In 2015 **Bass Pro Shops at the Pyramid** (1 Bass Pro Dr., 901/291-8200, www.basspro.com, 8am-10pm Mon.-Sat., 8am-7pm Sun.) opened what it modestly calls "one of the most dynamic, immersive retail stores in the world." This outdoor gear store includes a cypress swamp; 10 aquariums holding 600,000 gallons of water; the **Big Cypress Lodge,** a 103-room hotel (800/223-3333, www.big-cypress.com) with treehouse cabins; a spa; the Ducks Unlimited National Waterfowling Heritage Center; Uncle Buck's Fishbowl and Grill, a nautical-themed restaurant; the Memphis Beretta Gallery; a giant 28-story freestanding elevator; and more. Obviously, this isn't an average store. There are regular fish feedings (10am and 3pm daily), and you can access the top-floor observation deck and restaurant, **The**

Lookout, for a fee (11am-10pm Mon.-Fri., 11am-7pm Sun., adults $10, $5 for kids until 4pm). Views include the city, Big River Crossing and other bridges, Mud Island, and the mighty Mississippi.

MIDTOWN

You'll need a car (or take a Lyft or be up for a bike ride) to explore the attractions in midtown, which sprawls along Union, Poplar, and Madison Avenues as they head eastward from the city center.

SUN STUDIO

It is well worth your time to take a tour at the famous **Sun Studio** (706 Union Ave., www.sunstudio.com, 10am-6:15pm daily, adults $14, kids 5-11 free, under 5 not admitted), where Elvis Presley recorded his first hit, "That's All Right," and where dozens of blues, rock, and country musicians recorded during the 1950s. Founded by radioman and audio engineer Sam Phillips and his wife, Becky, the studio recorded weddings, funerals, events, and, of course, music. Phillips was interested in the blues, and his first recordings were of yet-unknown artists such as Rufus Thomas and Howlin' Wolf. In 1953, Elvis Presley came into the studio on his lunch break to record a $3 record of himself singing "My Happiness" for his mother. Phillips was not impressed with the performance, and it was not for another year—and thanks to the prodding of Phillips's assistant, Marion Keisker—that Phillips called Presley in to record some more. When Phillips heard Elvis's version of the blues tune "That's All Right," he knew he had a hit.

But the story of Elvis's discovery is just one of many that took place in the modest homemade Sun Studio, and this attraction is not just for Elvis fans.

Sun Studio

Midtown Memphis

SLAVE HAVEN
UNDERGROUND
RAILROAD
MUSEUM

NORTH
MEMPHIS

CHELSEA AVE

AYERS AVE

BREEDLOVE ST

N 11TH ST

THOMAS ST

UPTOWN

51

N 2ND ST

N 3RD ST

ROXIE'S
GROCERY

N MANASSAS ST

JACKSON AVE

14

A.W. WILLIS AVE

ST. JUDE CHILDREN'S
RESEARCH HOSPITAL

COZY
CORNER

1

NORTH PKWY

N WATKINS ST

ELEMENTO
NEAPOLITAN PIZZA

CROSSTOWN

N FRONT BLVD

ALCENIA'S

GLOBAL
CAFÉ

DANNY THOMAS
PAVILION

40

ALABAMA AVE

N DUNLAP ST

N BELLEVUE BLVD

ART BAR
PROUD MARY

OVERTON PARK AVE

POPLAR AVE

ADAMS AVE

VICTORIAN
VILLAGE

Morris
Park

MOLLY FONTAINE LOUNGE

SHELLCREST
SUNRISE MEMPHIS

POPLAR AVE

DOWNTOWN

EVELYN & OLIVE

JEFFERSON AVE

N CLEVELAND ST

EDGE ALLEY

MARSHALL
ARTS

MADISON AVE

S DANNY THOMAS BLVD

51

SUN STUDIO

Robert R.
Church
Park

BEALE ST

UNION AVE

BEST WESTERN
GEN X INN

MINGLEWOOD
HALL

DR. MARTIN LUTHER KING JR. AVE

EAST ST

S PAULINE ST

CUPBOARD
RESTAURANT

S LAUDERDALE ST

VANCE AVE

S CLEVELAND ST

BHAN THAI

PEGGY'S

CENTRAL
GARDENS

E.H. CRUMP BLVD

LAMAR AVE

78

MISSISSIPPI BLVD

240

WALKER AVE

Elmwood
Cemetery

S BELLEVUE BLVD

STAX MUSEUM OF
AMERICAN SOUL MUSIC

SOUTH
MEMPHIS

E MCLEMORE AVE

E MCLEMORE AVE

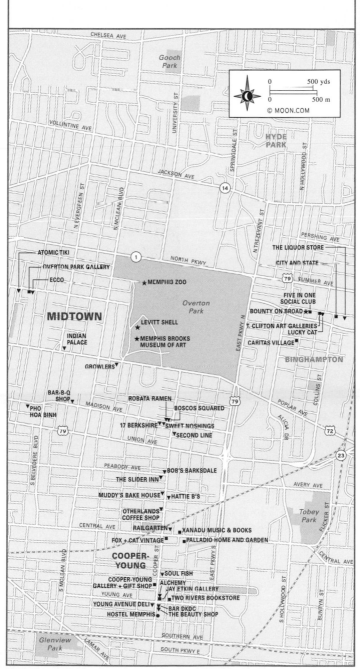

The tour of the studio leaves every hour on the half hour, and while you are waiting you can order a real fountain drink from the renovated snack bar or browse the shop's deep collection of recordings and paraphernalia. The studio is still in business; you can record here for $200 an hour for a five-hour block at night, and dozens of top-notch performers have, including Grace Potter, Beck, and Matchbox Twenty.

Tours are given hourly between 10:30am and 5:30pm during business hours and take approximately 90 minutes. Children under the age of five are not permitted on the tours. There are free shuttles from Graceland and the Rock 'n' Soul Museum to Sun Studio. Street parking is usually available near the studio.

LAUDERDALE COURTS/ UPTOWN SQUARE

One of the lesser-known Elvis attractions in Memphis is **Lauderdale Courts** (252 N. Lauderdale St., 901/523-8662, adults $10, rent the room for the night $250), the public housing complex where Presley lived with his parents from 1949 to 1953, before his rise to fame. The handsome brick building was saved from the wrecking ball in the 1990s thanks to its history with the King, and the apartment where the Presleys lived has been restored to its 1950s glory. The Lauderdale Courts Elvis suite is open for public tours during Elvis's Birthday Week in January and Elvis Week in August, plus 8am-5pm Monday-Friday, 9am-4pm Saturday, and 1pm-5pm Sunday when it isn't otherwise rented.

VICTORIAN VILLAGE

Set on a tree-lined block of Adams Avenue near Orleans Street is Victorian Village, where a half-dozen elegant Victorian-era homes escaped the "urban renewal" fate of other historic Memphis dwellings.

Woodruff-Fontaine House

Visitors can tour the **Woodruff-Fontaine House** (680 Adams Ave., 901/526-1469, www.woodruff-fontaine.org, noon-4pm Wed.-Sun., tours at noon, 1pm, 2pm, and 3pm, adults $15, seniors and military $12, children 6 and under $10), one of the street's most magnificent buildings. Built in 1870 for the Woodruff family and sold to the Fontaines in the 1880s, the house was occupied through 1930, when it became part of the James Lee Art Academy, a precursor to the Memphis Academy of Art. When the academy moved in 1959, the building became city property and stood vacant. Beginning in 1961, city residents raised funds to restore and refurnish the house with period furniture and accessories, and it opened as a museum in 1964. This period of

SIDE TRIP TO HENNING: ALEX HALEY'S TENNESSEE ROOTS

The tiny sawmill town of Henning, Tennessee, is an hour's drive northeast through the cotton fields from Memphis. It might be unremarkable except for the fact that it nurtured one of Tennessee's—and the nation's—greatest writers, Alex Haley.

The Alex Haley Museum and Interpretive Center (535 Haley Ave., 731/738-2240, www.alexhaleymuseum.org, 10am-5pm Tues.-Sat., by appointment only for groups of 15 or more Sun., adults $10, seniors $9, children $8, children under 5 free) illustrates the early childhood of the Pulitzer Prize-winning author. This is where Haley spent his first 10 years; he later returned during the summers to stay with his maternal grandparents, Will and Cynthia Palmer.

Today, visitors tour the kitchen where Cynthia Palmer told Haley stories of her ancestors, which he later used as inspiration for his masterwork, *Roots*. The museum has artifacts of the period, as well as family pictures and heirlooms. You also hear a recording of Haley describing Sunday dinners served in the family dining room. The home has been fully restored and is listed in the National Register. The museum was established with Haley's help and he was buried here in 1991.

Nearby, **Fort Pillow State Historic Park** (3122 Park Rd., 731/738-5581, www.tn-stateparks.com/parks/fort-pillow, visitors center 8am-4pm daily), with 20 miles of trails featuring restored Civil War fortifications, is another worthwhile stop.

Henning is 45 miles northeast of Memphis on U.S. 51. If you'd prefer to have someone else do the driving, **Heritage Tours of Memphis** (901/527-3427, www.heritagetoursinmemphis.com, prices vary per tour) will arrange outings.

urban renewal saw the demolition of many of Memphis's other old homes, and some of the house's furnishings were taken from homes that were later demolished; this is a good stop if you are interested in antiques. Period holiday décor, hung in November and December, is certain to put you in a Christmas mood. Tours last one hour and include all three floors and the basement; the 1st floor is wheelchair-accessible, but there is no elevator to access the different levels.

The **Magevney House** (198 Adams Ave., 901/523-1484, free admission first Sat. of each month 1pm-4pm) and the **Mallory-Neely House** (652 Adams Ave., 901/523-1484, www.memphismuseums.org, 10am-4pm Fri.-Sat., adults $10, seniors $9, children 3-12 $5) are two other historic homes in the district. The Magevney House is the oldest middle-class residence still standing in Memphis. It was built in 1836 by Irish immigrant Eugene Magevney. The Mallory-Neely House is of the same vintage and is

notable for the fact that it was not refurnished in more than 100 years and so remains remarkably true to the era in which it was built. Only the 1st floor is wheelchair-accessible; a video tour that replicates the **guided tour** (held every 30 minutes 10am-3pm Fri.-Sat.) is available in the carriage house, which also has a wheelchair-accessible restroom.

MEMPHIS BROOKS MUSEUM OF ART

Memphis's foremost art museum is located in Overton Park in midtown, a short drive from downtown. **Memphis Brooks Museum of Art** (1934 Poplar Ave., 901/544-6200, www.brooksmuseum.org, 10am-8pm Wed., 10am-4pm Thurs.-Fri., 10am-5pm Sat., 11am-5pm Sun., adults $7, seniors $6, students $3, children 6 and under free) is the largest fine-art museum in Tennessee, and its permanent collection comprises 8,000 works of art. This includes ancient African and Asian art, as well as 14th-century-present

SIDE TRIP TO BROWNSVILLE: TINA TURNER AND SLEEPY JOHN

Half welcome center, half museum, the **West Tennessee Delta Heritage Center** (121 Sunny Hill Cove, Brownsville, 731/779-9000, www.westtnheritage.com, 9am-5pm Mon.-Sat., 1pm-5pm Sun., free for self-guided tours or $7.50 for guided tours) is a good stop for understanding the special music, culture, and history of the delta region of Tennessee. With exhibits in three museums, it examines the musical heritage of the region, the ecology of the nearby Hatchie River, and cotton, the region's most important crop.

The scene-stealer at the museum complex is **Flagg Grove School,** which was once the childhood one-room schoolhouse of Anna Mae Bullock, better known as **Tina Turner.** Turner attended the African American school while growing up in nearby Nutbush (which provided the title for her hit "Nutbush City Limits"). The museum houses costumes, platinum and gold records, fan mail, an old yearbook, and other artifacts in sleek, modern displays in contrast with old wood floors, chalkboards, and wooden desks. On November 26, Turner's birthday, the center serves cake and has other festivities. The gift shop features quirky items that remind you of the megastar's rural roots: kudzu- and cotton ball-scented candles, for example.

Right next to the heritage center's museums is the **"Sleepy" John Estes Home,** a faded clapboard house that was relocated here so tourists could see where the blues legend was living when he died in 1977. Estes was born in Ripley, Tennessee, in 1904, but lived most of his life in Brownsville. A blues guitarist and vocalist, Estes had a distinctive "crying" vocal style and sounded like an old man, even on his early recordings. Estes made his recording debut in Memphis in 1929, and he recorded regularly until the United States joined World War II in 1941. Estes spent the end of his life blind and living in poverty.

The Heritage Center is located at exit 56, just off I-40, less than an hour's drive east of Memphis.

European art and 18th-century-present American art. There are 29 galleries at the Brooks, and special exhibitions have focused on the work of Annie Leibovitz, men's fashion in Africa, the silverwork of Paul de Lamerie, Activist Photographers of the Civil Rights Movement, and American Folk Art. The museum also has a shop and café, as well as an auditorium often used to screen films.

After decades of discussion, The Brooks (as locals call it) plans to move to a riverside downtown campus in 2024. While charming, the century-old Overton Park building can't accommodate the growth that the museum would like to experience. The new museum building—with a price tag of more than $110 million—will be connected to the Riverfront Greenway.

✪ CROSSTOWN CONCOURSE

A renovated and repurposed Sears warehouse has become a center of the arts community in midtown, **Crosstown Concourse** (1350 Concourse Ave., 901/507-8030, http://

crosstownarts.org, 10am-8pm Tues.-Fri., 10am-6pm Sat., noon-6pm Sun., hours may vary by business) is a diverse, high-energy space and a great place to hang out for the day. Among the charms of this all-in-one destination are a live music venue called the **Green Room**, artist studios and maker spaces, a weekend flea market, art galleries and public art exhibitions, pop-up shops, and an art-themed bar (aptly called **Art Bar**). All contribute to the creative vibe. There's also a park space, restaurants, a YMCA, CrossFit classes, and apartments. Even if you're not into the art or the shopping, you can appreciate the architecture and design that brought this space back to life. Even the outdoor planters are repurposed elements from the old warehouse.

MEMPHIS ZOO

The **Memphis Zoo** (2000 Prentiss Pl., 901/333-6500, www.memphiszoo.org, 9am-6pm daily Mar.-Oct., 9am-5pm daily Nov.-Feb., adults $18, seniors $17, children $13) has been expanding and is now the proud steward of two giant pandas, Le Le and Ya Ya; large cats; penguins; lions; tropical birds; and 500 other animal species. More hippos have been born here than at any other zoo and are featured in the Zambezi River Hippo Camp, where you can see them frolic in and out of the water. There are a number of seasonal exhibitions, including a jellyfish display and camel rides. The zoo is on the grounds of charming Overton Park; it's worth planning your trip to take advantage of several of this midtown gem's attractions at once. Zoo parking costs an additional $5 and is a point of considerable contention in the neighborhood. (Parking on the grass during zoo events upsets those who want to

see the magnificent Overton Park for other events and purposes. Be mindful when you visit.)

Tennessee residents with ID can get in free on Tuesdays after 2pm, except in March.

CHILDREN'S MUSEUM OF MEMPHIS

You will know the **Children's Museum of Memphis** (2525 Central Ave., 901/458-2678, www.cmom.com, 9am-5pm daily, $15, parking $4) by the large alphabet blocks outside spelling its acronym, CMOM. Bring children here for constructive, interactive, and educational play: They can sit in a flight simulator and real airplane cockpit, learn about railroad safety, climb a skyscraper, and more. The museum has more than 20 permanent exhibits and several traveling exhibits. Beat the Memphis summer heat at the museum's **H2Oh! Splash** park ($20 total combined with museum entry), which has 40 water sprayers in which children can frolic.

The Children's Museum is also home to the magnificent **Grand**

Children's Museum of Memphis

Carousel ($3/ride). Built in 1909 and moved to Memphis in 1923, it was part of Memphis childhoods for decades, until the Libertyland amusement park where it was house closed. Savvy community members saved it by protecting it and packing away for decades. It was fully restored and in 2017 reopened in the museum, surrounded by a new $4.5 million pavilion. The restoration includes Elvis's favorite horse, as well as modifications to make the carousel wheelchair-accessible. The carousel runs on the quarter hour, with the last ride making its spin at 4:45pm daily. Adults who are not accompanied by children are not permitted in the museum alone; however, they may go to the Grand Carousel, which is often rented for corporate events, weddings, and other private events. Even if you're not much of a merry-go-round fan, you will admire its craftsmanship.

SOUTH MEMPHIS
✪ STAX MUSEUM OF AMERICAN SOUL MUSIC

There is perhaps no place in Memphis that better tells the story of the city's legendary soul music than the **Stax Museum of American Soul Music** (926 E. McLemore Ave., 901/942-7685, www.staxmuseum.com, 10am-5pm Tues.-Sun., adults $13, seniors, students, and military $12, children 9-12 $10, children 8 and under free).

The museum tour starts with a short toe-tapping video that sets the scene for the musical magic that took place here during the 1960s. Exhibits include the sanctuary of an old clapboard Delta church, which illustrates the connection between soul and gospel music. You can also see Booker T. Jones's original organ, Otis Redding's favorite suede jacket, and Isaac Hayes's

Stax Museum of American Soul Music

1972 peacock-blue gold-trimmed Cadillac Eldorado, Superfly.

The museum also takes you through the studio's control room and into the studio itself, slanted floors and all. If you want to try your hand at singing, there is a karaoke machine, as well as a dance floor in case you can't help but move to the music. The Stax Museum is a must-see for music enthusiasts but also an educational journey for those who don't know the story behind some of America's most famous songs. It sits next door to the Stax Music Academy, a present-day music school that reaches out to neighborhood youth.

MASON TEMPLE CHURCH OF GOD IN CHRIST

On April 3, 1968, Martin Luther King Jr. gave his now-famous "I've Been to the Mountaintop" speech at **Mason Temple Church of God in Christ** (930 Mason St., 901/947-9300). He was assassinated the next day. Today, the church is a stop on the U.S. Civil Rights Trail and Memphis Heritage Trail. Built in 1941, the temple was the largest church building owned by a predominantly black religious denomination at the time. Now it's home to Church of God in Christ, the largest

South Memphis

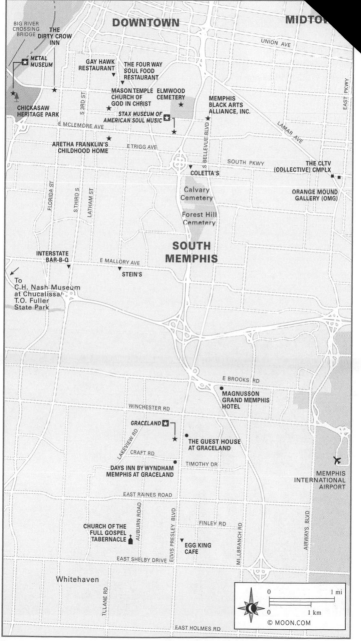

BIG RIVER CROSSING BRIDGE

THE DIRTY CROW INN

METAL MUSEUM

DOWNTOWN

MIDTOWN

UNION AVE

GAY HAWK RESTAURANT

THE FOUR WAY SOUL FOOD RESTAURANT

MASON TEMPLE CHURCH OF GOD IN CHRIST

ELMWOOD CEMETERY

STAX MUSEUM OF AMERICAN SOUL MUSIC

MEMPHIS BLACK ARTS ALLIANCE, INC.

CHICKASAW HERITAGE PARK

E MCLEMORE AVE

S 3RD ST

EAST PKWY

ARETHA FRANKLIN'S CHILDHOOD HOME

E TRIGG AVE

LAMAR AVE

S BELLEVUE BLVD

SOUTH PKWY

THE CLTV (COLLECTIVE) CMPLX

COLETTA'S

FLORIDA ST

S THIRD ST

LATHAM ST

Calvary Cemetery

ORANGE MOUND GALLERY (OMG)

Forest Hill Cemetery

SOUTH MEMPHIS

INTERSTATE BAR-B-Q

E MALLORY AVE

STEIN'S

To C.H. Nash Museum at Chucalissa/ T.O. Fuller State Park

E BROOKS RD

MAGNUSSON GRAND MEMPHIS HOTEL

WINCHESTER RD

GRACELAND

THE GUEST HOUSE AT GRACELAND

LACEVIEW RD

CRAFT RD

TIMOTHY DR

MEMPHIS INTERNATIONAL AIRPORT

DAYS INN BY WYNDHAM MEMPHIS AT GRACELAND

EAST RAINES ROAD

AUBURN ROAD

ELVIS PRESLEY BLVD

FINLEY RD

MILLBRANCH RD

AIRWAYS BLVD

CHURCH OF THE FULL GOSPEL TABERNACLE

EGG KING CAFE

EAST SHELBY DRIVE

Whitehaven

T. LANE RD

0   1 mi

0   1 km

© MOON.COM

EAST HOLMES RD

55

...own on Elvis ...ch the King's famous home, Graceland (3717 Elvis Presley Blvd., 901/332-3322 or 800/238-2000, www.graceland.com or www.elvis.com, 9am-5pm Mon.-Sat., 9am-4pm Sun. Mar.-Oct., 9am-4pm daily Nov., 9am-4pm daily Dec., 9am-4pm daily Jan.-Feb., adults $41, seniors and students $36.90, children 7-12 $21, children 6 and under free). Advance purchase tickets are recommended, particularly May-September.

The 200,000-square-foot (18,600-square-meter) complex houses a career museum, an automobile collection, and several other exhibits featuring everything from fashion to Elvis's army gear. Visitors can choose from four tour packages: The mansion-only tour takes about an hour and costs $41; the full-on Elvis Experience tour includes the automobile museum, the Graceland Archives Experience, and other special perks for $61. The Elvis Entourage VIP Tour, at $99, adds line-skipping privileges and a VIP shuttle and exhibit. A tour of Elvis's airplanes can be added to any of the aforementioned tours for $5. For $174 per person, groups of 8-10 looking for the top-tier experience can book the Ultimate VIP Tour, which includes all of the above, plus a self-guided tour of Elvis's private jets, access to a VIP lounge, access to keepsake merchandise, and a meal at Vernon's Smokehouse. Actor and Elvis fan John Stamos narrates an interactive multimedia digital tour that gives you access to archival audio, video, and photographs. Choose the tours

Graceland

African American Pentecostal group in the world.

✪ GRACELAND

Drive south from downtown on Elvis Presley Boulevard to reach the King's famous home, **Graceland** (3717 Elvis Presley Blvd., 901/332-3322 or 800/238-2000, www.graceland.com or www.elvis.com, 9am-5pm Mon.-Sat., 9am-4pm Sun. Mar.-Oct., 9am-4pm daily Nov., 9am-4pm daily Dec., 9am-4pm daily Jan.-Feb., adults $41, seniors and students $36.90, children 7-12 $21, children 6 and under free). Advance purchase tickets are recommended, particularly May-September.

The 200,000-square-foot (18,600-square-meter) complex houses a career museum, an automobile collection, and several other exhibits featuring everything from fashion to Elvis's army gear. Visitors can choose from four tour packages: The mansion-only tour takes about an hour and costs $41; the full-on Elvis Experience tour includes the automobile museum, the Graceland Archives Experience, and other special perks for $61. The Elvis Entourage VIP Tour, at $99, adds line-skipping privileges and a VIP shuttle and exhibit. A tour of Elvis's airplanes can be added to any of the aforementioned tours for $5. For $174 per person, groups of 8-10 looking for the top-tier experience can book the Ultimate VIP Tour, which includes all of the above, plus a self-guided tour of Elvis's private jets, access to a VIP lounge, access to keepsake merchandise, and a meal at Vernon's Smokehouse. Actor and Elvis fan John Stamos narrates an interactive multimedia digital tour that gives you access to archival audio, video, and photographs. Choose the tours

Graceland

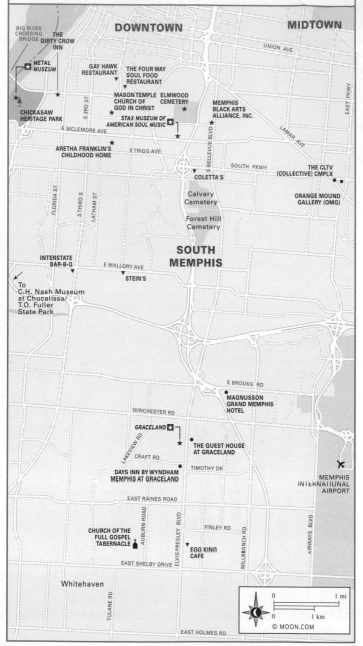

South Memphis

BIG RIVER CROSSING BRIDGE

THE DIRTY CROW INN

DOWNTOWN

MIDTOWN

UNION AVE

METAL MUSEUM

GAY HAWK RESTAURANT

THE FOUR WAY SOUL FOOD RESTAURANT

EAST PKWY

MASON TEMPLE CHURCH OF GOD IN CHRIST

ELMWOOD CEMETERY

MEMPHIS BLACK ARTS ALLIANCE, INC.

CHICKASAW HERITAGE PARK

E McLEMORE AVE

STAX MUSEUM OF AMERICAN SOUL MUSIC

LAMAR AVE

S BELLEVUE BLVD

ARETHA FRANKLIN'S CHILDHOOD HOME

E TRIGG AVE

SOUTH PKWY

THE CLTV (COLLECTIVE) CMPLX

COLETTA'S

FLORIDA ST

S THIRD S

LATHAM ST

Calvary Cemetery

ORANGE MOUND GALLERY (OMG)

Forest Hill Cemetery

SOUTH MEMPHIS

INTERSTATE BAR-B-Q

E MALLORY AVE

STEIN'S

To C.H. Nash Museum at Chucalissa/ T.O. Fuller State Park

E BROOKS RD

MAGNUSSON GRAND MEMPHIS HOTEL

WINCHESTER RD

GRACELAND

LAKEVIEW RD

THE GUEST HOUSE AT GRACELAND

CRAFT RD

TIMOTHY DR

MEMPHIS INTERNATIONAL AIRPORT

DAYS INN BY WYNDHAM MEMPHIS AT GRACELAND

EAST RAINES ROAD

AUBURN ROAD

ELVIS PRESLEY BLVD

FINLEY RD

MILLBRANCH RD

AIRWAYS BLVD

CHURCH OF THE FULL GOSPEL TABERNACLE

EGG KING CAFE

EAST SHELBY DRIVE

Whitehaven

TULANE RD

0   1 mi

0   1 km

© MOON.COM

EAST HOLMES RD

S 3RD ST

based on how hard-core of an Elvis fan you are.

Dining on-site includes barbecue at Vernon's Smokehouse, traditional American fare at Gladys' Diner, treats at Minnie Mae's Sweets, and grab-and-go items at Rock 'n' Go. They are fine options if you're peckish while touring, but there's certainly better food elsewhere in Memphis, so don't plan for these meals to be destination dining. In 2018, Graceland launched Graceland Excursions, motor coach tours of historical music-centric regions such as Tupelo (adults $99, children 5-12 $79) and the Mississippi Delta (adults $119, children $89).

The mansion tour, conducted by audio guide, includes the ground floor of the mansion (the upstairs remains closed to the public) and several outbuildings that now house exhibits about Elvis's life and career. High points include watching the press conference Elvis gave after leaving the army, witnessing firsthand his audacious taste in decor, and visiting the Meditation Garden, where Elvis, his parents, and his grandmother are buried. There is also a plaque in memory of Elvis's lost twin, Jesse Garon. The audio tour plays many of Elvis's songs, family stories remembered by Elvis's daughter Lisa Marie Presley, and several clips of Elvis speaking. Among the Graceland exhibits are: *Elvis: That's the Way It Is,* a documentary chronicling the legend's first Las Vegas performance; and *I Shot Elvis,* which features photos from the early years of his career and encourages museum guests to take a photo with a larger-than-life image of the King.

The exhibits gloss over the many challenges Elvis faced in his life—his addiction to prescription drugs, his failed marriage, and his unsettling affinity for firearms and younger women, among them. But they showcase Elvis's generosity, his dedication to family, and his fun-loving character. The portrait that emerges is sympathetic and human for a man who is so often portrayed as larger than life. For more information on Elvis' humble beginnings, a trip to the Elvis Presley Birthplace in Tupelo is informative and satisfying.

The Graceland automobile museum features 33 vehicles, including Presley's pink Cadillac, motorcycles, and a red MG from *Blue Hawaii,* as well as some of his favorite motorized toys, including a go-kart and dune buggy. His private planes include the *Lisa Marie,* which Elvis customized with gold-plated seat belts, suede chairs, and gold-flecked sinks. Other special Graceland exhibits include *The Country Road to Rock: The Marty Stuart Collection, Graceland Soundstage, Elvis' Tupelo Exhibit,* and *Icons: The Influence of Elvis Presley.*

The Graceland mansion was declared a National Historic Site in 2006. It attracts more than 650,000 visitors annually. The 2016 expansion also included Guest House at Graceland, a 450-room hotel with two restaurants and a 464-seat theater. Again, staying at the hotel and immersing oneself in all things Elvis may not be for everyone. If you are a hard-core fan, you will be satisfied. If you are merely curious and want to learn a little about the King because you are in Memphis, a shorter tour without the hotel stay is likely sufficient.

The ticket counters, shops, museums, airplanes, restaurants, and parking lots are on the west side of the boulevard, and here you board a shuttle van that crosses the highway and up the curved drive to the Graceland

SOULSVILLE

A lucky convergence of people, talents, and social forces led to one of Memphis's—and America's—most distinctive musical stories. **Stax Records** was founded in 1960 by Jim Stewart, an aspiring country fiddler, and his sister, Estelle Axton. The first two letters of the brother and sister's surnames came together to form Stax, a name now synonymous with the raw Memphis sound of performers like Rufus and Carla Thomas, Otis Redding, Sam and Dave, Isaac Hayes, Eddie Floyd, the Mar-Keys, the Staple Singers, and Booker T. & the MGs.

Stewart chose a closed movie theater in a working-class South Memphis neighborhood for his recording studio. He was on a tight budget, so he didn't bother to fix the sloped theater floor or angled walls, and the room's reverberating acoustics came to define the Memphis sound.

Motown was known as "Hitsville" for its smooth and palatable sound, so the artists at Stax began to call their neighborhood "Soulsville," a name that still refers to the area of South Memphis where Stax is located. The soul music that Stax recorded was raw and inventive, influenced by country, blues, gospel, and jazz.

The label's first hit was with WDIA-AM disc jockey Rufus Thomas and his daughter, Carla Thomas, who came in one day and recorded "Cause I Love You." The song became an overnight sensation.

Stax tapped into the talent of the neighborhood, and particularly the African American Booker T. Washington High School, which graduated such greats as the members of the Soul Children and the Mad Lads. As the Stax reputation developed, artists came from out of town to record, including a 21-year-old Otis Redding, who drove up from Georgia in hopes of making a record and made a career instead.

Stax also operated **Satellite Records,** right next door to the studio, and here Estelle Axton was able to quickly test-market new recordings on the neighborhood youngsters who came in for the latest music. Wayne Jackson, a member of the studio's house band, the Memphis Horns, recalls that Estelle and Jim would invite hundreds of young people from the neighborhood into the studio to listen to their newest recording. Based on the group's response, they would choose the single.

Stax was unique for its time as an integrated organization, where the love of music trumped racial differences. As the civil rights movement evolved, Stax artists turned to serious social themes in their music. In 1972, Stax artists organized **WattStax,** an outdoor black music festival in Los Angeles.

Between 1960 and 1975, when the Stax magic ran out, the studio produced 800 singles and 300 albums, including 243 Top 100 and 14 number-one R&B hits. Isaac Hayes's theme from the movie *Shaft* was the fastest-selling album in Stax history, and one of three Stax songs that went to number one on the pop charts. Other big Stax hits were Otis Redding's "(Sittin' on) The Dock of the Bay," the Staple Singers' "Respect Yourself," and Sam and Dave's "Soul Man."

Sadly, Stax was destroyed financially by a bad distribution deal with CBS Records in 1975 and the studio was closed. Its rare master tapes were sold at auction, and the studio where soul was born was demolished.

Thankfully, the story of Stax has not been forgotten. In 2001, ground was broken for a new Stax story, one that grew into the present-day music academy and the **Stax Museum of American Soul Music.**

mansion. The Graceland complex is surrounded by fast-food joints and a few souvenir shops that line the boulevard, but there's not a lot else in this part of town to attract tourists. If you don't have the time or the funds for a full tour, you can drive by, grab a street parking spot, and leave a memento to the King on the wall that surrounds the mansion.

✪ ELMWOOD CEMETERY

Elmwood Cemetery (824 S. Dudley St., 901/774-3212, www.

elmwoodcemetery.org, 8am-4:30pm daily), an 80-acre (32-hectare) cemetery southwest of the city center, is the resting place of 70,000 Memphians—both ordinary citizens and some of the city's most prominent leaders. It was founded in 1852 by 50 gentlemen who wanted the cemetery to be a park for the living as well as a resting place for the dead. They invested in tree planting and winding carriage paths so that the cemetery today is a pleasant, peaceful place to spend a few hours.

Elmwood Cemetery

The cemetery is the resting place of Memphians like Annie Cook, a well-known madam who died during the yellow fever epidemic of 1878; Marion Scudder Griffen, a pioneering female lawyer and suffragette; and musician Sister Thea Bowman. Thousands of anonymous victims of the yellow fever epidemic were buried here, as were both Confederate and Union casualties of the Civil War. Prominent citizens, including Robert Church Sr., Edward Hull Crump, and Shelby Foote, are also buried at Elmwood.

Visitors to the cemetery may simply drive or walk through on their own. But it is best to rent the one-hour audio CD guide ($10, available for rent 8am-3:30pm Mon.-Fri., 8am-noon Sat.), which takes you on a driving tour and highlights 50 people buried in the cemetery. Thanks to a well-written and well-presented narration, the cemetery tour comes closer than any other single Memphis attraction to bringing Memphis's diverse history and people to life. Maps are $5.

The cemetery offers occasional lectures and docent guided tours for $15 on select Saturdays at various times. Call ahead or check the website to find out if any are scheduled during your visit. Groups of 10 or more can schedule a tour for $15 per person, while smaller groups can schedule a private tour for $225. To find Elmwood, drive east along E. H. Crump Boulevard, turning south (right) onto Dudley, which leads to the single-lane bridge that marks the entrance to the cemetery. You may think you are in the wrong neighborhood en route; there's little signage to suggest you're about to find a green oasis in the city, but trust the maps and you'll find the bridge.

Tours of the 1,500 trees in the Carlisle S. Page Arboretum are also available.

CHURCH OF THE FULL GOSPEL TABERNACLE

A native of Arkansas and longtime resident of Michigan, Al Green first made his name as one of history's greatest soul singers, with hits like "Let's Stay Together," "Take Me to the River," and "Love and Happiness." Following a religious conversion in 1979, he dedicated his considerable talents to God and founded the **Church of the Full Gospel Tabernacle** (787

Hale Rd., 901/396-9192) in Memphis, where his Sunday sermons dripped with soulful gospel.

For almost 11 years, the Reverend Al Green left secular music, dedicating himself exclusively to God's music. He began his return to secular music in 1988, and in 1995 Green released the first of three new secular albums on Blue Note Records.

According to his official biography, *Take Me to the River*, Reverend Green faced some criticism when he returned to the secular scene. "I've got people in the church saying, 'That's a secular song,' and I'm saying, 'Yeah, but you've got Monday, Tuesday, Wednesday, Thursday, Friday, and Saturday to be anything other than spiritual. You've got to live those days, too!'" Reverend Green writes. In the book he says he has not neglected his duty to God: "The music is the message, the message is the music. So that's my little ministry that the Big Man upstairs gave to me—a little ministry called love and happiness."

Despite his rebirth as a secular soul performer, Al Green, now a bishop, still makes time for his church. He preaches regularly, but not every Sunday, and continues to sing the praises of God. The Sunday service at his Memphis church begins at 11:30am. Visitors are welcome, and you can come—within reason—as you are. Please show respect, though, by being quiet when it's called for and throwing a few bucks in the offering plate when it comes around. And don't forget that the church is a place of worship and not a tourist attraction. If you're not in town on Sunday, you can catch the weekly choir rehearsal on Thursday at 7pm. Don't bother to call ahead to find out if Reverend Green is preaching before you come

out: The staff can't confirm or deny his schedule.

❂ METAL MUSEUM

As the only museum in the country devoted to the art and craft of metalwork, the **Metal Museum** (374 Metal Museum Dr., 901/774-6380, www.metalmuseum.org, 10am-5pm Tues.-Sat., noon-5pm Sun., adults $6, seniors and military $5, students and children $4) is an unusual delight. Formerly called the National Ornamental Metal Museum, this complex is dedicated to preserving and displaying the craft. The permanent collection numbers more than 3,000 objects and ranges from contemporary American sculpture to works up to 500 years old. The museum hosts special exhibits several times a year, showcasing various aspects of metalwork.

blacksmithing demonstration at the Metal Museum

The museum itself is 40 years old, but it is housed on the grounds of a former Marine hospital that dates to 1798, so history is everywhere. Keep your eyes open—anything on these 3.5 acres may be a work of art, from the sculpture garden to the gates to signage.

There is also a working metalwork studio where you can take classes to try the craft for yourself, or just observe the pros, and the museum grounds on the bluff overlooking the Mississippi are an attraction in themselves. This is reputed to be the site where Spanish explorer Hernando de Soto and his men camped when they passed through the area in 1542.

Demonstrations may be available on weekend afternoons; call the museum to confirm. Sections of the museum and grounds may be difficult to navigate in a wheelchair, although staff is available to help. Call ahead as needed.

Directly across Metal Museum Drive is **Chickasaw Heritage Park** (sometimes referred to as DeSoto Park), which has two Native American ceremonial mounds. Unlike other burial mounds, which are sacred sites, you are allowed to walk to the top of these, where you'll find great views of the Mississippi River and the museum grounds. There's also a marker indicating that this is the place where Hernando de Soto may have first seen the Mississippi.

ARETHA FRANKLIN'S CHILDHOOD HOME

Fans of the Queen of Soul can drive by and pay respects at **Aretha Franklin's Childhood Home** (406 Lucy Ave.). Franklin was born in 1942 in the front bedroom of this small shotgun shack in South Memphis, which isn't renovated or open to the public. While there have been efforts to save it and turn it into a museum to honor her music and legacy, for now it remains as-is. If you drive by, remember this is private property in a residential

neighborhood: Aretha would want you to show some R-E-S-P-E-C-T.

C. H. NASH MUSEUM AT CHUCALISSA

A group of platform and ridge mounds along the Mississippi River is the main attraction at **Chucalissa Archaeological Site** (1987 Indian Village Dr., 901/785-3160, www.memphis.edu/chucalissa, 9am-5pm Tues.-Sat., 1pm-5pm Sun., adults $6, seniors and children 4-11 $4). The mounds were once part of a Choctaw Indian community that existed AD 1000-1550. The village was empty when Europeans arrived, and *chucalissa* means abandoned house.

The largest mound would have been where the chief and his family lived. The present-day museum, operated by the University of Memphis, consists of an exhibit about the Native Americans of the area and a self-guided tour around the mounds and courtyard area, where games and meetings would have been held. A 0.5-mile (0.8-mile) nature trail along the bluff overlooks the river. Call in advance to make a reservation for a group guided tour.

EAST MEMPHIS

East Memphis is home to old suburbs, gracious homes, and some excellent parks and other attractions.

THE DIXON GALLERY AND GARDENS

The Dixon Gallery and Gardens (4339 Park Ave., 901/761-5250, www.dixon.org, 10am-5pm Tues.-Sat., 10am-8pm third Thurs., 1pm-5pm Sun., adults $7, seniors and students $5, children 7-17 $3, children 6 and under free), a traditional art museum housed inside a stately Georgian-style

East Memphis

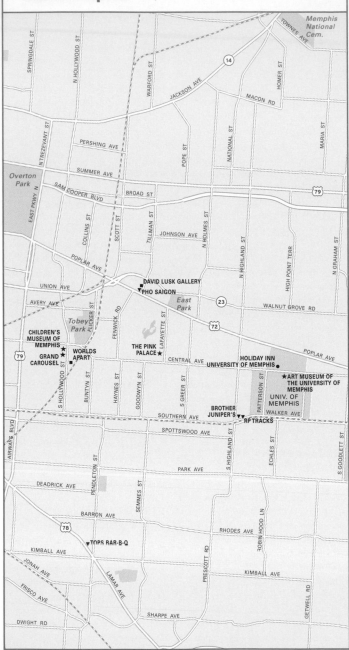

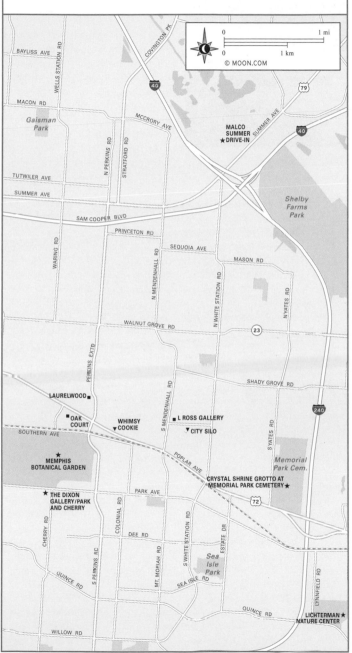

The Dixon Gallery and Gardens

home, has an impressive permanent collection of more than 2,000 paintings, many of them French impressionist and postimpressionist style, including works by Monet, Renoir, Degas, and Cézanne. It also mounts a half-dozen special exhibits each year; previous ones have showcased the art of Lester Julian Merriweather, Rodin, and Brian Russell.

The Dixon is an easy place to spend several hours, immersed first in art and then in walking the paths that explore the house's 17 acres (7 hectares) of beautifully tended gardens—a cutting garden, woodland garden, and formal gardens, among others. Signage inside the museum tells you exactly where the cut flowers in bouquets are growing in the garden, so you can find your favorites outside.

Admission to the Dixon is free on Saturday 10am-noon and pay what you wish on Tuesday. On-site restaurant **Park & Cherry** (lunch 11am-2pm Tues.-Sat., coffee 10am-4:30pm Tues.-Sat., 1pm-4.30pm Sun.) serves hot and cold sandwiches, salads, and espresso drinks.

MEMPHIS BOTANIC GARDEN

The 100-acre (40-hectare) **Memphis Botanic Garden** (750 Cherry Rd., 901/636-4100, www. memphisbotanicgarden.com, 9am-6pm daily summer, 9am-4:30pm daily winter, adults $10, seniors $8, children $5) is home to more than 140 different species of trees and more than two dozen specialty gardens, including the Sculpture Garden, Azalea Trail, and Iris Garden. Trails meander through the gardens, but for the greatest fun buy a handful of fish food and feed the fish and ducks that inhabit the pond at the Japanese Garden. The garden puts on a number of events, including blockbuster concerts, workshops, plant sales, wine tastings, and programs for children. **Fratelli's Café** (901/766-9900, 11am-2pm Mon.-Sat.) is a good option for lunch on-site.

CRYSTAL SHRINE GROTTO

Inside the mammoth Memorial Park Cemetery is one of Memphis's most offbeat sights: **The Crystal Shrine Grotto** (5668 Poplar Ave., 901/302-9980, www.memorialparkfuneraland-cemetery.com, 6am-10pm daily, free), described as the world's only man-made crystal cave. You experience this work of art by walking over a bridge and entering through a faux tree, after which you find yourself standing inside what seems like a geode, surrounded by biblical scenes documenting the life of Christ. The space is both kitschy and serene. The juxtaposition of the too-blue dyed water of the pond and the tinted concrete and colored lights and on the crystal is a lot to take in.

Even those who don't appreciate the cave's religious iconography may appreciate its craftsmanship. Made with five tons of crystals, the faux stone cavern is the work of artist Dionicio Rodríguez, who began the project in 1935. Rodríguez is known for faux bois, the sculpting of wood patterns from concrete. He died in 1995; in 1991 this site was added to the National Register of Historic Places.

Enter the cemetery from the Poplar Avenue side for the most direct route (north) to the grotto (note that the Poplar Avenue gate stays open until 10pm; Yates Road closes at 8pm). There are some signs inside the cemetery, and maps in the cemetery office. Be respectful of mourners who are at the cemetery, but don't feel uncomfortable about enjoying the grotto. Memphians consider a trip here a day at a park (the cool cave offers relief during hot summer days). R&B singer Isaac Hayes (1942-2008) is buried just across the path from the grotto.

PINK PALACE

A good destination for families, the **Pink Palace** (3050 Central Ave., 901/636-2362, www.memphismuseums.org, 9am-5pm Mon.-Thurs.,

9am-5pm and 6pm-9pm Fri., 9am-5pm Sat., noon-5pm Sun.) is a group of attractions rolled into one.

The **Pink Palace Museum** (adults $15, seniors $14, children 3-12 $10, children under 2 free, free after 1pm Tues.) is housed within the former mansion of Piggly Wiggly founder Clarence Saunders. Exhibits focus on the natural history of the mid-South region and the Memphis's development. You can also visit a replica of an early Piggly Wiggly store, the Country Store, and the Clyde Parke Miniature Circus. Don't miss the palace's refurbished grand staircase.

The Pink Palace is also home to the **Sharpe Planetarium,** which underwent a $1.5 million renovation in 2016. Starring attractions include the Autozone Dome, a 145-seat theater-in-the-round, and the **CTI 3D Giant Theater.** Ticket packages are available for all the Pink Palace attractions, as

The Crystal Shrine Grotto at Memorial Park Cemetery

well as the planetarium only (adults $8, seniors $7, children $6, with additional fees for 3-D films).

The annual **Enchanted Forest,** a holiday-themed village and Christmas destination for families, is open mid-November-December. It has an additional entry fee (adults $6, seniors and children under 12 $5).

LICHTERMAN NATURE CENTER

The **Lichterman Nature Center** (5992 Quince Rd., 901/636-2211, www.memphismuseums.org, 10am-3pm Tues.-Thurs., 10am-4pm Fri.-Sat., adults $9, seniors $8, children 3-12 $5, children 2 and under free, Tues. 1pm until close free to public) provides some 65 acres (26 hectares) for wandering in nature. Visitors enjoy native trees and flowers, including dogwood, lotus, and pine. Features include pleasant trails, picnic facilities, and a museum dedicated to the mid-South's ecosystem. Part of the Pink Palace collection of museums, this certified arboretum is a popular destination for families and school groups.

ART MUSEUM OF THE UNIVERSITY OF MEMPHIS

The **Art Museum of the University of Memphis** (142 CFA Building, 901/678-2224, www.memphis.edu/amum, 9am-5pm Mon.-Sat., free) houses excellent but small exhibits of ancient Egyptian and African art and artifacts, as well as a noteworthy print gallery. There are frequent special exhibitions. The museum is closed during university holidays and in between temporary exhibits. Parking is free after 4pm Friday and on weekends, otherwise it's $3 per hour or $15 per day in the parking garage.

DAVIES MANOR PLANTATION

Explore 32 acres (13 hectares) and see the oldest log home in Shelby County open to the public at **Davies Manor Plantation** (3570 Davieshire Dr., Bartlett, 901/386-0715, www.daviesmanorplantation.org, noon-4pm Tues.-Sat. Apr.-mid-Dec., adults $5, seniors $4, children and students $3, children 6 and under free, cash only) in suburban Bartlett, about a 30-minute drive northeast of the city. This historic plantation site includes a cotton patch, slave cabins, Civil War markers, and other artifacts left behind from a very different time in our nation's history. If you are traveling with kids, it is worth a stop. Special events include quilt shows.

TOURS
HISTORY TOURS

Heritage Tours of Memphis (901/527-3427, www.heritagetoursinmemphis.com, prices vary per tour) is the city's only tour company dedicated to presenting Memphis's African American history. Operated by Memphians Elaine Turner and Joan Nelson, Heritage Tours offers African American heritage and civil rights tours. The company can also arrange out-of-town tours to area attractions, such as the **Alex Haley Museum and Interpretive Center** (adults $40, students 4-17 $30) in Henning, Tennessee. Most local tours last about three hours.

The African American heritage tour includes stops at the W. C. Handy Home and Museum, Slave Haven Underground Railroad Museum, Beale Street Historic District, the National Civil Rights Museum/Lorraine Motel, St. Jude Hospital, Memphis Pyramid, and other historical monuments and parks.

The **Memphis Heritage Trail** (901/250-2700, www.memphisheritagetrail.com) was developed to honor the contributions of African Americans to the city's long history. Some sites can be visited and toured, and others have simple markers, but many stops are yet to be developed. The trail is distinct from the **U.S. Civil Rights Trail** (http://civilrightstrail.com), but there is some overlap. Memphis Heritage Trail maps are available online and at kiosks around town.

MUSIC TOURS

Music-themed tours are the specialty at **Backbeat Tours** (126 Beale St., 901/527-9415, www.backbeattours.com, from $20, tickets must be reserved in advance). You will travel on a reconditioned 1959 transit bus and be serenaded by live musicians. Tours include the Memphis Mojo Tour (adults $30, students $28, children 7-12 $15, children 6 and under free), which takes you to Memphis music landmarks like Sun Studio and the Stax Museum, and the Hound Dog Tour, which follows in Elvis Presley's Memphis footsteps. Backbeat can also take you to Graceland and offers two walking tours of Memphis (Mon.-Sat.

April-Nov., Sat. Feb. and March): the Memphis Ghost Tour (adult $20, children 7-12 $13, children 6 and under free), which explores the bloody and creepy side of the city's history, and a Memphis historical walking tour (adults $25, children 7-12 $15, children under 6 free).

RIVER TOURS

Memphis Riverboats cruises (901/527-2628, www.memphisriverboats.net, adults $20, seniors, college students, military, children 13-17 $17, children 3-12 $10, toddlers free) leave daily at 2:30pm from the Port of Memphis, located at the foot of Monroe Avenue on the riverfront. The afternoon tour lasts 90 minutes and takes you a few miles south of the city before turning around. Commentary relates some of the most famous tales of the river, but the biggest attraction of the tour is simply being on Old Man River. The views of the Memphis skyline from the water are impressive. Concessions are available on board. The company also offers two-hour dinner cruises at 7:30pm with a buffet meal, cash bar, and live music, starting at $45 per person. See the website for dates and times.

Nightlife

Memphis's vibrant, diverse personality is reflected in its entertainment scene. Blues, rap, R&B, and gospel are just some of the types of music you can hear on any given weekend. Alternative and indie rock find a receptive audience in Memphis, as do opera, Broadway productions, and the symphony. There's always a good excuse to go out.

Memphis may be the birthplace of the blues, but there's a lot more to the music scene than that. It's true that you can catch live blues at a Beale Street nightclub or in a city juke joint. But you can also find hard-edge rock, jazz, and acoustic music most nights of the week. The best resource for up-to-date entertainment listings is the free weekly **Memphis Flyer** (www.memphisflyer.com), which comes out on Wednesday morning and includes a detailed listing of club dates and concerts.

Big-name artists often perform at casinos in Tunica, which is just over the state line in Mississippi. Many of these shows are advertised in Memphis media outlets, or you can check out the upcoming events on the Tunica Convention and Visitors Bureau website (www.tunicatravel.com). Many neighborhood watering holes host local bands, often for ticket prices of less than $10. These spots often have good food and drinks, too, so there's no reason not to take a chance on an unknown band.

While the Johnny Cash Boyhood Home is just a short drive away in Little Rock, Arkansas, country music doesn't have much of a following in Memphis. Nashville or Tupelo are better sources for that beat. Instead, revel in the jazz, blues, and rock roots that make Memphis sing. There's a live show somewhere every night of the week, and a cold beer to go with it.

TOP EXPERIENCE

DOWNTOWN
LIVE MUSIC

If the **Center for Southern Folklore** (119 S. Main St., 901/525-3655, www.southernfolklore.com, 11am-6pm Mon.-Fri , ?pm-11pm Sat., 2pm-8pm Sun.) has concerts or activities planned during your stay, make plans to attend. This is one of the best places to hear authentic blues, with frequent live shows on Friday afternoon and in the Folklore Store most Friday and Saturday nights, starting around 8pm.

The Folklore Store also sells colorful and eclectic folk art, books, CDs, and traditional Southern food. A traditional sign stating "Be Nice or Leave" sets the tone as soon as you step inside (similar signs can be seen at bars all over town). The center is a nonprofit organization and well worth supporting. It has been documenting and preserving traditional Memphis and Delta blues music since the 1970s. The free self-guided tour of all things traditionally Southern leads you through Heritage Hall. This is also the location of concerts, lectures, and screenings of documentaries; the center offers group tours and educational programs and hosts the annual Memphis Music and Heritage Festival over Labor Day weekend.

Beale Street is ground zero for Memphis's blues music scene. While some people lament that Beale has become a sad tourist shell of its former self, it can still be a worthwhile place to spend your evening. Indeed, no other part of Memphis has as much music and entertainment encompassing such a small area. On a typical night, Beale Street is packed with a diverse crowd strolling from one bar to the next. Beer seems to run a close second to music as the street's prime attraction, with many bars selling directly onto the street through concession windows. The "Big Ass Beer" cups used by many establishments say it all.

Nearly all Beale Street bars have live music, but one of the most popular is **B. B. King's Blues Club** (143 Beale St., 901/524-5464, www.bbkings.com, 11am-midnight Mon.-Thurs., 11am-2am Fri.-Sat., 9am-midnight Sun., $3-5 cover on weekends, rarely on weekdays). Local acts and some nationally known performers take the stage. B. B. King's draws a mostly

B. B. King's Blues Club

bar. That serves Memphis barbecue instead of bangers and mash. And has beer-drinking pet goats on the premises. You have to see it to believe it. The vibe is St. Patrick's Day year-round, with live music and dueling pianos. Because it is on Beale Street, the music tends toward blues. Silky himself passed away in 2013, but his party plays on.

King's Palace Café (162 Beale St., 901/521-1851, 11am-10pm Sun.-Thurs., 11am-1am Fri.-Sat., www.kingspalace-cafe.com) specializes in live music, mostly jazz, with local blues and Cajun cuisine thrown in for good measure. Lots of wood paneling and red paint make the unpretentious bar and restaurant warm and welcoming.

Alfred's (197 Beale St., 901/525-3711, www.alfredsonbeale.com, 11am-3am Sun.-Thurs., 11am-5am Fri.-Sat., cover varies) has rock acts five nights a week. On Sunday evening, the 17-piece Memphis Jazz Orchestra takes the stage. The dance floor is one of the best on Beale Street.

tourist crowd, and it is a chain, but with the blues on full throttle, you probably won't care too much. Above B. B. King's, **Itta Bena** (http://ittaben-adining.com) offers fine dining with great views of the street scene below.

Also on Beale Street, **Blues City Café** (138 Beale St., 901/526-3637, www.bluescitycafe.com, 11am-3am Sun.-Thurs., 11am-5am Fri.-Sat., cover $3-5) books blues, plus other acts including doo-wop, zydeco, R&B, funk, and "high-impact rockabilly." The café-restaurant is one of the most popular on Beale Street, and its nightclub, **Rum Boogie Café** (182 Beale St., 901/528-0150, http://rumboogie.com, Sun.-Thurs 11am-1am, Fri.-Sat. 11am-2am, $3-4 cover charge in addition to food and drink tab), welcomes a variety of bands for lively performances of blues and R&B music seven nights a week. More than 200 guitars are on display (many of them feature the signature of a famous musician).

So **Silky O'Sullivan's** (183 Beale St., 901/522-9596, www.silkyosul-livans.com, 4 pm-midnight Mon., 11am-midnight Tues.-Thurs. and Sun., 11am-3am Fri.-Sat.) is kind of an Irish

BARS

The lobby bar at **The Peabody Hotel Memphis** (149 Union Ave., 901/529-4000, www.peabodymemphis.com, 10am-midnight Sun.-Thurs., 10am-2am Fri.-Sat., no cover) may be the best place in town to enjoy a relaxing drink, with comfortable seats, good service, and an unrivaled atmosphere.

In the South Main Arts District, **Earnestine and Hazel's** (531 S. Main St., 901/523-9754, www.carnestin-eandhazelsjukejoint.com, 5pm-3am Wed.-Sun.) is one of Memphis's most celebrated pit stops for a cold drink and a night out. Rumor is the joint is haunted, but folks come to this one-time brothel for one of the best juke-boxes in town, not the spirits. Take a seat upstairs and watch South Main Street below.

South Main Market is a collaborative space near downtown with vendors offering food, drinks, and retail goodies. The Civil Pour (409 S. Main St., 901/341-3838, http://the-southmainmarket.com/civil-pour, 8am-2pm and 4pm-close Tues.-Fri., 10am-close Sat., 10am-4pm Sun., $8-13, cards only, cash not accepted) offers the drinks portion of that equation. The bar is in an open corner of the food hall, and as a result doesn't have much of a vibe of its own, but it is one of the best places for a quality craft cocktail near downtown. Nonalcoholic juice beverages are served during daytime hours on weekdays.

The Blind Bear (119 S. Main St., 901/417-8435, http://blindbearmemphis.com, 3pm-3am Mon.-Fri., 11am-3am Sat.-Sun., $5-15) is part speakeasy, part pool hall, and part neighborhood hangout. Smoking is allowed here, so if that's not your jam, look for another watering hole. But if you don't mind, this is a great evening hang.

The **Green Beetle** (325 S. Main St., 901/527-7337, www.thegreenbeetle.com, 11am-11pm Sun.-Thurs., 11am-midnight Fri.-Sat. $10-15) has been quenching local thirsts since 1939. The location and vibe has changed, but the mission is the same. Today the grandson of the original owner serves a remarkable craft beer selection and great burgers. You can even come here for free poker classes.

If you like a velvet rope, a disco ball, and booties shaking, **Paula & Raiford's Disco** (14 S. Second St., 901/521-2494, 10pm-4am Fri.-Sat., $10-15 cover, cash only) is for you. Robert "Hollywood" Raiford opened his disco nearby in 1976 and ran it until 2007. In 2009 his daughter

Paula & Raiford's Disco

reopened the Memphis institution, adding her name, at the current location. Hollywood passed away in 2017, but Paula is keeping it going—with many family members working the door. Paula doesn't let anyone get away with anything: There are no drugs, no weapons, and no one gets in for free (seriously, staff shirts spell it out). Expect great people-watching and better music. The cover price increases after midnight.

MIDTOWN

LIVE MUSIC

The 1970s heyday of **Lafayette's Music Room** (2119 Madison Ave., 901/207-5097, www.lafayettes.com, 11am-10pm Mon, 11am-10:30pm Tues.-Wed., 11am-midnight Thurs., 11am-2am Fri.-Sat., 11am-midnight Sun., ticket prices vary) was brief, but memorable. It was shuttered for nearly four decades, its memory kept alive by old-timers telling tales of the acts they saw here, including KISS and Billy Joel. Since reopening in 2014, Lafayette's has hosted live music seven days a week, from jazz to rock to blues (of course). Its Overton Square location welcomes a steady stream of locals and tourists. The crowd is a little older than at some other midtown venues and the lineup may include more recognizable names.

"Minglewood" is referenced in blues music going back to 1928. Even the Grateful Dead name-checked it. **Minglewood Hall** (1555 Madison Ave., 901/312-6058, www.minglewoodhall.com, box office 11am-3pm Mon.-Fri. and 4pm show days, door times and prices vary by show) is a live music venue that honors that tradition. Yes, people still play the blues here, but all sorts of other genres as well, with a number of national names on the bill. Depending on the lineup, Minglewood Hall has more locals and fewer tourists in the audience than Beale Street.

In the same Minglewood complex, **B-SIDE** (1555 Madison Ave., 901/347-6813, 3pm-3am Mon.-Fri., 6pm-3am Sat.-Sun., $7-10 cover) is a relative newcomer to the live music scene. With a capacity of about 100 people, this is a nice, affordable venue for local music. The bar offers generous pours and a decent local craft beer selection.

Onix (1680 Madison Ave., 901/552-4609, http://onixrestaurant.com, 11am-10pm Mon.-Thurs., 11am-midnight Fri.-Sat.) is a midtown staple for live jazz. Walls are adorned with art from local artists. There's a full menu with trout, tilapia, and other solid American dishes, but the music is the draw.

The moniker **Bar DKDC** (964 S. Cooper, 901/272-0830, bardkdc.com, 5pm-2:30am Mon.-Sat., $6-13.75) is an acronym: Don't Know, Don't Care. It's a popular live music venue for locals who want to hear something other than blues. There's a definite hipster vibe, but you'll be welcomed even if you aren't wearing skinny jeans. It's

Minglewood Hall

BREWS IN BLUFF CITY

Memphis residents love their beer. There's never been a shortage of places to pop a cold one. Now the number of places that make beer in the city continues to increase. Check out a few of these local microbreweries.

- The **Memphis Made Brewing Co.** (768 S. Cooper St., 901/207-5343, http://memphismadebrewing.com, 4pm-10pm Thurs.-Fri., 1pm-10pm Sat., 1pm-7pm Sun.) has some serious beer cred. Head brewer/cofounder Drew Barton was former head brewer at French Broad Brewery in North Carolina. Cofounder Andy Ashby also helped launch the Cooper-Young Beerfest. The brewery puts out three year-round brews plus a handful of seasonals. Try them in the taproom. There's no food on the menu, but local food trucks often stop by, and Aldo's Pizza is next door.

- Take a tour of **High Cotton Brewing Co.** (598 Monroe Ave., 901/543-4444, http://highcottonbrewing.com, 4pm-9pm Tues.-Fri., noon-10pm Sat., noon-8pm Sun.) on Saturday at 3pm. The cost is $12 and includes a pint glass and samples. Or come by for a drink and live music in the taproom throughout the week.

- Tours and brews that have been given nods from national magazines like *Men's Journal* are available at **Wiseacre Brewing Co.** (2783 Broad Ave., http://wiseacrebrew.com, 4pm-10pm Mon.-Thurs., 1pm-10pm Fri.-Sat.). The brewery was founded by brothers Kellan and Davin Bartosch, after the name their grandmother used to call them. Tours with samples are offered Saturday at noon; reserve a ticket ($15) online in advance.

- **Crosstown Brewing Taproom** (1264 Concourse Ave., no phone, www.crosstownbeer.com, 4pm-8pm Mon.-Tues., 4pm-10pm Wed.-Thurs., noon-10pm Fri.-Sat., noon-8pm Sun.) offers quirky themed beers that reflect the identity of the Crosstown community. A rotating selection of food trucks and local restaurants that deliver supplement the taproom beers.

owned by Karen Carrier, who also helms restaurants **The Beauty Shop** and **Mollie Fontaine Lounge**.

The Hi-Tone (412 N. Cleveland, 901/490-0335, 5pm-3am daily, www.hitonememphis.com, ticket prices vary) is committed to bringing good live music to Memphis, with all kinds of acts, from soulful acoustic sets to high-energy rockers. The commitment pays off: it's one of the best places to see live music in town. The cover charge for local shows is a few bucks, but tickets for bigger-name acts can run $20 and more. The bar serves respectable burgers and finger foods, excellent martinis, and lots of beer.

BARS

If you want your tropical drinks in a themed glass, served with Polynesian meatballs, you've come to the right place at **Atomic Tiki** (1545 Overton Park Ave., 901/279-3935, www.atomic-tikimemphis.com, 5pm-midnight Tues.-Fri., $6-12). Happy hour (5pm-7pm) is particularly popular with the midtown locals.

Outdoor table tennis, sand volleyball, and an outdoor stage make Railgarten (2166 Central Ave., 901/504-4342, http://railgarten.com, 11am-close Tues.-Sun., $8.75-$17.25) an appealing tiki bar, particularly in the long, hot summers. The location used to be a railroad substation (hence the name), so there's a lot of space, which includes a kid-friendly play area. They get ice cream, you get cocktails, everyone gets happy.

Located in the hip Cooper-Young neighborhood, the friendly **Young Avenue Deli** (2119 Young Ave., 901/278-0034, www.youngavenuedeli.com, 11am-3am daily, kitchen closes at 2am, no cover) attracts a diverse crowd, from young hipsters to older neighborhood denizens. Choose from 36 different beers on tap and 100-plus in cans and bottles. It occasionally books live acts.

The **Blue Monkey** (2012 Madison Ave., 901/272-2583, www.bluemonkeymemphis.com, 11am-3am daily, no cover) is a midtown favorite for a night out. Grab a pizza or the signature hot wing rolls and a beer, shoot some pool, and rock out to the live band. There's a second location downtown (513 S. Front St., 901/527-6665).

If beer's your thing, check out the growler station at **Joe's Wines &**

Liquor (1681 Poplar Ave., 901/725-4252, www.joeswinesandliquor.com, 8am-11pm Mon.-Sat., 10am-5pm Sun.). Behind this iconic neon retro signage you'll find 20 beer taps and 10 wine taps.

Murphy's (1589 Madison Ave., 901/726-4193, www.murphysmemphis.com, 11am-3am Mon.-Sat., noon-3am Sun., no cover) is a neighborhood bar with a menu of pub grub and burgers, plus a nice patio. It attracts a late-night crowd of servers and bartenders from other joints who come by when they get off work.

There's more to do than just watch the game at **Rec Room** (3000 Broad Ave., 901/209-1137, www.recroom-memphis.com, 5pm-11pm Mon.-Thurs., 4pm-2am Fri., noon-2am Sat., noon-11pm Sun., no cover). In addition to the oversized TV screens, you can get your game on with foosball, Ping-Pong, vintage video games, and board games. Partying with a group? Rent a living room ($10/hour Mon.-Thurs., $25/hour Fri.-Sat.) equipped with a 20-foot projection screen to play video games together. Kids are

Bar DKDC

JUKE JOINTS

In Memphis, there are only two reasons to go to a juke joint full of blues: because you feel good or because you feel bad. Beale Street is a reliable source seven nights a week, and your visit to Memphis wouldn't be complete without checking out its scene. But if you want to sneak away from the tourist crowd and catch some home-grown talent, check out a real Memphis juke joint. Live music is typical on Friday and Saturday nights and sometimes Sunday, but it gets scarce during the week. Generally music starts late (11pm) and finishes early (3am). Don't be surprised if the person you've engaged in conversation sitting next to you gets called to the stage sometime during the evening and delivers a beautiful song.

Remember that it's in the nature of things for these clubs to come and go, and often they don't have telephones. Or websites. Or signage. The following listings were current as of this writing, but they are always subject to change. Asking a local is a great way to find the juke joint that will be jumping when you are in town.

- **Wild Bill's** (1580 Vollintine Ave., 901/409-0081): A legendary club in Memphis. The patriarch himself passed away in the summer of 2007, but what he established carries on. It's the quintessential juke joint: small and intimate, with an open kitchen dishing out chicken wings, and ice-cold beer served in 40-ounce bottles. It closed briefly in 2017 and came back in 2018. It's home to the Wild Bill Band.

- **CC's Blues Club** (1427 Thomas St., 901/526-5566): More upscale. More mirrors. But a great dance floor, and don't you dare come underdressed. Security guards patrol the parking lot.

- **1884 Lounge at Minglewood Hall** (1555 Madison Ave., 901/312-6058): This small room is inside a historic music venue mentioned in a 1928 song, "Minglewood Blues," that has been recorded by artist after artist, including the Grateful Dead.

- **Mr. Handy's Blues Hall** (174 Beale St., 901/528-0150): New Orleans has Preservation Hall. Memphis has Handy's Blues Hall. Everyone bad-raps Beale Street, but this tiny spot, connected to Rum Boogie Café, is the real deal. You'll feel like you are at the end of a country road in Mississippi.

- **Big S Grill** (1179 Dunnavant St., 901/775-9127): Since the 1960s, this unassuming white house has been a place where the music plays, the beer flows, and the barbecue cooks slowly.

welcome before 6pm if escorted by an adult; after 6pm, it's 21 and up.

The 2nd floor of the funky Crosstown Concourse is home to **Art Bar** (1350 Concourse Ave., 901/507-8030, 5pm-1am Tues.-Sat., $12-18), an offbeat space where the colorful drinks are paired with the art on the walls. Drinks are made with local ingredients when possible.

LGBTQ BARS

Perhaps because of its population of artists and musicians, perhaps because of its racial diversity, Memphis is generally an inclusive place. Several of the city's most popular gay and lesbian bars are in midtown.

Dru's Bar (1474 Madison Ave., 901/275-8082, http://drusbar.com, 1pm-midnight Sun.-Wed., 1pm-3am Thurs.-Sat., $5 cover after 9pm Fri.-Sat.) is a welcoming bar known for its weekly Drag Time and Beer Bust. There are also frequent happy hours, trivia and karaoke, darts, a patio, and a reliable jukebox. The beer is cold and the liquor is BYO. Like many Memphis gay and lesbian clubs, it doesn't get going until late, after other clubs have closed.

The Pumping Station (1382 Poplar Ave., 901/272-7600, www.thepumpingstationmemphis.com, 4pm-3am Mon.-Fri., 3pm-3am Sat.-Sun., no cover) is one of the city's favorite gay bars, with a full bar and craft beers on tap. The outdoor beer garden, the Backdoor Lounge, is the only place where you can smoke. It is housed in a building that once allowed a Jewish couple, evicted from another location, to open a liquor store, and is proud of its inclusive historical roots.

Housed in a Victorian home decorated in a hodgepodge of styles, **Mollie Fontaine Lounge** (679 Adams Ave., 901/524-1886, www.molliefontainelounge.com, 5pm-3am Wed.-Sat., $8-11) is intended to welcome a hodgepodge of guests. While not specifically an LGBTQ bar, its accept-everyone vibe has made it a de facto one. Order upscale cocktails, relax with live jazz music, and eat tasty Mediterranean- and Middle Eastern-inspired tapas

The food is upmarket and delicious, but people come for the bar and the crowd.

SOUTH MEMPHIS

You'll probably think you've found a real dive bar at **Dirty Crow Inn** (855 Kentucky St., 901/207-5111, 11am-3am Mon.-Sun., $5.50-$11.50). Once inside, you'll see it's nicer than the parking lot suggests. It's a must-visit. There's a jukebox inside and an outdoor deck with live music. The bartenders give great advice about what to do in the city and the wings, poutine, and chicken sandwiches can't be beat.

EAST MEMPHIS

Memphis isn't known for comedy clubs, but if you want that traditional stand-up experience, **Chuckles Comedy House** (1770 Dexter Springs Loop, Cordova, 901/421-5905, www.chucklescomedyhouse.com, 8pm Thurs.-Sun., ticket prices vary by show) is your best bet.

Arts and Culture

Perhaps more than any other city in Tennessee, Memphis has a thriving and innovative visual arts scene. Native son William Eggleston is considered the father of color photography as fine art. Photojournalist Ernest Withers, who documented the civil rights movement, and fashion photographer Jack Robinson Jr. also have Memphis connections. From 1936 until its closure in 2020, the **Memphis College of Art** (MCA) contributed to that tradition, with faculty, students, and alumni living and working

in Bluff City. Even without MCA, artists and art educators are continuing to make Memphis a city where the arts are important. Affordable real estate—increasingly difficult to find in Nashville and Chattanooga—still exists in Memphis, meaning studios and gallery spaces dot the city. Performing arts, including dance and theater, also thrive in Memphis. **ArtsMemphis** (901/578-2787, www.artsmemphis. org) provides funding for more than 80 local arts groups. It's a reliable source of information about upcoming events.

DOWNTOWN
GALLERIES

With more than 1.8 million photographic images, the **Withers Collection Museum and Gallery** (333 Beale St., 901/523-2344, www.thewitherscollection.com, noon-10pm Tues.-Thurs., noon-11pm Fri.-Sat., 2pm-9pm Sun., $10 adults, $7 students and seniors) is one of the world's leading archives of images about the U.S. civil rights movement. Memphis native Ernest Withers (1922-2007) was a freelance photojournalist who documented the fight for equality. You can look at the historical images in changing themed exhibitions and also purchase prints for sale at this site on the Memphis Heritage Trail.

Historical photographs of Memphis and the Mississippi Delta's past—including fashion and celebrities of the 1960s and 1970s—are on display at **Robinson Gallery** (400 S. Front St., 901/576-0708, http://robinsongallery.com 11am-5pm Mon.-Fri.), primarily the work of former *Vogue* photographer Jack Robinson Jr. While Robinson lived and worked in New York at the apex of his career, he was a native of Meridian, Mississippi, and brought his understanding of the region to his art.

Marshall Arts (639 Marshall Ave., 901/406-6978, www.marshallarts-memphis.org) comprises 15 studios housed in a former auto body shop. **Sue Layman Designs** (125 East G. E. Patterson, Ste. 103, 901/409-7870, http://suelaymandesigns.com) features bright abstract and whimsical works in a showroom in the South Main Arts District. Both are open by appointment only, but it's worth a phone call to see contemporary work.

The **South Main Arts District** (www.gosouthmain.com) near downtown is home to a number of small, independently owned arts businesses and is a good place to learn about the city's rich African American history as well as contemporary art. One of its gems, **Art Village Gallery** (410 S. Main St., 901/521-0782, www.artvillagegallery.com, 11am-5pm Tues.-Sat.), has been a mainstay of the neighborhood since 1991. Owners Ephraim and Sheila Urévbu have a mission to showcase diversity through art. In addition to the art gallery, the space houses a small retail shop with candles and other gift items. **Trolley Night,** the last Friday of the month, is *the* night to gallery hop and shop on South Main. The event starts at 6pm and runs till the musicians go home.

PERFORMANCE

Major performance venues include the **Cannon Center for the Performing Arts** (255 N. Main St., 901/576-1200, www.thecannoncenter.com, box office noon-5pm Mon.-Fri. and two hours before showtime) and the magnificent **Orpheum Theatre** (203 S. Main St., 901/525-3000, www.orpheum-memphis.com, box office 9am-5pm Mon.-Fri.). The latter, built in 1890 as an opera house, regularly books major artists and Broadway performances.

MIDTOWN
GALLERIES

Changing exhibitions by local contemporary artists are part of the mission of **Crosstown Arts** (1350 Concourse Ave., No. 280, 901/507-8030, www.crosstownarts.org, 10am-8pm Tues.-Fri., 10am-6pm Sat., noon-6pm Sun.), which is located in the mammoth Crosstown Concourse. Check the calendar for specific events and exhibitions, or just head over before or after a meal, knowing you'll find something interesting no matter when you show up. Crosstown Arts also hosts live music, dance, and lectures. The **Broad Avenue Arts District** (www.broadavearts.com) in midtown is another good place to find galleries, studios, and arts-related events. Many midtown galleries are open late for strolls the first Friday of every month.

Yes, you can buy objects made by local artists at **Five in One Social Club** (2535 Broad Ave., 901/308-2104, www.fiveinone.org, 11am-6pm Sun.-Wed., 11am-8pm Thurs.-Sat.), and you should. But you can also get crafty yourself, thanks to an ever-changing list of workshops and classes. Many are just a few hours long, so you don't need to be a local to learn how to make stained glass or master screen printing. On the same street, **T. Clifton Art Galleries** (2571 Broad Ave., 901/323-2787, www.tcliftonart.com, 10am-5pm Tues.-Sat.) focuses on contemporary art and art glass.

Flicker Street Arts District is worth exploring if you're into

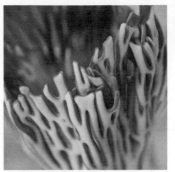

art at T. Clifton Art Galleries

architecture, fashion, gardening, or history. The **Flicker Street Art Studio** (74 Flicker St., 901/767-2999, http://flickerstreetstudio.com) hosts art classes for kids and adults. The **Urban Earth Garden Center** (80 Flicker St., 901/323-0031, http://urbanearthmemphis.com, 10am-5pm Tues.-Fri., 9am-5pm Sat., 1pm-4pm Sun.) is a retail shop and teaching space. The **Memphis Fashion Design Network** (www.memphisfashiondesignnetwork.com) is housed in the neighboring Flicker Street Quonset huts, which are in the process of being added to the National Register of Historic Places.

David Lusk Gallery (97 Tillman St., 901/767-3800, http://davidluskgallery.com, 10am-5:30pm Tues.-Fri., 11am-4pm Sat.), which has a second location in Nashville, likes to say it represents "thinkers" from across the country. Indeed, the artwork you'll find here, near Flicker Street, is likely to be thought-provoking, such as that of photography icon (and Memphis native) William Eggleston and Nashville airbrush artist Brandon Donohue.

In the Cooper-Young neighborhood, you'll find **Jay Etkin Gallery** (942 S. Cooper St., 901/550-0064,

Broad Avenue Arts District

www.jayetkingallery.com, 11am-5pm Tues.-Sat.), which focuses on contemporary and ethnographic works of art, as well as vintage African tribal art. The minimalist look and feel of the gallery space often contrasts the vibrant works on display.

Overton Park Gallery (1581 Overton Park Ave., 2nd floor, 901/484-6154, www.overtonparkgallery.com, 11am-6pm Tues.-Sat.) focuses on the works of contemporary artists from the mid-South, including painters and photographers.

The nonprofit **Caritas Village** (2509 Harvard Ave., 901/327-5246, www.caritasvillage.org, 9am-8pm Mon.-Sat.) is a community space as well as an art space, where locals can come to create. Caritas hosts several exhibitions annually, as well as literary events and theater works.

PERFORMANCE

For theater, check out dynamic Memphis institution **Playhouse on the Square** (66 S. Cooper St., 901/726-4656, www.playhouseonthesquare.org, box office 10am-5pm Tues.-Sat., 1pm-5pm Sun.), which is home to several of the city's acting companies and stages 15-20 different performances every year. It also offers theater classes, school performances, and pay-what-you-can shows.

TheatreWorks (2085 Monroe Ave., 901/274-7139, www.theatreworksmemphis.org) and **Evergreen Theatre** (1705 Poplar Ave., 901/274-7139) encourage nontraditional work by resident companies that include Our Own Voice Theatre Troupe, Bluff City Tri-Art Theatre Company, Cazateatro, Emerald Theatre Company, FreakEngine, and Inner City South.

Ballet Memphis (901/737-7322, www.balletmemphis.org) performs classical dance at the Playhouse on the Square, the Orpheum, and other venues throughout the city. The **New Ballet Ensemble** (901/726-9225, www.newballet.org) puts on performances around the city.

EAST MEMPHIS
GALLERIES

While many Memphis galleries are focused on newcomers, **L Ross Gallery** (5040 Sanderlin Ave., Ste. 104, 901/767-2200, lrossgallery.com, 10am-5pm Tues.-Fri., 11am-3pm Sat.) specializes in established artists who focus on contemporary expressionism.

Located inside the Memphis Jewish Community Center, **Shainberg Art Gallery** (6560 Poplar Ave., 901/259-9230, 8am-9:30pm Mon.-Thurs., 8am-5:30pm Sun.) hosts exhibitions that change monthly. Expect work of Tennessee artists and craftspeople. Some exhibitions, but not all, have a Jewish theme.

Contemporary **Gallery Ten Ninety One** (7151 Cherry Farms Rd., Cordova, 901/458-2521, 9am-4pm Mon.-Fri.) is located inside the WKNO Digital Media Center, home to the local PBS affiliate.

PERFORMANCE

The **Memphis Symphony Orchestra** (610 Goodman Rd., 901/537-2525, www.memphissymphony.org, box office 9am-5pm Mon.-Fri.) performs a varied calendar of works year-round in its home at the **Cannon Center for the Performing Arts** (2155 N. Main St.). The symphony was founded in 1952 and today has more than 850 musicians, staff, and volunteers. The box office is in Newport Hall on the University of Memphis campus.

Opera Memphis (Clark Opera

Memphis Center, 6745 Wolf River Blvd., 901/202-4533, www.operamemphis.org) performs traditional opera at a variety of venues around town, including the historic Playhouse on the Square and the Germantown Performing Arts Centre. Throughout September the company performs "pop-up" operas at different locations around the city.

Theatre Memphis (630 Perkins Ext., 901/682-8323, www.theatrememphis.org, box office 10am-5pm Tues.-Fri., plus 6pm-curtain on performance weekdays, noon-curtain Sat. Sun.) is a community theater company that has been in existence since the 1920s. It stages about 12 shows annually at its theater in midtown.

SOUTH MEMPHIS
GALLERIES

Referred to as "the collective," **CLTV at the CPLX** (2234 Lamar Ave.,

615/482-2777, www.thecltv.org, noon-8pm Wed.-Sun.) is a collaborative art space in Orange Mound with a focus on the work of black artists who are Memphis natives. In addition to the exhibits, the CPLX hosts occasional retail pop-ups and sells pieces at its Corner Store retail space (literally a corner of the gallery). Next door is **The Orange Mound Art Gallery** (2232 Lamar Ave., 901/231-4095, 2pm-6pm Tues.-Sat., 3pm-6pm Sun.), called OMG for short, which is also focused on African American artists, although not necessarily local or contemporary works. Both spaces are tucked into an unassuming strip mall behind a fast-food joint. Signage is not noticeable from the street, so you need to turn into the mall parking lot to find them.

Housed in a 1910 firehouse, the **Memphis Black Arts Alliance** (985 S. Bellevue Blvd., 901/948-9522, http://mbaafirehouse.org, 10am-2pm

CLTV at the CPLX

Mon.-Fri.) has been a place for African American visual and performing artists to share their works since 1982. Browse the small gallery space and scan the theater calendar for scheduled performances.

CINEMA

For most of us, the drive-in movie is a thing gone by, something our parents or grandparents talk about fondly. But in Memphis, more than 2,000 cars can park at **Malco Summer Drive-In** (5310 Summer Ave., 901/767-4320, www.malco.com, $7.50 for a double feature, kids under 10 free) to watch a movie on a big screen, enjoying sound coming loud and clear through the car speakers. Named for the street, and not the season, the drive-in has four screens and your choice of first-run flicks. Lines get long on summer nights, so plan to arrive early to get a prime spot. The concession stand is affordable, but you are welcome to bring food in if you prefer. Don't forget to shut off your headlights before the movie starts!

There are a number of other large-screen theaters, including the **Malco Paradiso Cinema** (584 S. Mendenhall Rd., 901/682-1754) and **Malco Studio on the Square** (2105 Court Ave., 901/725-7151) in midtown. The magnificent 1890 **Orpheum Theatre** (203 S. Main St., 901/525-3000, www.orpheum-memphis.com) occasionally shows art films and second-run movies. For $8 for adults and $6 for kids, it's a good deal in a great space.

FESTIVALS AND EVENTS

With music fests, cooking competitions, and block parties taking place year-round, there's never a dull time of year to visit Memphis. May is an all-out citywide party. Memphis does enjoy a beer or a cocktail, so you'll likely see alcohol served, even at family-friendly events. Added bonus: many of events are free or have low admission costs.

SPRING

In early May, the Memphis-based Blues Foundation hosts the annual **Blues Music Awards** (www.blues.org), the Grammys of the blues world. Per the foundation, a nominee announcement, as well as ticket information for the event, is released each year in mid-December on its website.

Memphis in May (www.memphisinmay.org), the city's largest annual event, is really many major festivals rolled into one. The **Beale Street Music Festival,** which takes place at Tom Lee Park on the river, kicks things off with a celebration of Memphis music. Expect a lot of wow-worthy performers, plus many more up-and-coming talents. The festival has grown over the years, and it is now a three-day event with four stages of music going simultaneously. In addition to music, the festival offers excellent people-watching, lots of barbecue, cold beer, and festivity. You can buy daily tickets or a three-day pass for the whole weekend. The **Great American River Run,** a half marathon and 5K race (www.memphisinmay.org/events/great-american-river-run), takes place then, too.

In mid-May, attention turns to the **World Championship Barbecue Cooking Contest,** a four-day celebration of pork, pigs, and barbecue that takes place in Tom Lee Park. In addition to the barbecue judging, there is entertainment, hog-calling contests, and other piggy antics. If you're not part of a competing team (or friends with one), you can buy barbecue from vendors who set up in the park.

The **Memphis International Festival** pays tribute to a different country each year with one week of exhibits and presentations about its music, food, culture, and history.

The month wraps with **901Fest**, a closing party with music, fireworks and plenty of locally made food and drinks. Book your hotel rooms early for Memphis in May; many hotels, particularly those in downtown, sell out.

Forty-six-foot-long (14-meter-long) boats with dragon heads and tails race at Mud Island River Park each May during the **Duncan-Williams St. Jude Dragon Boat Races** (www.st.jude. org/dragonboat). Proceeds benefit the St. Jude's Research Hospital.

David Acey and his wife, Yvonne, have been leaders in the Memphis civil rights movement for more than 50 years. In 1986 they started the **Africa in April Festival** (Robert R. Church Park, 901/947-2133, http://africain-april.org, $5 admission), three days of food, arts and crafts, and fashion to promote cultural awareness in Memphis. Each year features a different theme, often honoring a different African country. African dignitaries, such as the king and queen of Togo, have come to Memphis for this event.

While barbecue gets all the attention, hot wings are just as essential to Memphis cuisine. Nowhere is this clearer than the **Southern Hot Wing Festival** (www.southernhotwing-festival.com), held each April at the University of Memphis. More than 70 teams compete in the blind judging competition.

Each March, **Memphis Black Restaurant Week** (www.blackres-taurantweek.com) promotes African American-owned restaurants with special menus and promotional deals. Participating restaurants have included The Four Way and Sage.

SUMMER

Don't let the name fool you: **Carnival Memphis** (901-458-2500, www.carni-valmemphis.org) is a Mardi Gras-style celebration, not a fairgrounds-esque event. It features a parade, fireworks, a ball, and more. This festival, once called Cotton Carnival, was segregated for decades but since the mid-1980s has been racially integrated. This celebration raises funds for local children's charities. Like carnivals elsewhere in the South, Carnival Memphis consists of several events, including the Crown & Sceptre Ball, Princess Ball, and a luncheon for businesses. Carnival members (who pledge $75-2,500 in fees) get discounted tickets or tickets included in their membership, depending on their contribution. Public ticket prices are released annually on the website.

The annual candlelight vigil at Graceland on August 15, the anniversary of Elvis's death, has grown into a whole week of Elvis-centric activities throughout Memphis. More than 30,000 people visit Graceland during **Elvis Week** (http://graceland.com/elvis-week), and during the vigil his most adoring fans walk solemnly up the Graceland drive to pay their respects at his grave. Special concerts, tribute shows, and movies are shown during the week as the city celebrates its most famous son even more than usual.

FALL

Organized by the Center for Southern Folklore, the **Memphis Music and Heritage Festival** (901/525-3655, www.southernfolklore.com), held over Labor Day weekend, sticks close to the roots of Memphis music. Performers include gospel singers, bona fide bluesmen and -women, rockabilly superstars, and much more. Performances take place in the center's shop and concert hall (119 S. Main St.), making them more intimate than those at other blockbuster music festivals.

End-of-summer fairs are a tradition for Southern communities. The 10-day **Mid-South Fair** (662/280-9120, www.midsouthfair.org) in September is a bonanza of attractions: livestock shows, rodeos, agricultural judging, concerts, beauty pageants, exhibitions, carnival rides, funnel cakes, and cotton candy. The fair is held at **Landers Center** (4560 Venture Dr. Southaven) in northern Mississippi, about 30 miles (48 km) south of Memphis.

In mid-September, the Cooper-Young neighborhood throws its annual one-day jamboree at the **Cooper-Young Festival** (www.cooperyoungfestival.com). This street carnival features an arts and crafts fair, live music, and food vendors.

The annual **Southern Heritage Classic** (www.southernheritageclassic.com) is one of the South's big football games. But the match of two historically black college rivals, Jackson State University and Tennessee State University, is more than just a game—it is a serious citywide festival that lasts three days in September.

For decades **Gonerfest** (www.goner-records.com/gonerfest/), sponsored by the Goner Records label, has welcomed up-and-coming rock-and-roll, garage, and punk bands from across the globe to Memphis, where they drink beer, eat barbecue, and play loud music. Expect an international crowd and an all-night party.

WINTER

The colder weather welcomes a number of sporting events, including the **St. Jude Marathon and Half Marathon** (800/565-5112, www.stjudemarathon.org) in December, which is a qualifying race for the Boston Marathon. The **AutoZone Liberty Bowl** (www.libertybowl.org, 901/795-7700) welcomes two major college football teams to town in late December.

Taking place over the weekend closest to Elvis Presley's January 8 birthday, the **Elvis Birthday Celebration** (www.elvis.com) draws Elvis fans with special performances, dance parties, and a ceremony at Graceland proclaiming Elvis Presley Day.

Shopping

Memphis doesn't have a reputation as a world-class shopping center. However, a population teeming with creatives means its streets are chock-full of places to find one-of-a-kind goods, particularly in midtown's **Broad Avenue Arts District** and downtown in the **South Main Arts District.** Memphis is a city where the men's clothing shopping is as interesting—or more so—than that for women's clothing. If you want to go home dressing like the King, Memphis can make that happen.

DOWNTOWN

Any of the half-dozen shops along Beale Street sell souvenirs of the city. **Memphis Music** (149 Beale St., 901/526-5047, www.memphismusic-store.com, 10am-midnight Mon.-Sat., 10am-10pm Sun.) has a good selection of CDs and DVDs for music fans. For a unique gift or something practical for yourself, **A. Schwab** (163 Beale St., 901/523-9782, www.a-schwab.com, noon-5pm Mon.-Wed., noon-7pm Thurs., 10am-9pm Fri.-Sat., noon-6pm Sun., later summer hours) is your best choice and is lots of fun to boot.

Open since 1946, **Lansky Bros.** is known as the "Clothier to the King," as it dressed Elvis Presley and lots of other musicians. Its fashions are neither dated nor stodgy. It has two downtown locations, one in the Peabody Hotel (149 Union Ave., 901/529-9070, www.lanskybros.com, 9am-6pm Sun.-Wed., 9am-9pm Thurs.-Sat.) and the other in the Hard Rock Café (126 Beale St., 901/425-3960, 11am-7pm Sun.-Wed., 11am-9pm Thurs.-Sat.).

historic photo from Lansky Bros., the "Clothier to the King"

Bright **South Main Book Juggler** (548 S. Main St., 901/249-5370, www.southmainbookjuggler.com, 10am-6pm Tues.-Sat., 10am-3pm Sun.) stocks new and used books, with an emphasis on local interest. Your dog is welcome to tag along while you browse.

Perhaps you think it odd that you could get a cup of coffee, a haircut, and your next piece of art under one roof, but at **Stock and Belle** (387 S. Main St., 901/734-2911, http://salon387memphis.com, 10am-7pm Mon.-Fri., 10am-5pm Sat.) it all works. This Instagram-worthy shop in the South Main Arts District stocks letterpress prints, accessories, and more.

Inside Primas Bakery and Boutique is **Shop Mucho** (523 South Main St., 901/352-4193, www.primasbakeryandboutique.com, 6am-6pm Tues.-Fri., 11am-6pm Sat., 10am-3pm Sun., $2-36), a quirky art, clothing, and gift shop with a focus on Latin American-made goods.

MIDTOWN

Goner Records (2152 Young Ave., 901/722-0095, noon-7pm Mon.-Fri., noon-7pm Sat., 1pm-5pm Sun., www.goner-records.com) is not just a record store, and not just a record label—it's a Memphis landmark and a neighborhood hangout. The label hosts the annual Gonerfest music festival every fall. One of the city's best record stores, **Shangri-La Records** (1916 Madison Ave., 901/274-1916, www.shangri.com, noon-7pm Mon.-Fri., 11am-6pm Sat., 1pm-5pm Sun.) has an indie vibe, specializing in Memphis music.

Head out to Central Avenue between Cooper and East Parkway for the greatest concentration of antiques stores. **Flashback** (2304 Central Ave., 901/272-2304, www.

Goner Records

flashbackmemphis.com, 10:30am-5:30pm Mon.-Sat., 1pm-5pm Sun.) sells both vintage furniture and clothes, including a whole lot of Levi's jeans. **Palladio Home and Garden** (741 S. Cox St., 901/276-3806, http://palladiomemphis.com, 10am-5pm Mon.-Sat.) has lots of locations in Memphis, divided into categories like home décor, antiques, and garden supplies, and includes studio space for artists and a cafe. Most of the locations are in midtown and are close to one another. One of those locations, **Palladio Antiques and Arts** (2169 Central Ave., 901/276-3808, http://palladiomemphis.com, 10am-5pm Mon.-Sat.), works with more than 75 dealers to promote a diverse cross-section of styles.

The Cooper-Young neighborhood is mostly about restaurants, bars, and houses, but the **Cooper-Young Gallery + Gift Shop** (889 S. Cooper St., 901/729-6305, www.cooperyoung. gallery, 10am-6pm Tues.-Sat., noon-5pm Sun.) is working on starting a retail revolution. Find locally designed fabrics, one-of-kind of art, books, gifts, and charming conversation with owners who love their craft and their community.

Also in Cooper-Young, **Burke's Book Store** (936 S. Cooper St., 901/278-7484, www.burkesbooks. com, 10am-6pm Mon.-Wed., 10am-9pm Thurs.-Sat., 11am-6pm Sun.) has more than a century of history in Memphis, with many owners and almost as many locations. Author Corey Mesler and his wife, Cheryl, now own the shop and will help you find what you need. Browse new, used, and rare books to your heart's content.

Perhaps the linchpin of the Broad Avenue Arts District, **City and State** (2625 Broad Ave., 901/249-2406, www. cityandstate.us, 7am-6pm Mon.-Fri., 8am-6pm Sat., 8am-2pm Sun.) sells charming Memphis-themed T-shirts, well-made leather goods, books, jewelry, and, in an adjacent space, coffee.

Timeless style is the organizing principle at **Fox + Cat Vintage** (2153 Central Ave., 901/409-6117, www.foxandcatvintage.com, 11am-6pm Tues.-Sat., 2pm-6pm Sun.), a meticulous boutique chock-full of clothing, shoes, handbags, and jewelry of past eras.

Across the street from the Crosstown Concourse, **Proud Mary** (433 N. Cleveland St., 901/249-2532, 11am-6pm Tues.-Sun.) stocks vintage and handmade jewelry, clothing, and art.

If listening to Elvis or the blues in Memphis has you motivated to play music of your own, **Xanadu Music & Books** (2200 Central Ave., 901/274-9885, 11am-6pm Mon.-Thurs., 11am-7pm Fri.-Sat.) is the place to find a used instrument and quirky art made from old instruments and other objects, as well as new and used books.

Find new and used sci-fi and fantasy books at **Two Rivers Bookstore** (2172 Young Ave., 901/630-8088, www.tworiversbookstore.com, 11am-7pm Mon.-Fri., noon-5pm Sat.-Sun.).

Midtown's **Oak Court** (4465 Poplar Ave., 901/681-0642, http://oakcourtmall.com, 10am-9pm Mon.-Sat., noon-6pm Sun.) has department stores, including Macy's and Dillard's, as well as an occasional food truck parking lot event that brings in some offbeat eats.

EAST MEMPHIS

Indie bookstore **Novel** (387 Perkins Ext., 901/922-5526, www.novelmemphis.com, 9am-9pm Mon.-Sat., 10am-5pm Sun.) offers new releases, events, and other things for book lovers. **Libro** (901/800-2656, 9am-8pm Mon.-Sat., 11am-2pm Sun.), its lovely on-site restaurant, is more than a standard café.

Laurelwood (422 S. Grove Park Rd., 901/682-8436, www.laurelwoodmemphis.com, individual store hours vary) is an outdoor mall with a cross-section of local and chain shops, including a bookstore, yoga studio, bake shop, and children's shops.

Located in Germantown, the east side's town suburb, **Wolfchase Galleria** (2760 N. Germantown Pkwy., 901/372-9409, www.simon.com/mall/wolfchase-galleria, 10am-9pm Mon.-Sat., noon-6pm Sun.) is the Bluff City's most popular, if standard, indoor shopping mall. There's a movie theater and many restaurants. The only **IKEA** (7900 IKEA Way, 888/888-4532, www.ikea.com, 11am-8pm Sun.-Thurs., 10am-9pm Fri.-Sat.) store in Tennessee is across I-40 from Wolfchase.

Discounted furniture, home décor, and other random finds can be yours if you're willing to sift through the displays at **Worlds Apart** (322-324 S. Hollywood St., 901/529-0844, 9am-5pm Mon.-Fri., 10am-4pm Sat.). Near the Children's Museum of Memphis, this outlet has many great finds stacked upon other great finds. Be prepared to load it up and take it with you if you love it.

If bargain-hunting is your thing, you may find your next treasure at the Junior League of Memphis's **Repeat Boutique Thrift Store** (3586 Summer Ave., 901/327-4777, www.jlmemphis.org/repeat-boutique, 10am-5pm Tues.-Sat.).

Sports and Recreation

With a professional basketball team, an excellent downtown baseball stadium, and lots of city parks (including many with a river view), Memphis is a great city in which to both watch sports and get active yourself.

PARKS
DOWNTOWN

Named for the legendary blues composer W. C. Handy, **Handy Park** (200 Beale St.), on Beale Street between 3rd Street and Rufus Thomas Boulevard, seems a tad out of place among Beale's nightclubs and restaurants. But the park is a site of historical importance, if only because of the statue of its namesake that guards its gates. The park hosts occasional outdoor concerts and festivals, and at other times you will find places to sit and a handful of vendors.

Across the street from the Metal Museum, on the banks of the Mississippi River, is **Chickasaw Heritage Park** (Metal Museum Drive, 901/576-4200, dawn-dusk daily). This is where Hernando de Soto and his crew are said to have met Chief Chisca of the Chickasaw Indians and first crossed the river in 1541, although some historians say that is more legend than fact. You can also see two Native American mounds built between 400-700 AD and 1000-1500 AD. You are permitted to climb these mounds (and sled in the winter, when there is snow). It's worth a visit for history fans. The park's walking trails and great views of river make it a worthy addition to a visit to the Metal Museum across the street. To get there, take exit 12C off of

I-55 North. It is about a five-minute drive from downtown.

The mile-long **Big River Crossing** (www.bigrivercrossing.com, 6am-10pm daily, free) is the country's longest active pedestrian bridge (good for bikes and trains, too—just not cars!). The bridge, which opened in 2016, is illuminated with LED lights that dance every hour on the hour. It connects to a 10-mile corridor that is part of the **Big River Trail System** (www.bigrivertrail.com), attracting cyclists, runners, walkers, and others to pop over to Arkansas for the day. This is one of the best options for seeing river views. Heavy rains can temporarily flood some of the trails on the Arkansas side. To get to the base of the bridge from Memphis, head to Channel 3 Drive and Virginia Avenue West. There is street parking and some lot parking in nearby **Martyrs Park.**

UPTOWN

Tom Lee Park (Riverside Dr.), a long, narrow 30-acre (12-hectare) grassy park that overlooks the Mississippi, is a popular venue for summertime festivals and events, including Memphis in May's World Championship Barbecue Cooking Contest. It is also used year-round for walking and jogging and by people who simply want to look out at the giant river. The park is named for Tom Lee, an African American man who saved the lives of 32 people when the steamboat they were on sank in the river in 1925. Lee, who pulled people out of the river and into his boat, *Zev,* could not even swim. An outmoded monument erected at the park in 1954 calls Lee "a very worthy

Chickasaw Heritage Park

negro." A $70 million renovation is in the works to expand the greenway near Tom Lee and better leverage this riverside park's remarkable location. The Memphis Brooks Museum of Art will be part of this connected greenway when it moves downtown in 2024.

Located on the northern side of downtown Memphis, **Court Square** (62 N. Main St.), three blocks from the waterfront along Court Avenue, is a pleasant city park surrounded by historical buildings. Court Square is one of four parks that were included when the city was planned in 1819. There are benches and trees, and it is a wireless Internet hot spot.

Memphis Park (N. Front St.), on Front Street between Court and Jefferson Streets, commemorates Civil War soldiers who died in the Battle of Memphis, as well as soldiers who died in World War I. In 2018 the city sold several parks, including this one, to a Memphis nonprofit so that it could legally have a statue of Confederate president Jefferson Davis removed from

the park, an action that remains controversial to some. The statue removal came five years after the park was renamed: It was called Confederate Park until 2013. This is where many residents gathered to watch the Battle of Memphis in 1862, and it remains a good place from which to view the river below.

MIDTOWN

Located in midtown Memphis, **Overton Park** (1914 Poplar Ave., www.overtonpark.org) is one of the best all-around parks the city has to offer. This 342-acre (138-hectare) park has a nine-hole golf course, nature trails through the woods, bike trails, an outdoor amphitheater now called the Levitt Shell, and lots of green, open spaces. The park shares space with the Memphis Zoo and the Memphis Brooks Museum of Art, making the area a popular destination for city residents and visitors. Patience may be required when looking for a parking spot during an event at Overton.

Overton Park

The Madison Avenue trolley passes **Health Sciences Park** (799 Madison Ave.), along Madison Avenue between North Manassas and North Dunlap Streets. This ample city park was formerly named Forrest Park after the controversial Nathan Bedford Forrest. Forrest, a slave trader, Confederate general, and the first grand wizard of the Ku Klux Klan, has an uncomfortable position of prominence in the whole of western Tennessee. In 2013 the City of Memphis renamed the park and in 2018 it sold several parks, including this one, to a nonprofit so that it could legally have the statue of Forrest removed. Given the name change and the controversy, many locals just refer to this as "the park near the UT med school."

SOUTH MEMPHIS
Southwest of the city center, about a 15-minute drive from the airport, is **T. O. Fuller State Park** (1500 Mitchell Rd., 901/543-7581, http://tnstateparks.com, visitors center 8am-sunset fall and winter, 8am-7pm spring and summer), the first state park east of the Mississippi River open to African Americans, and the second in the nation. Amenities at the 1,138-acre (460-hectare) park include sheltered picnic areas, tennis courts, a golf course, a swimming pool ($5 per day), basketball courts, a softball field, 8.5 miles (13.7 km) of hiking trails, and a full campground, making urban camping—devoid of traffic noise and light pollution—an option. The park's Environmental Interpretive Learning Center functions as an educational center for the local community, and its indoor conference room and outdoor classroom are available for rental.

EAST MEMPHIS
Located near the University of Memphis and Oak Court Mall, **Audubon Park** (4145 Southern Ave.) has an 18-hole golf course, indoor tennis courts, walking trails, picnic areas, and other sports facilities. The

Memphis Botanic Garden is located here.

Memphis residents celebrate the fact that their largest city park, **Shelby Farms** (6903 Great View Dr. N., www.shelbyfarmspark.org), is five times the size of New York's Central Park. The visitors center, lakefront stage, pavilions, boathouse, and trails are all the result of a $70 million renovation. You can go mountain biking, horseback riding, in-line skating, walking, or running along some of the many trails or take advantage of fishing, rafting, canoeing, or sailing on any of the park's six lakes. It has a wheelchair-accessible trail, areas for picnicking, and a shooting range. You can also explore the park from above with **Go Ape!** (www.goape.com) via a network of rope ladders, bridges, and zip lines near Pine Lake. Because most of its 4,500 acres (1,800 hectares) are pleasantly undeveloped, you'll often feel like you have Shelby Farms to yourself, despite the more than 500,000 people who visit annually.

Shelby Farms was originally set aside to be the county penal farm, and although it was not used in this way, the county jail is on the western edge of the park. Shelby Farms is on the eastern side of the city, just outside the I-40/I-240 loop that circles Memphis. It is easily accessible from exits 12 and 14 off I-40 and exit 13 off I-240, or via Walnut Grove Road from midtown.

BIKING

Most cyclists in the city bike as a form of recreation, rather than transportation. The City of Memphis has established five bike routes that circle the city and various neighborhoods. These routes are marked and have designated parking and restroom facilities at the start. They are not bike paths—you share the road with cars—and normal safety measures are necessary.

The **Memphis Hightailers Bicycle Club** (www.memphishightailers.com) organizes weekly rides for various levels, with distances ranging 20-100 miles (30-160 km). For bike rentals, gear, and advice about riding in and around the city, go to **Peddler Bike Shop** (3548 Walker Ave., 901/327-4833, www.peddlerbikeshop.com, 9am-6pm Mon.-Fri., 9am-5pm Sat., 1pm-5pm Sun.), where owner Hal Mabray will happily help you get geared up to ride. A used-bike rental will cost about $15 for one hour, $26 for two hours, and $60 per day. Peddler also has locations in downtown Memphis; Germantown, Tennessee; and Southaven, Mississippi.

There are a number of parks near Memphis that are bike friendly. **Meeman-Shelby Forest State Park** (910 Riddick Rd., 901/876-5215, http://tnstateparks.com), north of the city, has 5 miles (8 km) of paved bike paths, and cyclists use the main park roads for more extensive riding. Bicyclists will also find trails and bike rentals at

Shelby Farms

AutoZone Park

Shelby Farms (6903 Great View Dr. N., www.shelbyfarmspark.org).

It is also noteworthy that the **Mississippi River Trail** (www.nps. gov), a bicycle route that runs 3,000 miles (4,800 km) from the headwaters of the Mississippi River in Minnesota to the Gulf of Mexico, runs through Memphis and on to Mississippi.

GOLF

The City of Memphis (http://memphistn.gov) operates award-winning 18-hole golf courses at **Audubon Park** (4160 Park Ave., 901/683-6941), with gently rolling hills; **Fox Meadows** (3064 Clarke Rd., 901/362-0232), which is easy to walk but has several challenging holes; **Galloway Park** (3815 Walnut Grove, 901/685-7805); **Davy Crockett Golf Course** (4380 Range Line Rd., 901/358-3375); and **Pine Hill Park** (1005 Alice Ave., 901/775-9434), a great course for walkers. There are three public 9-hole courses: one at **Riverside Park** (465 S. Parkway W., 901/576-4296),

one at **Overton Park** (2080 Poplar Ave., 901/725-9905), and one at **Whitehaven** (750 E. Holmes Rd., 901/396-1608). Greens fees on the public courses are under $20.

The semiprivate Audubon-certified **Mirimichi** (6129 Woodstock Cuba Rd., 901/259-3800, www.mirimichi. com, $25-59) in Millington is about a 30-minute drive from downtown.

SPECTATOR SPORTS
BASKETBALL

In 2001, Memphis realized the dream of many in the mid-South when the Vancouver Grizzlies announced they would be moving south. The National Basketball Association (NBA) team played its first two seasons in Memphis at the Pyramid before the massive $250 million FedEx Forum opened for the 2004-2005 season. The arena is one of the largest in the NBA and hosts frequent concerts and performances by major artists.

The **Grizzlies** have yet to win any titles, but they keep fans coming back.

Ticket prices range from under $20 to several hundred dollars. For ticket information, contact the **FedEx Forum box office** (191 Beale St., 901/205-2640, www.fedexforum.com, 10am-5:30pm Mon.-Fri.) or purchase through Ticketmaster. The NBA season runs October-April.

BASEBALL

From April to October, the **Memphis Redbirds** (901/721-6000, www.memphisredbirds.com, $9-75) play AAA ball at the striking **AutoZone Park** in downtown Memphis. The stadium is bounded by Union Avenue, Madison Avenue, and 3rd Street, and is convenient to dozens of downtown hotels and restaurants. The Redbirds are an affiliate of the St. Louis Cardinals. Cheap tickets ($9) buy you a seat on the grassy berm, or you can pay a little more for seats in the stadium or boxes. The Redbirds are owned by a nonprofit organization that also operates community and youth programs in the city.

RACING

The **Memphis International Raceway** (550 Victory Ln., 901/969-7223, www.racemir.com) is a short drive from downtown Memphis in Millington, northeast of the city center. The park includes a 0.75-mile (1.2-km) NASCAR oval, a 0.25-mile (0.4-km) drag racing strip, and a 1.8-mile (2.9-km) road course. It hosts more than 200 race events every year, including a stop in the Xfinity Series circuit.

Millington is about a 30-minute drive north of Memphis. From the west, take I-40 east toward Nashville. From the east, take I-40 west toward Memphis.

Restaurants

Eating may be the best thing about visiting Memphis. The city's culinary specialties start—but don't end—with barbecue. Plate-lunch diners around the city offer delectable cornbread, fried chicken, greens, fried green tomatoes, peach cobbler, and dozens of other Southern specialties on a daily basis. And to make it even better, such down-home restaurants are easy on your wallet. For those seeking a departure from home-style fare, Memphis has dozens of fine restaurants—some old established eateries, others newcomers that are as trendy as those in any major American city.

Not sure where to start? Try a **Tastin' 'Round Town food tour** (901/870-1824, www.tastinroundtown.com). Choose from barbecue for $65 or Taste of Memphis for $54. These walking tours are multi-restaurant experiences that let you sample some of the city's best.

Memphis also has a decent **food truck** scene with nearly 40 trucks around town, and a food truck park near the airport (3803 Winchester Rd., 10:30am-3pm Mon.-Fri.).

DOWNTOWN

SOUTHERN

Tucked inside an unassuming storefront across from the valet entrance to the Peabody Hotel is **Flying Fish** (105 S. 2nd St., 901/522-8228, 11am-10pm daily, $8-20), your first stop for real fried catfish in Memphis. If catfish isn't your thing, try the grilled or boiled shrimp, fish tacos, frog legs, or oysters. The baskets of fried seafood come with fries and hush puppies, and the grilled plates come with grilled veggies, rice, and beans. The tangy coleslaw is a must. The atmosphere is laid-back; place your order at the window and come and get it when the coaster they give you starts to vibrate. The checkered tables are well stocked with hot sauce and saltines. There's also a Flying Fish in downtown Little Rock.

It would be a mistake to visit Memphis and not stop at ✪ **Gus's World Famous Fried Chicken** (310 Front St., 901/527-4877, 11am-9pm Sun.-Thurs., 11am-10pm Fri.-Sat., $6-12) for some of its delicious fried bird. The downtown location is a franchise of the original Gus's, which is a half-hour drive northeast out of town along U.S. 70, in Mason. It is no exaggeration to say that Gus's cooks up some of the best fried chicken out there: It is spicy, juicy, and hot. It's served casually wrapped in brown paper. Sides include coleslaw, baked beans, and fried pickles. The restaurant also serves grilled-cheese sandwiches. The service in this small establishment is slow but friendly, oo come in with a smile on. It is not unusual for there to be a line out the door.

Soul food egg rolls? Yes, **Sage Memphis** (94 S. Main St., 901/672-7902, http://sagememphis.com, 11am-10pm Tues.-Wed., 11am-midnight Thurs., 11am-2am Fri.-Sat., 11am-5pm Sun., 11am-3pm Mon.) puts new twists on traditional tastes. Chef Eli Townsend draws customers to the downtown eatery, which has a hopping late-night bar scene, for his fusion culinary creations.

✪ BARBECUE

Barbecue is serious business in Memphis. On the northern fringe of downtown Memphis is one of the city's most famous and beloved barbecue joints: **Cozy Corner** (735 N. Parkway, 901/527-9158, www.cozycornerbbq.com, 11am-8pm Tues.-Sat., $5-20). Cozy Corner is tucked into a storefront in an otherwise abandoned strip mall; you'll smell it before you see it. Step inside to order barbecue pork, sausage, or bologna sandwiches. Or get a two-bone, four-bone, or six-bone rib dinner plate, which comes with your choice of baked beans, coleslaw, or barbecue spaghetti, plus slices of Wonder bread to sop up the juices. One of Cozy Corner's specialties is its barbecued Cornish hens—a preparation that is surprising but delicious. Sweet tea goes perfectly with the tangy and spicy barbecue.

CONTEMPORARY

The Majestic Grille (145 S. Main St., 901/522-8555, www.majesticgrille.com, 11am-10pm Mon.-Thurs., 11am-11pm Fri., 11am-2:30pm and 4pm-11pm Sat., 10am-2pm and 4pm-9pm Sun., $8-48) serves a remarkably affordable yet upscale menu at brunch, lunch, and dinner. Located in what was once the Majestic Theater, the restaurant's white tablecloths and apron-clad waiters lend an aura of refinement. But with main courses starting at just $8-9, this can be a bargain. Flatbread pizzas feature asparagus, spicy shrimp, and smoked sausage, and sandwiches include burgers and clubs. Specialties include pasta, barbecue ribs, grilled salmon, and steaks. Don't pass on dessert, served in individual shot glasses, with offerings such as chocolate mousse, key lime pie, and carrot cake.

It is impossible to pigeonhole **Automatic Slim's** (83 S. 2nd St., 901/525-7948, www.automaticslims-memphis.com, 11am-close Mon.-Fri., 9am-close Sat.-Sun., brunch $11-16, dinner $16-22), except to say that this Memphis institution consistently offers fresh, spirited, and original fare. Named after a character from an old blues tune, Automatic Slim's uses lots of strong flavors to create its eclectic menu; Caribbean and southwestern influences are the most apparent. Take a seat and in two shakes you'll be presented with soft bread and pesto-seasoned olive oil for dipping. Start with buffalo fries or coconut shrimp, or come for brunch and an Oreo waffle. Automatic Slim's is a welcome departure from barbecue and Southern food when you're ready. Its atmosphere is relaxed, and there's often a crowd at the bar, especially on weekends, when there's live music on tap.

Long the city's standard-bearer for fine French cuisine, **Chez Philippe** (149 Union Ave., 901/529-4000, 5pm-10pm Wed.-Sat., $98-135, three-course afternoon tea 1pm-3:30pm Wed.-Sat., $45-55/$30 kids), located in the Peabody Hotel, serves traditional French dishes with a Southern touch. Entrées include grouper, bass, pork, and venison. Chez Philippe offers a prix fixe menu: Four course meals are $98; seven courses are $135.

Located in an old distillery in the South Main Arts District, **Gray Canary** (301 S. Front St., 901/249-2932, http://thegraycanary.com, 4pm-10pm Tues.-Thurs., 4pm-11pm Fri.-Sat., 3pm-9pm Sun., $19-56) is one of Memphis's high-end dining experiences. The emphasis is on small plates with a global twist, fresh seafood, and craft cocktails. The kitchen is the brainchild of chefs Andrew

Ticer and Michael Hudman, who also own Hog & Hominy and Catherine & Mary's. Complementary valet parking is available.

INTERNATIONAL

Catherine & Mary's (272 S. Main St., 901/254/8600, www.catherineand-marys.com, 4pm-10pm Mon.-Thurs., 4pm-11pm Fri.-Sat., 10:30am-3pm Sun., $10-35) is a downtown addition from James Beard Award-nominated chefs Andy Ticer and Michael Hudman. The cuisine is Italian—Tuscan and Sicilian, more specifically—from the salumi board to the simple, hearty pasta preparations. On the 1st floor of the historical **Hotel Chisca**, the restaurant is a stunner, with big open spaces and amazing art on the walls. The scene is good for people-watching. However, service can be dismissive, particularly for solo diners. Hotel Chisca, part of the Memphis Heritage Trail, was built in 1913 and is where Elvis gave his first radio interview; it has been repurposed as an apartment building.

Looking for a quick, affordable bite to eat? **Maciel's** (45 S. Main St., 901/526-0037, www.macielstaco-shop.com, 11am-8pm Mon.-Thurs., 11am-10pm Fri.-Sat., 11am-3pm Sun. brunch, $3-14) is just one of several options that won't break the bank. Try tacos, salads, and tortas inspired by the flavors of the Mexican state of Michoacán. There's a second location near the University of Memphis (525 S. Highland St., 901/504-4584, 11am-9:30pm Mon.-Thurs., 11am-10pm Fri.-Sat.).

DINERS AND DELIS

You can order deli sandwiches, breakfast plates, and a limited variety of plate lunches at the **Front Street**

EVERYTHING OLD IS NEW AGAIN

In lots of cities all the talk is about the new restaurants. Whatever just opened has a line around the block. And, yes, in the Bluff City new places get buzz, but locals really love a restaurant that has stood the test of time. In fact, a number of eateries claim to be the oldest in town, albeit with a number of different qualifiers. Here's a look at six of Memphis's time-tested dining spots.

- **The Little Tea Shop** (69 Monroe Ave., 901/525-6000): This downtown diner has served sandwiches and salads with a smile since 1918.

- **The Green Beetle** (325 S. Main St., 901/527-7337, www.thegreenbeetle.com): While it has changed locations and owners, this tavern served its first cold beer in 1939, leading to its claim to be the oldest in Memphis. The burger is dang fine.

- **The Arcade** (540 S. Main St., 901/526-5757, www.arcaderestaurant.com): Popular with tourists thanks to its retro look and downtown location, this classic diner has been generating a buzz since opening in 1919.

- **Coletta's** (1063 S. Parkway East, 901/948-7652, www.colettas.net): Open since 1923, this Italian restaurant claims to have invented the Memphis barbecue pizza.

- **Dyer's** (205 Beale St., 901/527-3937, www.dyersonbeale.com): Since 1912 Dyer's has been frying burgers in the same, strained-daily grease. They say that's what makes them so delicious.

- **Front Street Deli** (77 S. Front St., 901/522-4824, www.frontstreetdelimemphis.com): Featuring standards named after movies, the city's oldest deli—open since 1976—is a newcomer compared to the others on this list.

Deli (77 S. Front St., 901/522-4824, www.frontstreetdelimemphis.com, 7am-3pm Mon.-Fri., 8am-3pm Sat., $6-9). The deli, which claims to be Memphis's oldest, serves breakfast and lunch. One of its claims to fame is that scenes from the movie *The Firm* were filmed here.

For the best burgers on Beale Street, go to **Dyer's** (205 Beale St., 901/527-3937, www.dyersonbeale.com, 11am-close Sun.-Thurs., 11am-close Fri.-Sat., $5-18). The legend is that the secret of Dyer's burgers is that it has been using the same grease (strained daily) since it opened in 1912. Only in Tennessee could century-old grease be a selling point. True or not, the burgers here are especially juicy. Dyer's also serves wings, hot dogs, milk shakes, and a full array of fried sides.

Part beer bar, part coffee shop, **Tamp & Tap** (122 Gayoso Ave., 901/207-1053, www.tampandtap.com, 7am-6pm Mon.-Fri., 8am-6pm Sat.-Sun.) serves the latest from Memphis breweries alongside espresso drinks, plus breakfast options and sandwiches.

Calling itself Memphis's first gastropub, **South of Beale** (361 S. Main St., 901/526-0388, www.southofbeale.com, 11am-11pm Mon.-Thurs., 11am-midnight Fri.-Sat., 11am-10pm Sun., $8-22) has burgers, cocktails, beer, and a gouda mac-and-cheese that drives people wild.

Founded in 1919 and still operated by the same family, the **Arcade** (540 S. Main St., 901/526-5757, www.arcaderestaurant.com, 7am-3pm Sun.-Wed., 7am-10pm Thurs.-Sat., $5-10) is said to be Memphis's oldest restaurant. With its vintage decor, it feels like a throwback to an earlier time. The menu is diverse, with pizzas, sandwiches, and plate-lunch specials during the week, and breakfast served anytime. The chicken spaghetti special is a stick-to-your-ribs favorite.

The Arcade restaurant

A tiny outpost in uptown, **Roxie's Grocery** (520 N. 3rd St., 901/525-2817, 7am-9pm Mon.-Fri., 7am-10pm Sat., 8am-10pm Sun., $1-9) serves one of the best burgers in Memphis, hand-formed patties that are accompanied by chili cheese fries.

COFFEE AND BAKED GOODS

At **Primas Bakery and Boutique** (523 South Main St., 901/352-4193, www.primasbakeryandboutique.com, 6am-6pm Tues.-Fri., 11am-6pm Sat., 10am-3pm Sun., $2-36), two cousins offer a small selection of baked goods and sweets (hence the name: "primas" means "cousins" in Spanish). The charming shop in the South Main Arts District also sells Latin American-made gifts, clothing, and accessories.

Cupcakes, cookies, and other goodies that satisfy a sweet tooth can be found at **Two Girls and a Whip** (363 South Front St., 901/472-2253, www.twogirlsandawhip.com, 9am-5pm Tues.-Thurs., 9am-7pm Fri., 10am-4pm Sat., $3, $30-75 for custom cakes) downtown.

For coffee, pastries, and fruit smoothies, **Bluff City Coffee** (505 S. Main St., 901/405-4399, www.bluffcitycoffee.com, 6:30am-6pm Mon.-Sat., 8am-6pm Sun., $2-8) is your best bet in this part of the city. Located in the South Main Arts District, the shop is decorated with large prints of vintage photographs and has free Wi-Fi. There's a second location in Cooper-Young (945 S. Cooper St., 901/249-3378).

UPTOWN

✪ **The Little Tea Shop** (69 Monroe Ave., 901/525-6000, 11am-2pm Mon.-Fri., $5-$10) serves traditional plate lunches throughout the week. Choose from daily specials like fried catfish, chicken potpie, and meat loaf, with your choice of vegetable and side dishes, by ticking off boxes on the menu. Every meal (except sandwiches) comes with fresh, hot cornbread that might as well be the star of the show. This is stick-to-your-ribs Southern cooking at its best, so come hungry. If you have room, try the peach cobbler or pecan ball for dessert. The staff's welcoming yet efficient style makes this perfect for a quick lunch. They'll treat you like a regular even if you've never walked in the door before.

Alcenia's (317 N. Main St., 901/523-0200, www.alcenias.com, 11am-5pm Tues.-Fri., 9am-3pm Sat., $9-13), in the Pinch District, is among Memphis's best Southern style restaurants. Known for its plate lunches, fried chicken, and pastries, Alcenia's has a style unlike any other Memphis eatery, witnessed in its offbeat decor of '60s-style beads, folk art, and wedding lace. Proprietor B. J. Chester-Tamayo is all love, and she pours her devotion into some of the city's best soul food. Try the spicy cabbage and deep-fried chicken, or the salmon croquette, and save room for Alcenia's famous bread pudding for dessert. Chicken and waffles is the Saturday morning specialty.

Although aficionados will remind you that the ribs served at the ✪ **Rendezvous** (52 S. 2nd St., 901/523-2746, www.hogsfly.com, 4:30pm-10:30pm Tues.-Thurs., 11am-11pm Fri., 11:30am-11pm Sat., $8-20) are not technically barbecue, they are one of the biggest barbecue stories in town. Covered in a dry rub of spices and broiled until the meat falls off the bones, these ribs will knock your socks off. If you prefer, you can choose Charlie Vergos's dry-rub chicken or boneless pork loin. Orders come with baked beans and coleslaw, but beer is really the essential accompaniment to any Vergos meal. The door to Rendezvous is tucked in an alley off Monroe Avenue. The interior, decorated with antiques and yellowing business cards, is casual, noisy, and lots of fun.

The **Blue Plate Café** (113 Court Square 3., 901/523-2050, 8am-2pm daily, $4-10) serves hearty breakfasts, plate lunches, and traditional home-style cooking. Its newsprint menu imparts wisdom and declares that every day should begin with a great breakfast. It's not hard to comply at the Blue Plate. Eggs come with homemade biscuits and gravy, and your choice of grits, hash browns, or pancakes. For lunch, try a meat-and-three or vegetable plate, slow-cooked white-bean soup, or a grilled peanut butter and banana sandwich. Locals swear by the

fried green tomatoes. There is also a Blue Plate Café in an old house in midtown (5469 Poplar Ave., 901/761-9696, 7am-2pm daily).

With a biscuit and gravy bowl on the menu, **Sunrise Memphis** (670 Jefferson Ave., 901/552-3144, http://sunrise901.com, 6am-3pm daily, $5-10) cements itself as one the city's favorite breakfast and lunch spots. While there are some healthier salads and veggie burgers available, people come here for the eggs, grits, and other traditional breakfast fare. Sunrise is a popular working lunch spot, too

You'll be welcomed into a bright, sunny space as soon as your set foot into **Cafe Keough** (12 S. Main St., 901/509-2469, www.cafekeough.com, 7am-5pm Mon.-Fri., 9am-4pm Sat.-Sun., $2-12). This uptown coffee shop has a French bistro feel, plus a few innovative items, such as matcha lattes.

MIDTOWN
SOUTHERN

Just follow the crowds to the **Cupboard Restaurant** (1400 Union Ave., 901/276-8015, www.thecupboardrestaurant.com, 7am-8pm daily, $7-12), one of Memphis residents' favorite stops for plate lunches. The Cupboard moved from its downtown location to an old Shoney's about a mile outside of town to accommodate the throngs who stop here for home-style cooking. The Cupboard gets only the freshest vegetables for its dishes like okra and tomatoes, rutabaga turnips, steamed cabbage, and green beans. The meat specials change daily but include things like fried chicken, chicken and dumplings, hamburger steak with onions, and beef tips with noodles. The cornbread "coins" are exceptionally buttery, and the bread is baked fresh daily. For dessert, try the lemon icebox pie.

The Woman's Exchange Tea Room (88 Racine St., 901/327-5681, 10am-4pm Mon.-Fri., 10am-2pm Sat., $8-15) feels like a throwback. Located one block east of the Poplar Street viaduct, the Woman's Exchange has been serving lunch since 1936, and the menu has not varied much over the years. The specials change daily and includes a choice of two to four entrées, or a four-vegetable plate, except on Saturday when there's one choice. Classics like chicken salad, salmon loaf, beef tenderloin, and seafood gumbo are favorites, and all lunches come with a drink and dessert. The dining room looks out onto a green garden, and the atmosphere is homey, not stuffy. The Exchange also sells gifts, housewares, and other knickknacks.

Before hanging her own shingle more than a decade ago, the namesake owner of **Peggy's Heavenly Home Cooking** (326 S. Cleveland St., 901/474-4938, 11am-7pm Tues.-Thurs., 11am-9pm Fri., 9am-6pm Sat., noon-6pm Sun., $12-18) worked at the Peabody Hotel. Peggy Brown drew locals to her new spot with fried chicken and catfish, greens, black-eyed pies, and cakes. Her recipes use more seasonal vegetables than some other soul food favorites.

One of chef Kelly English's restaurants, the French Creole **Restaurant Iris** (2146 Monroe Ave., 901/590-2828, http://restaurantiris.com, 5pm-10pm Mon.-Sat., last seating 9:30pm, $30-42) is one of Memphis's favorites, located in a former home in Overton Square. The restaurant's dishes change frequently. A typical dinner menu might include surf and turf (New York strip steak stuffed with blue cheese

and fried oysters) and shrimp and grits with andouille sausage.

An outpost of the Nashville hot-chicken chain, **Hattie B's** (596 Cooper St., 901/424-5900, http://hattieb.com, 11am-10pm Mon.-Thurs., 11am-11pm Fri.-Sat., 11am-4pm Sun., $9-12) serves the iconic spicy chicken on white bread with a pickle, just like it is supposed to be. Memphis is more about fried chicken, while it is Nashville that loves it hot, but Hattie B's has been packed since it opened in Bluff City.

A collection of four metal silos comprises **Carolina Watershed** (141 E. Carolina Ave., 901/504-4749, www.carolinawatershed.com, 4pm-midnight Fri., 10:30am-midnight Sat., 10:30am-8pm Sun., $8-13.50), a weekend-only restaurant and bar. The environment is a rehabbed backyard, complete with waterfalls, so you'll be sitting on picnic tables as you feast on pulled pork cheese fries, fried catfish po'boys, and fried chicken.

Memphis residents have a soft spot for New Orleans, and nowhere is that clearer than at **Second Line** (2144 Monroe Ave., 901/590-2829, www.secondlinememphis.com, 11am-close daily, $9-26). This Overton Square restaurant features jambalaya, gumbo, the classic roast beef "debris" piled high on a po'boy, and even a vegetarian debris.

Shareable small plates and classic Southern "big plates" combine to make **Alchemy** (940 S. Cooper St., 901/726-4444, http://alchemymemphis.com, 4pm-2am Mon., 4pm-11pm Tues.-Thurs., 4pm-2am Fri.-Sat., 10:30am-2:30pm and 4pm-10pm Sun., $7-21) a neighborhood favorite. The extensive wine and spirits list attracts folks for a post-work cocktail.

With a biscuit and gravy bowl on

Central BBQ

the menu, **Sunrise Memphis** (670 Jefferson Ave., 901/552-3144, http://sunrise901.com, 6am-3pm daily, $5-10) cements itself as one the city's favorite breakfast and lunch spots. While there are some healthier salads and veggie burgers available, people come here for the eggs, grits, and other traditional breakfast fare. Sunrise is a popular working lunch spot, too.

✪ BARBECUE

Central BBQ (2249 Central, 901/272-9377, www.cbqmemphis.com, 11am-9pm daily, $5-27) appeals to both those who love dry rub and those who want their sauces. Can't decide between the pulled pork, the brisket, and other local favorites? Easy solution: Get the combo platter. Central has several locations around town

In Memphis everything can be served "barbecue," even spaghetti. At the **Bar-B-Q Shop** (1782 Madison Ave., 901/272-1277, http://thebar-b-qshop.com, 11am-9pm Mon.-Sat., $10-24) barbecue spaghetti is a specialty,

not an afterthought (and sold by the quart for takeout). The ribs are also popular.

CARIBBEAN

Jamaican and Southern cooking come together at **Evelyn & Olive** (630 Madison Ave., 901/748-5422, www.evelynandolive.com, 11am-9pm Tues.-Thurs., 11am-10pm Fri., noon-10pm Sat., $5-14), a South Main Arts District eatery. The storefront is unassuming (and a little off-putting, perhaps, with limited street-side windows), but go inside and feast on jerk chicken, key lime pie, and more.

CONTEMPORARY

One of Memphis's most distinctive restaurant settings is an old beauty shop in the Cooper-Young neighborhood. ✪ **The Beauty Shop** (966 Cooper St., 901/272-7111, www.thebeautyshoprestaurant.com, 11am-2pm and 5pm-10pm Mon.-Thurs., 11am-2pm and 5pm-11pm Fri.-Sat., 10am-3pm Sun., lunch $5-14, dinner

$23-28) takes advantage of the vintage beauty parlor decor to create a great talking point for patrons and food writers alike. The domed hair dryers remain, and the restaurant has put the shampooing sinks to work as beer coolers. At lunch, the Beauty Shop offers a casual menu of sandwiches and salads. For dinner, the imaginative cuisine of Memphis restaurateur Karen Blockman Carrier, who also owns Mollie Fontaine Lounge and Bar DKDC, takes over.

cuisine at The Beauty Shop

Bounty on Broad (2519 Broad Ave., 901/410-8131, www.bountyonbroad. com, 5pm-9:30pm Mon.-Thurs., 5pm-10pm Fri., 11am-2pm and 5pm-10pm Sat., 11am-2pm Sun., $17-42) serves family-style dishes with a farm-to-table slant. High-quality meats are a focus, but there are plenty of seafood and veg-centric plates, too. Note: Cash is not accepted, just credit cards.

ITALIAN
Ecco on Overton Park (1585 Overton Park, 901/410-8200, www. eccoonovertonpark.com, 11am-2pm and 4:30pm-9pm Tues.-Thurs., 11am-2pm and 5:30pm-9:30pm Fri., 10am-2pm and 5:30pm-9:30pm Sat., $12-33) channels all the comforts of a European café with dishes such as chicken cacciatore, pasta puttanesca, and duck marsala. Drink as the Italians do with an Aperol spritz or sip a bit of Spain with a bottle of rosé from Rioja.

Inside the Crosstown Concourse, **Elemento Neapolitan Pizza** (1350 Concourse Ave., 901/672-7527, http:// elementopizza.com, 11am-9pm Mon.-Thurs., 11am-10pm Fri.-Sat., $6-13) serves from-scratch pizzas cooked in head-turning white tile pizza ovens. The thin Neapolitan-style pies aren't everyone's taste, but if they are yours, these are done well.

LATIN AMERICAN
The exterior of ✪ **The Liquor Store** (2655 Broad Ave., 901/405-5477, www. thebroadliquorstore.com, 8am-2pm Mon., 8am-9pm Tues.-Sat., 8am-4pm Sun., $4-15) matches its name, but inside is one of the city's best restaurants and bars. The menu is loaded with flavorful Cuban food and drinks, not to mention house-made PopTarts and tres leches cake. The décor is Instagram friendly, with analog clocks, turning cake displays, and bright, tropical colors and motifs.

It's the regulars who are happy at the **Happy Mexican Restaurant and Cantina** (385 S. 2nd St., 901/529-9991, www.happymexican.com, 11am-10pm Mon.-Thurs., 11am-11pm Fri.-Sun., $7-17). Serving generous portions of homemade Mexican food for lunch and dinner, Happy Mexican is destined to become a downtown favorite. The service is efficient and friendly, and the decor is cheerful but not over the top. It's just a few blocks south of

The Liquor Store

the National Civil Rights Museum. There are two additional locations in the greater Memphis area.

Owned by a Mexico City native who has made Memphis his home, **Las Tortugas Deli Mexicana** (6300 Poplar Ave., 901/623-3882, www.delimexicana.com, 10:30am-8pm Mon.-Sat., $5-20) serves up full-flavored Mexican dishes, such as the namesake tortuga sandwiches, at reasonable prices. The crab tacos and *elote* are local favorites. There's a second location in Germantown (1215 S. Germantown Rd., 901/751-1200).

ASIAN

The **India Palace** (1720 Poplar Ave., 901/278-1199, www.indiapalacememphis.com, 11am-2:30pm and 5pm-9:30pm Mon.-Fri., 11am-3pm and 5pm-10pm Sat.-Sun., $11-17) is a regular winner in readers' choice polls for Indian food in Memphis. At $11, the lunchtime buffet is filling and economical, and the dinner menu features vegetarian, chicken, and seafood dishes. The dinner platters are generous and tasty.

Robata Ramen & Yakitori Bar

(2116 Madison Ave. 901/410-8290, www.robatamemphis.com, 11am-9pm Sun., 11am-2pm and 5pm-11pm Mon.-Thurs., 11am-2pm and 5pm-midnight Fri., 11am-midnight Sat., $7-15) is equal parts fun and affordable, with an array of *yakitori* (bite-size meats and veggies that are skewered, then grilled) sold by the piece and a create-your-own ramen menu.

Dumplings, ramen, and rice bowls are the order of the day at **Lucky Cat** (2583 Broad Ave., 901/208-8145, www.luckycatmemphis.com, 5pm-9pm Tues.-Thurs., 5pm-10pm Fri.-Sat., $4-14), a cozy eatery in the Broad Avenue Arts District. This is a popular spot, so be prepared to wait.

Pho Binh (1615 Madison Ave., 901/276-0006, 11am-9pm Mon.-Sat., $4-9) is one of the most popular Vietnamese restaurants in town. You can't beat the value of the lunch buffet, or you can order from the dizzying array of Chinese and Vietnamese dishes, including spring rolls, vermicelli noodle bowls, rice, and meat dishes. There are a lot of vegetarian options.

The atmosphere at **Bhan Thai** (1324 Peabody Ave., 901/272-1538, www.bhanthairestaurant.com, 11am-2:30pm Tues.-Fri., 5pm-9:30pm Sun.-Thurs., 5pm-10:30pm Fri.-Sat., $14-25) in midtown is almost as appealing as the excellent Thai food served there. Set in an elegant 1912 home, Bhan Thai makes the most of the house's space, and seating is spread throughout several colorful rooms and on the back patio. Choose from dishes like red snapper and roasted duck curry. The Bhan Thai salad is popular, with creamy peanut dressing and crisp vegetables.

Immigrants from Sudan, Nepal, and Syria offer their takes on their

Yes, Memphis is known for barbecue, but it has another culinary specialty that may be more omnipresent: hot wings. A claim oft repeated (but not substantiated) is that more hot wings are sold in Memphis than anywhere else in the world.

What makes for a good hot wing? Some like them hot. Others smoked, fried, or sweet. Some dip them in ranch dressing, others blue cheese. You'll find them all over town. There's even the annual **Southern Hot Wing Festival** (www.southernhotwing-festival.com) each April. Here are a few places to give them a try. Most offer quantities of 100 pieces or more (not priced here), if you're looking for a mess of wings to take to a picnic or a party.

- **Ching's Hotwings** (1264 Getwell Rd., 901/743-5545, 11am-10pm Mon.-Sat., noon-6pm Sun., $3-17): Near the University of Memphis, Ching's specializes in "honey hot," a seasoning that's both spicy and sweet.

- **Alex's Tavern** (1445 Jackson Ave., 901/278-9086, noon-3am Sun.-Sat., $7-25): This midtown institution serves crispy, vinegar-y, made-to-order wings (as well as a very popular burger).

- **Crumpy's Hot Wings** (1671 S. 3rd St., 901/512-5552, 10:30am-10pm Mon.-Thurs., 10:30am-11pm Fri.-Sat., noon-7pm Sun., $3-40): The garlic-parmesan wings here are an unusual twist on the Memphis classic. Try them at several locations (6250 E. Shelby Dr., 901/368-6777; 671 South Highland St., 901/443-5857).

- **These Damn Wings** (2711 Lamar Ave., 901/305-6118, www.thesedamnwings.com, 11am-3am Mon.-Thurs., 11am-4am Fri.-Sat., noon-8pm Sun., $5-25): This stop in the Orange Mound neighborhood allows you to add wings to other entrees for just $1.

- **Uncle Lou's Fried Chicken** (3633 Millbranch Rd., 901/332-2367, www.unclelous-friedchicken.com, 10:30am-8pm Mon.-Sat., 11am-5pm Sun., $3-30): These buffalo wings have been featured on the Food Network's *Diners Drive Ins & Dives*.

cuisines at **Global Café** (1350 Concourse Ave., no phone, www.globalcafé.com, 11am-9pm Tues.-Thurs. and Sun, 11am-10pm Fri.-Sat., $6-17), a friendly cafeteria-style eatery in the Crosstown Concourse complex. Dumplings, meat and rice dishes, desserts, and a full bar tempt palates and encourage sampling and conversation. The Concourse has patio seating in addition to the small indoor tables and bar seating.

VEGETARIAN

Raw and vegan food delivery service **Raw Girls Memphis** (www.raw-girls-memphis.myshopify.com) also runs two food trucks that dole out cold-pressed juices, snacks, soups, salads, and sandwiches. Eats are as clean as

they get—free of gluten, dairy, and refined sugar, a boon for those navigating food allergies or sensitivities—and feature organic, locally grown produce to boot. Look for the trucks (8am-6:30pm Tues.-Sat., noon-6pm Sun., $7-14) parked in midtown (242 S. Cooper) and East Memphis (5502 Poplar Ave.).

Located inside Ballet Memphis in Overton Square, **Mama Gaia** (2144 Madison Ave., 901/214-2449, 10:30am-8pm Mon.-Sat., $4-14) focuses on organic, vegetarian quick dishes, such as bowls, sandwiches, pizzas, and juices.

DINERS AND CAFES

Wood paneling and other classic diner décor make **Bob's Barksdale**

(237 Cooper St., 901/722-2193, 7am-2pm Mon.-Sun., $2.50-8.25) seem like a movie set. A loyal customer base flocks to this midtown staple for hearty breakfasts.

A bar and restaurant with a popular patio, **The Slider Inn** (2117 Peabody Ave., 901/725-1155, www.thesliderinn. com, 11am-3am Mon.-Sun., $5-13) is a Memphis weekend institution. Grab an order of wings, a burger, and a Jameson slush and get to know the locals. Vegan sliders are a good option for those who eschew meat. The owners also helm **Bardog** (73 Monroe Ave., 901/275-8752, www.bardog. com), a popular downtown bar.

One of the funkiest places you can find in midtown—and that's saying something—**Otherlands Coffee Shop** (641 S. Cooper St., 901/278-4994, http://otherlandscoffeebar.com, 7am-8pm Mon.-Sun., $2-7) is a café, art gallery, live music venue, gift shop, and neighborhood hangout. The menu is heavy on organic, with lots of vegetarian and vegan options. The outdoor patio is dog friendly.

Connected to High Cotton Brewing Co. in the South Main Arts District, **Edge Alley** (600 Monroe Ave., 901/425-2605, www.edge-alley.com, 7am-8pm Tues.-Thurs., 7am-9pm Fri., 9:30am-9pm Sat., 9:30am-4pm Sun., $7-19) is a charming, off-the-radar eatery. The menus are chock-full of healthy, simple dishes with a nod to the hip, such as avocado toast and chicken salad on brioche. The space is bright, clean, and welcoming, but bringing your laptop and working for hours is discouraged. This is a talk-to-your-friends kind of place, not a coffee shop.

Edge Alley restaurant

BAKED GOODS

Overton Square's **Sweet Noshings** (2113 Madison Ave., 901/288-4753, 11:30am-9:30pm Mon.-Thurs., 11:30am-11pm Fri.-Sat., noon-9:30pm Sun., $3-12) is the candy store for the kid in all of us. Come for coffee, ice cream, and candy. Sweet Noshings makes many (many) varieties of flavored popcorn, which is a treat that is particularly popular in Memphis. (Yes, the "Memphis Mix" popcorn does have a barbecue flavor to it.)

If you are judicious about your sugar consumption, midtown's **17 Berkshire** (2094 Trimble Place,

Sweet Noshings

Muddy's Bake Shop

901/729-7916, www.17berkshire.com, 11am-7pm Tues.-Sat., noon-5pm Sun., $2-35) is the place to indulge. This small, artful bakery and chocolate shop feels like it could be in Paris rather than Overton Square, with its attention to detail and appreciation of all things sweet. The hot chocolate is not just a beverage, it's an expcrience.

The cupcakes and pies at **Muddy's Bake Shop** (585 S. Cooper St., 901/443-4144, www.muddysbakeshop.com, 6:30am-9pm Mon.-Fri., 7am-9pm Sat., $5-42) are a Memphis obsession. Try the rich and creamy Prozac cake—you know, chocolate is better than antidepressants. There's a second location at Laurelwood in East Memphis (5101 Sanderlin Ave., 901/683-8844, 10am-9pm Mon.-Thurs., 10am-10pm Fri.-Sat.).

SOUTH MEMPHIS
SOUTHERN

Gay Hawk Restaurant (685 S. Danny Thomas Blvd., 901/947-1464, 11:30am-3pm Mon.-Fri.,11:30am-5pm Sun., $6-10) serves country-style food that sticks to your ribs and warms your soul. Chef Lewis Bobo declares that his specialty is "home-cooked food," and it really is as simple as that. The best thing about Gay Hawk is the luncheon buffet, which lets newcomers to Southern cooking survey the choices and try a little bit of everything. The Sunday lunch buffet table practically sags with specialties like fried chicken, grilled fish, macaroni and cheese, greens, and much, much more. Save room for peach cobbler.

You'll find some of the best fried chicken in Memphis—crispy on the outside, moist on the inside—at **Stein's** (2248 S. Lauderdale St., 901/775-9203, 10:30am-3pm Mon.-Fri., noon-4pm Sun., closed Sat., $8-14). This cafeteria-style neighborhood institution serves a meat (the aforementioned fried chicken, baked chicken, Salisbury steak, and more), plus two sides, corn breads, and pies and cakes. The room is chock-full of regulars, plus folks picking up to-go

Clarence Saunders opened the first **Piggly Wiggly** here in Memphis, at 79 Jefferson Street, in 1916, thus giving birth to the modern American supermarket. Until then, shoppers went to small storefront shops where they would ask the counter clerk for what they needed: a pound of flour, a half-dozen pickles, a block of cheese. The clerk went to the bulk storage area at the rear of the store and measured out what the customer requested.

Saunders's big idea was self-service. At the Piggly Wiggly, customers entered the store, carried a basket, and were able to pick out prepackaged and priced containers of food that they paid for at the payment station on their way out.

Suffice to say, the Piggly Wiggly idea took off, and by 1923 there were 1,268 Piggly Wiggly franchises around the country. Saunders used some of his profits to build a massive mansion east of the city out of pink Georgia limestone, but he was never to live in the Pink Palace, which he lost as a result of a complex stock transaction.

Today, Saunders's **Pink Palace** is home to the **Pink Palace Museum,** which includes, among other things, a replica of the original Piggly Wiggly supermarket.

orders. Despite the cafeteria-style line, the pace here is slow; don't expect to get in and out quickly, just enjoy your food. Don't panic if you get there close to opening time and the door is locked; again, sometimes things run a little slow. It's worth the wait. This is a good stop before or after a tour of Graceland or a drive by Aretha Franklin's birthplace.

Since 1946, **The Four Way** (998 Mississippi Blvd., 901/507-1519, http://fourwaymemphis.com, 11am-7pm Tues.-Sat., 10am-5pm Sun., $4-10) has been an important part of Memphis life. Even when the city was segregated, this was a place where blacks and whites were welcomed to dine together. Martin Luther King Jr. ate here when he was in town, and it was also a favorite of Elvis Presley. Today's diners still love the soul food favorites: country-fried steak, turkey and dressing, pickled beets, and mac and cheese. Sundays are popular for to-go orders as well as in-house dining, so lines can be long.

✪ BARBECUE

Jim Neely's **Interstate Bar-B-Q** (2265 S. 3rd St., 901/775-2304, www.interstatebarbecue.com, 11am-10pm Mon.-Wed., 11am-11pm Thurs., 11am-midnight Fri.-Sat., 11am-7pm Sun., $5-23) was once ranked the second-best barbecue in the nation, but the proprietors have not let it go to their heads; this is still a down-to-earth, no-frills eatery. Large appetites can order a whole slab of pork or beef ribs, but most people will be satisfied with a chopped pork sandwich, which comes topped with coleslaw and smothered with barbecue sauce. Families can get the fixings for 6, 8, or 10 sandwiches sent out family style. For an adventure, try the barbecue spaghetti or barbecue bologna sandwich. If you're in a hurry, Interstate has a drive-up window, and if you are really smitten, you can order pork, sauce, and seasoning in bulk to be frozen and shipped to your home.

Coletta's (1063 S. Parkway East, 901/948-7652, www.colettas.net, 11am-10pm Mon.-Thurs., 11am-11pm Fri., noon-11pm Sat., 1pm-9pm Sun., $8-18) has three claims to fame: It's one of Memphis's oldest restaurants, it says it invented the Memphis barbecue pizza, and it was home to Elvis's favorite pizza. There's a second location in East Memphis (2850 Appling Rd., 901/383-1122).

DINERS

You can guess the focus of the restaurant by its name: **Egg King Cafe** (4458 Elvis Presley Blvd., 901/249-3690, http://eggkingcafe.com, 6am-3pm Mon.-Sat., 7am-3pm Sun., $4-10) serves all the breakfast standards. Waits can be long during peak times, but this is a reliable, affordable breakfast stop in an area without a lot of remarkable restaurants.

EAST MEMPHIS
✪ BARBECUE

The mustard slaw at **Leonard's Pit Barbecue** (5465 Fox Plaza Dr., 901/360-1963, www.leonardsbarbecue.com, 11am-2:30pm Sun.-Thurs., 11am-4pm Fri.-Sat., $5-20) is an essential side dish to complement the classic Memphis barbecue.

Since 1952, **Tops Bar-B-Q** (2748 Lamar Ave., 901/743-3480, http://topsbarbq.com, 8:30am-8:45pm Mon.-Thurs., 8:30am-9:45pm Fri.-Sat., 8:30am-7:45pm Sun., $9-14) has been preparing pork shoulder over charcoal and hickory wood in open pits. Some folks swear the burgers are even better than the shoulder sandwich. Tops also has brisket, which is less common on Memphis barbecue menus (it's more of a Texas barbecue item). There are a dozen locations around the metro area.

You can get absolutely anything barbecued in Memphis. At **RP Tracks** (3547 Walker Ave., 901/327-1471, http://rptracks.com, 11am-3am Mon.-Sat., 10am-3am Sun., $5-12) that anything is tofu. Barbecue tofu nachos and buffalo tofu appetizers are among the local favorites.

CONTEMPORARY

To many minds, Memphis dining gets no better than ✪ **Erling Jensen,**

The Restaurant (1044 S. Yates Rd., 901/763-3700, www.ejensen.com, 5pm-10pm daily, $39-51). Danish-born Erling Jensen is the mastermind of this fine-dining restaurant that has consistently earned marks as Memphis residents' favorite. Understated decor and friendly service are the backdrop to Jensen's dishes, which are works of art. The menu changes with the seasons and is based upon availability, but usually it includes about four different seafood dishes and as many meat and game choices. Black Angus beef and buffalo tenderloin are some of the favorites. Meals at Jensen's restaurant should begin with an appetizer, salad, or soup—or all three. The jumbo chunk crab cakes with smoked red-pepper sauce are excellent. Reservations are a good idea at Erling Jensen, and so are jackets for men. Expect to spend upwards of $80 for a four-course meal, $60 for two courses. Add more for wine.

Memphis's premier steak house is **Folk's Folly** (551 S. Mendenhall Rd., 901/762-8200, www.folksfolly.com, 5:30pm-10pm Mon.-Sat., 5:30pm-9pm Sun., $30-70), just east of Audubon Park. Diners flock here for prime aged steaks and seafood favorites. For small appetites, try the 8-ounce filet mignon for $36; large appetites can gorge on the 28-ounce porterhouse for $72. Seafood includes lobster, crab legs, and wild salmon. The atmosphere is classic steak house: The lighting is low, and there's a piano bar, called Cellar Lounge, on the property.

Some say **Acre Restaurant** (690 S. Perkins, 901/818-2273, www.acre-memphis.com, 11am-1pm and 5pm-9pm Mon., 11am-1pm and 5pm-10pm Tues.-Sat., $24-38) is Memphis's best. Certainly, it has one of the best wine lists in town. The menu combines

Southern and Asian flavors with locally grown and raised ingredients in a modern setting.

Where else in the world can you enjoy the offbeat combination that is **Jerry's Sno-Cones** (1657 Wells Station Rd., 901/767-2659, 11am-9pm Mon.-Sat. spring-summer, 11am-8pm Mon.-Sat. fall, 11am-7pm Mon.-Sat. winter)? Choose from more than 70 varieties of shaved ice, plus burgers, pretzels, funnel cakes, ice cream sundaes, and more. Cash only.

ITALIAN

Andrew Michael Italian Kitchen (712 W. Brookhaven Cir., 901/347-3569, www.andrewmichaelitaliankitchen. com, 4pm-10pm Tues.-Sat., $25-35) is home to chefs Andrew Ticer and Michael Hudman, finalists in 2015 and semifinalists in 2019 for the James Beard Foundation Awards. They learned the nuances of Italian cooking from their grandmothers as well as from travels throughout Italy. Ticer and Hudman also own Hog & Hominy, Gray Canary, and Catherine & Mary's.

Libro (387 Perkins Ext., 901/800-2656, www.novelmemphis.com, 9am-8pm Mon.-Sat., 11am-2pm Sun., $14-18) is more than a bookstore café. Located inside Novel, this eatery has pastas, salads, entrées, a great wine list, and cocktails that elevate it to Italian restaurant status.

CAFES AND DINERS

It is a bit of a drive from downtown to Laurelwood, where **City Silo** (5101 Sanderlin Ave., 901/729-7687, www. thecitysilo.com, 7am-8pm Mon.-Thurs., 7am-9pm Fri.-Sat., $4-13) is tucked away in an unassuming strip mall. But if you're looking for organic, vegetarian- and vegan-friendly dishes,

and a staff that accommodates healthy eaters, it is worth the 25-minute drive. The hearty lunch bowls will keep you full till dinner.

The café at the Dixon Gallery and Gardens, **Park & Cherry** (4339 Park Ave., 901/761-5250, 10am-4:30pm Tues.-Sat., 1pm-4:30pm Sun., $7-10), makes delicious salads and hot sandwiches that are perfect for when you're feeling peckish. The ingredients are fresh and the service friendly, and you'll still have room for a heavier meal later.

Brother Juniper's (3519 Walker Ave., 901/324-0144, http://brotherjunipers.com, 6:30am-1pm Tues.-Fri., 7am-12:30pm Sat., 8am-1pm Sun., $2-14) is a popular breakfast and coffee shop with a San Francisco-style hippie vibe.

BAKED GOODS

Cute is the watchword at **Whimsy Cookie** (4704 Poplar Ave., 901/343-0709, www.whimsycookieco.com, 10am-6pm Mon.-Sat., $2-42), a pink confection of a building as sweet as its cookies. The menu includes all

Gibson's Donuts

manner of desserts, but the cake-like signature cookie is the reason to go.

Is there anything better than a doughnut shop that never closes? **Gibson's Donuts** (760 Mt. Moriah Rd., 901/682-8200, 24 hours daily, $2-8) has been a Memphis staple since 1967. Try the Crumb, which is just is as it sounds: a doughnut made from rolling it in the crumbs of other doughnuts. The pineapple fritter is so popular it often sells out. Prices are reduced after 11pm.

Accommodations

There are thousands of cookie-cutter hotel rooms in Memphis, but travelers who want a little something different can find alternatives to the major chains. If you plan to see all the major sights, stay in downtown Memphis. With the city at your doorstep, you'll have a better experience both day and night, without spending most of your time in a car.

If you want more of a neighborhood feel, or are on a budget, the farther from the city center, the cheaper the room. Midtown hasn't yet seen an explosion of hotels, although that is likely on its way. Airbnb, VRBO, and other short-term rentals are good options for staying outside of downtown, particularly if you're traveling with a few other folks and would like to have a kitchen and not eat every meal out. Backlash about short-term rentals disrupting residential neighborhoods isn't as acute in Memphis as it is in Nashville, but it never hurts to remember to be considerate of those around you. Remember that certain neighborhoods, particularly around Graceland, aren't ideal for strolling around at night.

DOWNTOWN
$100-150
The 71-room **Comfort Inn Memphis Downtown** (100 N. Front St., 901/526-0584, $189-194) is within easy walking distance of all the city-center attractions. Rooms aren't anything special, but the staff is often quite friendly; guests get free breakfast, Internet access, and indoor parking; and there's an outdoor pool. Ask for a room facing west, and you'll have a nice view of the Mississippi River. Parking is $12 a day.

$150-200
The **Talbot Heirs Guesthouse** (99 S. 2nd St., 901/527-9772, www.talbotheirs.com, $130-275), in the heart of downtown, offers a winning balance of comfort and sophistication. Each of the inn's eight rooms has its own unique decor—from cheerful red walls to black-and-white chic. All rooms are thoughtfully outfitted with a full kitchen and modern bathroom, television, radio and CD player, sitting area, desk, and high-speed Internet. Little extras, like the refrigerator stocked for breakfast, go a long way. Book early because the Talbot Heirs is often full, especially during peak summer months.

The bar stays open 'til 3am, there are board games and turntables, and…

well, at every turn it's clear that the **Moxy** (40 N. Front St., 901/522-0841, $150-180, valet parking $20/day and off-site parking $17/day) is targeting a younger hotel guest. If that's you, this Marriott offshoot, which opened in 2019, might be your style.

OVER $200

The **Westin Memphis Beale Street** (170 Lt. George W. Lee Ave., 901/334-5900, $185-499) is located across the street from FedEx Forum and one block from Beale Street. The hotel's 203 guest rooms are plush and modern, each with a work desk, high-speed Internet, MP3-player docking station, and super-comfortable beds. The location can be noisy when Beale Street is in full swing. Expect to pay $30 a day to park (self-parking or valet).

Arrive Memphis (Main St. and E. Butler, http://arriveenterprises.com/arrive-memphis) brings style to a historical building in the South Main Arts District. The 62-room hotel is housed in a space once owned by the Memphis College of Art. Amenities include large meeting spaces, restaurants, and a happening bar.

In the heart of the South Main Arts District, **Memphis Central Station Hotel** (544 S. Main St., 888/225-9664, http://valorhospitality.com/hotel/central-station-a-curio-by-hilton) has resurrected an old train station with style. Amenities at the 123-room hotel include a listening room (with both live music and a vinyl collection), bar, and restaurant.

UPTOWN

$100-150

The most affordable Memphis accommodations are in chain hotels. One solid choice is the **Sleep Inn at Court**

Square (40 N. Front St., 480/568-6713, $179-299), with 124 simple but clean and well-maintained rooms. Guests have access to a small fitness room, free parking, and a free continental breakfast. For those with a bigger appetite, the Blue Plate Café is just across the square. It's a five-block walk to Beale Street from Court Square, but the trolley runs right past the front door of the hotel. Parking will run you $18-30 each night.

$150-200

Near AutoZone Park and a lot of restaurants is **Doubletree Downtown Memphis** (185 Union Ave., 901/528-1800, $134-299). A 272-room hotel set in the restored Tennessee Hotel, the Doubletree maintains a touch of the old grandeur of the 1929 hotel from which it was crafted. Rooms are large, and there's an outdoor swimming pool and fitness room. Valet parking is $28 per night.

If you want to be in the middle of things but can't afford to stay at the swanky Peabody, consider the **Holiday Inn Memphis-Downtown** (160 Union Ave., 901/525-5491, starting from $252). Located across the street from the Peabody and near AutoZone Park, this Holiday Inn routinely gets good reviews from travelers. Parking will set you back $25 per day.

If the ✪ **Hotel Indigo Memphis Downtown** (22 N. B. B. King Blvd., 901/527-2215, www.ihg.com, $160-315, parking on-site $20/night) has a retro feel, it is because this swanky hotel was once the first Holiday Inn in Memphis. They've kept lots of the vintage mid-century charm, but upgraded with Frette linens and a pool in the center of the action.

Ducks march at the Peabody Hotel.

OVER $200

⚙ **The Peabody Hotel Memphis** (149 Union Ave., 901/529-4000 or 800/732-2639, www.peabodymemphis.com, $300-500) is the city's signature hotel. Founded in 1869, the Peabody was the grand hotel of the South, and the hotel has preserved some of its traditional Southern charm. Tuxedoed bellhops greet you at the door, and all guests receive a complimentary shoeshine. The 464 rooms and 15 suites are nicely appointed with plantation-style furniture, free wireless Internet, and in-room safes, as well as all the amenities typical of an upper-tier hotel. Several fine restaurants are located on the ground floor, including the lobby bar, which is the gathering place for the twice-daily red carpet march of the famous Peabody ducks. Both self-parking ($24 per day) and valet ($33 per day) are available for guests, and the hotel is also pet friendly.

One of Memphis's more unusual hotels is the **River Inn of Harbor Town** (50 Harbor Town Sq., 901/260-3333, www.riverinnmemphis.com, $300-680). A 28-room boutique hotel on Mud Island, the River Inn offers great river views and an unusual location that is just minutes from downtown. Set in the mixed residential and commercial New Urbanist community of Harbor Town, the River Inn provides guests with super amenities, like a fitness center, reading rooms on each floor, free parking, several restaurants including a rooftop bar, and a 1.5-mile (2.4-km) walking trail. Even the most modest rooms have luxurious extras like fireplaces, chocolate truffle and wine turndown service, and gourmet breakfast. The River Inn offers the best of both worlds—a relaxing and quiet getaway that is still convenient to the center of Memphis.

With a name and look that aims to pay homage to the hues of Memphis and one of its best-known citizens, **Hu. Hotel** (79 Madison Ave., 866/446-3674, http://huhotelmemphis.com,

River Inn of Harbor Town

$195-235, valet parking $28/night) offers a modern aesthetic in an old beaux arts bank building. Formerly the Madison Hotel, Hu. Hotel now features a check-in at the coffee shop (the barista will hand you your key), sleek and minimalist guest rooms, and a rooftop bar with great views of the mighty Mississippi, Big River Crossing, and AutoZone Park. It honors Hu Brinkley, the grandson of one of the founders of Memphis, and an icon in his own right. He raised the money to build the Lyceum Theatre and served in the state legislature and as vice mayor.

It is hard to describe the **Big Cypress Lodge** (1 Bass Pro Dr., 800/223-3333 and 901/620-4600, www.big-cypress.com, $385-800) without making it sound a little crazy. First of all, this 103-room hotel is inside a giant pyramid that houses a Bass Pro Shops retail store. Opulent rooms are designed to look like tree houses and duck-hunting cabins. Rooms overlook a cypress swamp filled with alligators and fish and the retail shopping of the Bass Pro store. But for all its quirkiness, this hotel, which opened

in 2015, is a luxury resort, with all the associated amenities, including a spa and a bowling alley. Expect to pay a $20 resort fee plus $15 per day for parking.

MIDTOWN

Midtown hotels are cheaper than those in downtown. By car, they are convenient to city-center attractions, and all of midtown is right outside your door.

UNDER $100

For affordable accommodations in in Cooper-Young, check in to **Hostel Memphis** (1000 S. Cooper St., 901/273-8341, http://hostelmemphis.com, $25-55). Options include single-sex and coed dorm rooms for $25 per night or private rooms for $55 (all bathrooms are shared). The hostel offers Wi-Fi, continental breakfast, bike storage, and access to common areas.

$100-150

The **Best Western Plus Gen X Inn** (1177 Madison Ave., 901/692-9136, www.bestwestern.com, $98-200) straddles downtown and midtown Memphis, about 2 miles (3.2 km) from the city center along the Madison Avenue trolley line. Gen Xers can get downtown on the trolley in about 15 minutes, with a little luck. The hotel, which has free parking and breakfast, is also accessible to the city's expansive medical center and the attractions around Overton Park. These rooms are standard hotel style, enhanced with bright colors, flat-panel plasma TVs, and a general aura of youthfulness. The whole hotel is nonsmoking, and guests enjoy a good continental breakfast and a special partnership with the downtown YMCA for gym use. This is a good choice for travelers who want to be near downtown but are on a budget, particularly those with a car. No pets are permitted.

The **Holiday Inn-University of Memphis** (3700 Central Ave., 901/678-8200, www.holidayinn.com, $130-165) is part of the university's hospitality school. All rooms are suites, with a wet bar and microwave, sitting room, and spacious bathrooms. The lobby contains an exhibit on Kemmons Wilson, the Memphis-born founder of Holiday Inn, who is credited with inventing the modern hotel industry. It is about 6 miles (10 km) from downtown Memphis.

OVER $200

The five rooms available in **The James Lee House** (690 Adams Ave., www.jamesleehouse.com, 901/359-6750, $245-450) may be in one of the most opulent homes you've had the pleasure to stay in. The building dates to the 19th century, but the inn's amenities, such as wireless internet and private gated parking, are 21st century.

You can sleep where Elvis slept at ✪ **Lauderdale Courts** (252 N. Lauderdale St., 901/523-8662, $250). The onetime housing project where Elvis and his parents lived after they moved to Memphis from Mississippi is now a neat midtown apartment complex. The rooms where the Presleys lived have been restored to their 1950s greatness, and guests can use the working 1951 Frigidaire. The rooms are decorated with Presley family photographs and other Elvis memorabilia. You can rent Lauderdale Courts No. 328 for up to six nights. It sleeps up to four adults. The rooms are not rented during Elvis Week in August or his birthday week in January, when the suite is open for public viewing.

SOUTH MEMPHIS

There are two reasons to stay in South Memphis: the airport and Graceland. But even if you are keenly interested in either of these places, you should think twice about staying in this part of town. You will need a car, as some of these neighborhoods are seedy and South Memphis is not within walking distance of anything of interest. Book early for **Elvis Week** in August.

UNDER $100

Expect Elvis kitsch at the **Days Inn at Graceland** (3839 Elvis Presley Blvd., 901/410-3967, $75-95), one of the most well-worn properties in the venerable Days Inn chain. Tune in to free nonstop Elvis movies or swim in a guitar-shaped pool. There is a free continental breakfast.

The **Magnuson Grand Memphis Hotel** (1471 E. Brooks Rd., 901/207-7924, www.magnusonhotels.com, $38-125) is a tidy, safe oasis in an otherwise unappealing part of town. Before its remodel, being close to Graceland and the airport were the only draws of this budget hotel. It remains affordable, but now it has the added perk of being clean, with updated rooms and bathrooms, plus a restaurant and bar. There's a decent outdoor pool, a small fitness room, and a lovely lobby.

$150-200

Opened in 2016, **The Guest House at Graceland** (3600 Elvis Presley Blvd., 901/443-3000, http://guesthousegraceland.com, from $178) is a 430-room Elvis-themed hotel. The property has 20 themed suites, the design of which was supervised by Priscilla Presley herself. The hotel has two full-service, albeit average, restaurants and a grab-and-go café, plus an outdoor pool and a 464-seat theater for performances and films (starring Elvis, of course). The decor is sleek and contemporary, but you still get plenty of Elvis kitsch. Pets weighing less than 35 pounds are welcome with an additional $50 daily cleaning fee per dog. If you remember the old Heartbreak Hotel on this property, you will be pleasantly surprised by this upgrade, with clean rooms, modern décor, and decent amenities. But the primary appeal of the Guest House is its proximity to Graceland. If that's not of interest, there's not a lot of other reason to stay here.

CAMPING

You can pitch your tent or park your RV just a 15-minute drive from downtown Memphis at **T. O. Fuller State Park** (1500 Mitchell Rd., 901/543-7581, http://reserve.tnstateparks.com, $25).

The park has 45 tent and RV sites, each with a picnic table, fire ring, grill, lantern hanger, and electrical and water hookups.

On the north side of Memphis, **Meeman-Shelby Forest State Park** (910 Riddick Rd., Millington, 901/876-5215, http://reserve.tnstateparks.com, $25-27) is a half-hour drive from downtown. Stay in one of six lakeside cabins, which you can reserve up to one year in advance; book at least one month in advance to avoid being shut out. The two-bedroom cabins can sleep up to six people. Rates are $100-125 per night, depending on the season and day of the week. There are also 49 tent/RV sites ($25-27), each with electrical and water hookups, picnic tables, grills, and fire rings. The bathhouse has hot showers.

Information and Services

INFORMATION

VISITORS CENTERS

The city's visitors center is the **Tennessee Welcome Center** (119 Riverside Dr., 901/543-6757, www.tnvacation.com, 7am-9pm daily), located on the Tennessee side of the I-40 bridge. The center has lots of brochures and free maps and staff who can answer your questions. It also has a picnic area and pet-walking area.

Although it is not designed to be a visitors center per se, the **Memphis Convention and Visitors Bureau** (47 Union Ave., 901/543-5333, www.memphistravel.com,. 8:30am-5pm Mon.-Fri.) is a resource for visitors during the week. You can collect maps and ask questions. The bureau also produces videos highlighting city

attractions and restaurants, which are available on many hotel televisions.

The free maps provided at the concierge desk of the Peabody Hotel are particularly well marked and useful. If you want to explore further, or if you plan to drive yourself around the city, it is wise to get a proper city map or GPS. Rand McNally publishes a detailed Memphis city map, which you can buy from bookstores or convenience marts in downtown.

EMERGENCY SERVICES

Dial 911 in an emergency for fire, ambulance, or police. The downtown police department is the **North Main Station** (444 N. Main St., 901/636-4099). Police patrol downtown by car, on bike, and on foot.

Several agencies operate hotlines for those needing help. They include **Emergency Mental Health Services** (855/274-7471), **Shelby County Crime Victims & Rape Crisis Center** (901/222-4350), **Poison Emergencies** (800/222-1222), **Alcoholics Anonymous** (901/454-1414), and the **Better Business Bureau** (901/759-1300).

HOSPITALS

Memphis is chockablock with hospitals. Midtown Memphis is also referred to as Medical Center for the number of hospitals and medical facilities there. Here you will find the **Regional Medical Center at Memphis** (877 Jefferson Ave., 901/545-7100), a 325-bed teaching hospital affiliated with the University of Tennessee; and the **Methodist University Hospital** (1265 Union Ave., 901/516-7000), the 617-bed flagship hospital for Methodist Healthcare.

In East Memphis, **Baptist Memorial Hospital** (6019 Walnut Grove Rd., 901/226-5000) is the cornerstone of the huge Baptist Memorial Health Care System, with 771 beds.

Transportation

GETTING THERE

AIR

Memphis International Airport (MEM, 2491 Winchester Rd., 901/922-8000, www.flymemphis.com) is 13 miles (21 km) south of downtown Memphis. There are two popular routes to Memphis from the airport. Take I-240 north to arrive in midtown. To reach downtown, take I-55 north and exit on Riverside Drive. The drive takes 20-30 minutes.

The airport's main international travel insurance and business services center (901/922-8090) is in the ticket lobby of Terminal B and is open 9am-5pm daily. Here you can exchange foreign currency, buy travel insurance, conduct money transfers, and buy money orders and travelers checks. There is free Wi-Fi throughout the airport from Boingo, with premium paid service available for streaming video or downloading large files.

Airport Shuttle

TennCo Express (901/527-2992, www.tenncoexpress.com) provides an hourly shuttle service from the airport to many downtown hotels. Tickets are $20 one-way and $30 round-trip and can be purchased at the ground-level shuttle stop. Look for the shuttle parked in the third lane near column 14 outside the airport terminal. Shuttles depart every 30 minutes 7:30am-9:30pm. For a hotel pickup, call at least a day in advance or reserve online.

CAR

Memphis is at the intersection of two major interstate highways: I-40, which runs east-west across the United States, and I-55, which runs south from St. Louis to New Orleans.

Many people who visit Memphis drive here in their own cars. The city is 130 miles (210 km) from Little Rock, 200 miles (320 km) from Nashville, 300 miles (485 km) from St. Louis, 380 miles (610 km) from Atlanta, 410 miles (660 km) from New Orleans, and 560 miles (900 km) from Chicago.

BUS

Greyhound (800/231-2222, www. greyhound.com) runs daily bus service to Memphis from around the United States. Direct service is available to Memphis from surrounding cities, including Jackson and Nashville, Tennessee; Tupelo and Jackson, Mississippi; Little Rock and Jonesboro, Arkansas; and St. Louis, Missouri. The Greyhound station (3033 Airways Blvd., 901/395-8770) is open 24 hours a day.

TRAIN

Amtrak (800/872-7245, www.amtrak. com) runs the City of New Orleans train daily between Chicago and New Orleans, stopping in Memphis on the way. The southbound train arrives daily at Memphis's Central Station at 6:27am, leaving at 6:40am. The northbound train arrives at 10:20pm every day, departing at 10:40pm. It is an 11-hour ride overnight between Memphis and Chicago, and about 8 hours between Memphis and New Orleans.

The Amtrak station (901/526-0052) is in Central Station (545 S. Main St.) in the South Main Arts District of downtown. Ticket and baggage services are available at the station daily 5:45am-11pm.

GETTING AROUND

DRIVING

Driving is the most popular and easiest way to get around Memphis. Downtown parking is plentiful if you are prepared to pay; an all-day pass in one of the many downtown parking garages costs anywhere from $12 to $25, depending on events that day.

Traffic congestion peaks predictably at rush hours and is worst in the eastern parts of the city and along the interstates. But traffic isn't the problem it is in Nashville; Memphis commutes are considered more reasonable.

PUBLIC TRANSPORTATION
Buses

The **Memphis Area Transit Authority** (901/274-6282, www. matatransit.com) operates dozens of buses that travel through the greater Memphis area. For information on routes, call or stop by the North End Terminal on North Main Street for help planning your trip. The bus system is not used frequently by tourists. A daily pass is available for $3.50, a seven-day pass is $16, and a 31-day pass is $50.

Sun Studio runs a **free shuttle** between Sun Studio, the Rock 'n' Soul Museum at Beale Street, and Graceland (www.memphisrocknsoul. org/sunstudioshuttle). The first run stops at the Guest House at Graceland at 9:55am, Graceland at 10am, Sun Studio at 10:15am, and the Rock 'n' Soul Museum at 10:30am. Runs continue throughout the day on an hourly schedule. The last run picks up at the Guest House at 5:55pm, Graceland Plaza at 6pm, and Sun Studio at 6:15pm. The shuttle is a 12-passenger black van painted with the Sun Studio logo. The ride is free, but consider tipping your driver. The published schedule is a loose approximation, so it's a good idea to get to the pickup point early in case the van is running ahead. You can call 901/521-0664 for more information.

Trolleys

Public trolleys (or hybrid bus shuttles when the trolleys are being serviced) run for about 2 miles (3.2 km) along Main Street in Memphis from the Pinch District in the north to Central Station in the south (red line), and circle up on a parallel route along Riverfront Drive and Front Street (green line). Another trolley line (yellow line) runs about 2 miles (3.2 km) east on Madison Avenue, connecting the city's medical center and midtown with downtown. The Main Street trolleys run every 20 minutes at most times, but the Madison Avenue trolleys only run until 6pm on weekday evenings and 6:30pm on Saturday evenings, with no service on Sundays.

Memphis trolley

The trolley system, run by the **Memphis Area Transit Authority** (901/274-6282, www.matatransit.com), is useful, especially if your hotel is on either the northern or southern end of downtown or along Madison Avenue. Brochures with details on the routes and fares are available all over town, or you can download one online. The trolleys are simple to understand and use; if you have a question, just ask your driver.

Fares are $1, and trolleys accept both cash and transit passes on board. Daily FastPasses are usable on both trolleys and fixed-route buses and can be purchased at the North End Terminal at the northern end of the Main Street route.

TAXI AND RIDE-SHARE

Memphis has a number of taxi companies, and you will usually find available cabs along Beale Street and waiting at the airport. Otherwise, you will need to call for a taxi. Some of the largest companies are **Yellow Cab** (901/577-7777, www.yellowcabofmemphis.com), **City Wide Taxi** (901/722-8294, http://citywidetaxi.net), and **Metro Cab** (901/322-2222). Expect to pay $25-35 for a trip from the airport to downtown; most fares around town are under $10. Taxis accept credit cards. App-based ride-sharing services like Uber and Lyft (approximately $17 from the airport to downtown) operate in Memphis and have agreements with the local government to allow them to make stops at the airport and other destinations.

Ride-sharing services that use an app and contracted drivers in their own vehicles are becoming a popular solution in cities. **Lyft** (www.lyft.com) or **Uber** (www.uber.com) serve Memphis, Little Rock, Hot Springs, Oxford, Tupelo, and other nearby cities.

BICYCLE

With more than 60 stations around town, **Explore Bike Share** (901/292-0707, explorebikeshare.bcycle.com) is a great way to see Memphis on two wheels. Pay $1.25 for every 15 minutes as you go, or by a $5 day pass or $10 for a weekly pass. The system is set up with an app and a credit card, but you can arrange to pay with cash by calling ahead. Stations are all over the city, but concentrated downtown and midtown.

To rent bicycles, or get parts and repairs for your existing bike, try **Peddler Bike Shop** (3548 Walker Ave., 901/327-4833, http://peddler-bikeshop.com, 9am-6pm Mon.-Fri., 9am-5pm Sat., 1pm-5pm Sun.), which has three other locations in the greater Memphis area. **Bike Plus** (9445 Poplar Ave., Germantown, 901/755-7233, http://bikesplus.net, 10am-6pm Mon.-Fri., 10am-5pm Sat.) is another full-service shop for repairs and rentals, with a second location in Bartlett (7124 Hwy.64/Stage Rd., Suite 115).

EXCURSIONS

With its location on the bluffs of

the Mississippi River, Memphis is at the far western end of Tennessee. But if you're using Memphis as a jumping-off point for further exploration, it's not really the end—it's just the beginning.

To the south is Mississippi. Music lovers will want to follow the **Mississippi Blues Trail**, which begins in Memphis. This meandering route stops at places significant to the history and evolution of this local art form. You can follow the entire trail or see it in in pieces, focusing on the locales of most interest to you, from the restaurants and

Excursions From Memphis

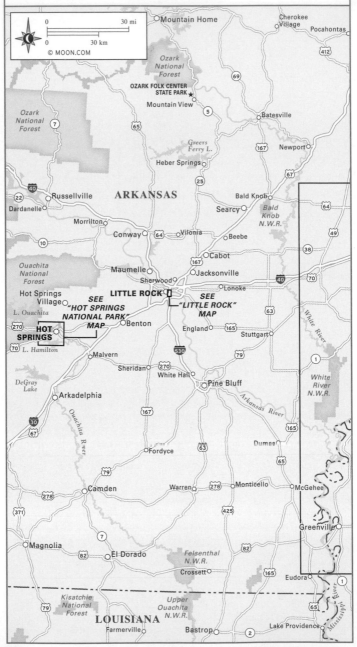

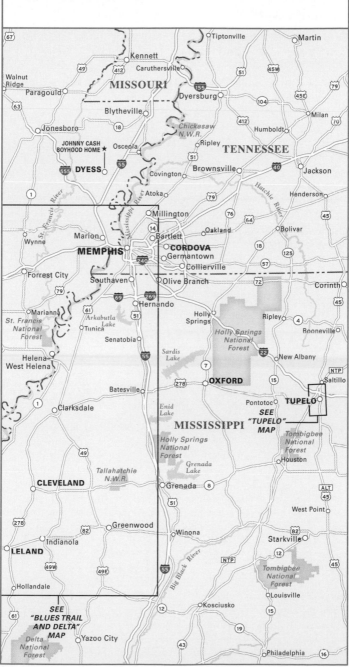

HIGHLIGHTS

✪ **BEST PLACE TO LEARN ABOUT THE BLUES:** The role of the Delta in American music is beautifully laid out to see—and more importantly, to hear—in the **Grammy Museum Mississippi** (page 125).

✪ **BEST PLACE TO SEE WHERE THE LEGEND BEGAN:** The **Elvis Presley Birthplace** is a popular stop, not just for fans of the King of Rock 'n' Roll, but for anyone who appreciates music history (page 128).

✪ **PLACE WHERE YOU'LL HEAR "HOTTY TODDY" AS A GREETING:** Explore the historical and collegiate charms of the **University of Mississippi**—more affectionately known as Ole Miss (page 136).

✪ **BEST PLACE TO BETTER UNDERSTAND** *THE SOUND AND THE FURY*: Gain insight into author William Faulkner's creative inspiration at his family home, **Rowan Oak** (page 138).

✪ **BEST PLACE THAT SHOWS HOW A FEW PEOPLE CAN CHANGE THE WORLD:** The nation took some significant steps toward greater equality thanks to nine brave students at **Little Rock Central High School** (page 143).

✪ **BEST PLACE TO PEEK INSIDE OTHER PEOPLE'S HANDBAGS:** Women's history is told through the fashionable accessories at **ESSE Purse Museum** in Little Rock (page 146).

✪ **MOST HISTORIC PLACE TO GET WET:** In Hot Springs, the restored and repurposed **Bathhouse Row** gives a glimpse into the history of the national parks and provides modern-day relaxation (page 160).

clubs where live music fills the room to the birthplaces of blues greats. Elvis Presley fans should head to his birthplace in **Tupelo** to see the spots that were formative in his youth. Fans of another native son, William Faulkner, will be interested in **Oxford,** which is a center of intellectual life thanks to the University of Mississippi, as well as a great place to cheer on college sports.

To the west is Arkansas. From the banks of the Arkansas River, **Little Rock** offers a gateway to outdoor recreation, as well a landmark in civil rights history, a presidential library, museums, and a thriving foodie scene.

Nestled in the Ouachita Mountains (pronounced WAH-shu-tah), **Hot Springs** is known as America's first resort, thanks to its 143-degree thermal water. Come to explore, relax, and recharge. Trips to these two Arkansas destinations can easily be combined or explored separately.

PLANNING YOUR TIME

These excursions are easy to reach…as long as you have a car. The Mississippi Blues Trail, Oxford, and Tupelo can be explored in one loop to the south; Little Rock and Hot Springs are an easy loop to the west.

As with all **road trips,** the number of adventures you can experience expands when you have more time. Each of these cities—Oxford, Tupelo, Little Rock, and Hot Springs—can be explored in a **long weekend.** If you have more time, plan on a more leisurely pace. Plan on four days minimum to explore the Mississippi Blues Trail, unless you want to spend all your time in the car.

Music fans should prioritize the Mississippi Blues Trail and Tupelo. **Foodies** and devotees of **Southern literature** should make Oxford first on their list. Those who love the **great outdoors** should head to Little Rock and Hot Springs. **History fans** should know that there's something significant and essential in every excursion: Tupelo has Civil War sites; Little Rock was a center of the U.S. civil rights movement; Hot Springs is known as America's first resort.

All of these destinations have four-season charms, although **summer** can be hot and humid in Mississippi. **Ole Miss football games** are a sought-after ticket in Oxford, so hotel rooms are hard to come by; check the schedule in advance. Hot Springs, in particular, is lovely year-round, with **spring wildflowers,** colorful **fall foliage,** and **winter snow.** Summer means more crowds. Autumn is a dream and includes the annual Hot Springs Documentary Film Festival in October.

Mississippi Blues Trail

There are nearly 200 sites included as part of the **Mississippi Blues Trail** (www.msbluestrail.org). Visiting all of them would be a considerable undertaking, but some diehard blues fans make the pilgrimage. Several of the sites are in Memphis, making it a good starting place for the exploration. The must-see stops covered in this guide delve into the history and influence of blues greats like Muddy Waters and B. B King. However, there are many more, some mere markers or plaques about artists from the town or what happened on that spot—even blues fans might want to skip some. If you're only casually acquainted with the blues, it's likely that this side trip isn't for you. But embarking on this trip may convert you!

This section covers 170 miles of the Blues Trail, with stops in Tunica, Friar's Point, Clarksdale, Indianola, and Leland. Driving from Memphis south to Leland will take just over three hours, not including time for sightseeing and meals, so you'll want to plan on at least two days, with an overnight stay in Leland before you turn back to Memphis.

Make sure your car has good speakers and your phone is charged up, because you'll be in the mood to listen to a lot of music.

TUNICA

Tunica is best known as a gateway to the casinos just over the state line. But the **Gateway to the Blues Museum** (13625 U.S. 61 N., 888/488-6422, www.tunicatravel.com, 8:30am-5pm Mon.-Fri., 10am-5pm Sat., 1pm-5pm Sun., adults $10, children 12 and under $5)

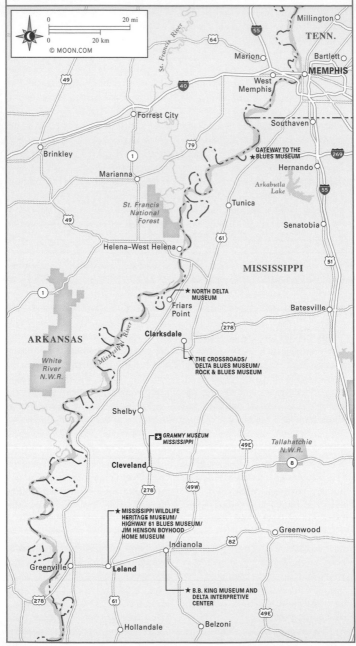

The Blues Trail and the Delta

offers a different kind of excitement. This 3,500-square-foot museum has six different galleries where you can learn about the history of the blues and how the local geography contributed to the genre. There's even an exhibition where you can record your own blues song (delivered via email). Housed in an old railroad station, the museum is connected to the **Tunica Visitors Center,** where you can get information about the area and browse the gift shop.

GETTING THERE

Tunica is 30 miles southwest of downtown Memphis. It's a 40-minute drive down U.S. 61 to get there.

FRIARS POINT

Music is in the water in tiny Friars Point. Robert Nighthawk, considered one of the foremost blues guitarists, lived here off and on for years, even working the town into song lyrics. Nighthawk's Blues Trail marker is right outside historic **Hirsberg Drug Store,** where many legendary musicians, including Robert Johnson, have played. Country legend Conway Twitty was also born here (as Harold Lloyd Jenkins).

Friars Point is home to the **North Delta Museum** (748 2nd St., 662/383-2233, 9am-2pm Mon.-Fri., adults $4, children under 7 $2), a small local heritage museum with lots of blues-related artifacts. The museum is closed for renovation; call ahead to see if it has reopened.

GETTING THERE

Friars Point is about a 45-minute drive south of Tunica along U.S. 61. After about 25 miles on U.S. 61, turn right onto Friars Point Road. Continue for about 8 miles, turn right onto Sheriff Ridge Avenue, then turn left onto Washington Street after two blocks. Make a right onto 2nd Street to get to the North Delta Museum.

CLARKSDALE

At the intersection of Old U.S. 49 and Old U.S. 61, Clarksdale is often referred to as **The Crossroads.** Legend goes that bluesman Robert Johnson sold his soul to the devil here in exchange for his musical talent. Today, the intersection (Desoto Ave. and N. State St./MS-161) is marked by a crossroads sign with giant guitars. This Mississippi Delta town was also important to civil rights history. In 1958, Martin Luther King Jr. visited the town for the first major meeting of what would become the Southern Christian Leadership Conference (SCLC).

SIGHTS

On your way into Clarksdale from Friars Point, you can take a short detour and drive by the former site of **Muddy Waters's House at Stovall Farms** (4146 Oakhurst Stovall Rd., 662/624-2153), where the legend was born. The sign is just past the entrance to the farm. From Friars Point, take Friars Point Road south for about three miles to MS-1 South. After about two miles, turn left onto Old River Road, which will soon turn into Oakhurst Stovall Road. Follow this for two miles to reach the cabin. Continue on Oakhurst Stovall Road for four miles to reach Clarksdale.

Created in 1979 and made a standalone museum in 1999, the **Delta Blues Museum** (1 Blues Alley, 662/627-6820, www.deltabluesmuseum.org, 9am-5pm Mon.-Sat. Mar.-Oct., 10am-5pm Mon.-Sat. Nov.-Feb., adults $10, children 6-12 $8, children under 6 free) is the state's oldest music museum. It's housed in an old train depot, originally built in 1918 for the Yazoo and Mississippi Railroad lines, and has both permanent and changing exhibitions. Muddy Waters's cabin has been relocated here from its original site a few miles northwest.

Next door is the **Ground Zero Blues Club** (387 Delta Ave., 662/621-9009, www.groundzerobluesclub.com, 11am-2pm Mon.-Tues., 11am-11pm Wed.-Thurs., 11am-2am Fri.-Sat., closed Mon.-Tues. in late fall and winter), a restaurant and bar with live music in a juke joint atmosphere. It is partly owned by actor and Mississippi Delta advocate Morgan Freeman, and the menu includes barbecue, catfish, and tamales, a favorite dish in this region.

Music memorabilia from 1920 to 1970 is on display at the **Rock & Blues Museum** (113 E. 2nd St., 662/524-5144, www.blues2rock.com, 10am-5pm Thurs.-Tues., $5). This small museum is a good place to see (and hear) how blues music connects to other genres.

FESTIVALS AND EVENTS

If you really want to get your feet tapping, consider coming to Clarksdale for the **Sunflower River Blues & Gospel Festival** (www.sunflowerfest.org) in August or the **Juke Joint Festival** (www.jukejointfestival.com) in April. Hotel rooms are at a premium then, so plan ahead.

ACCOMMODATIONS

If you want to stay overnight in Clarksdale, do so at the historic ✪ **Riverside Hotel** (615 Sunflower Ave., 662/624-9163, $70-110), where Muddy Waters, Duke Ellington, and Ike Turner have all stayed. The rooms of the brick-front building are clean but not fancy, with simple lamps, beds,

Ground Zero Blues Club

U.S. 61 is often called the Blues Highway, and some say it rivals Route 66 as the most famous road in American music history. Dozens of blues artists have recorded songs about **Highway 61.** The first was Roosevelt Sykes's "Highway 61 Blues," recorded back in 1932. Bob Dylan even named an album after it in 1965.

The original route is now known as Old Highway 61, while the newer one is part of the U.S. highway system. The old route (west of the new road) was winding and, in the state of Mississippi, largely unpaved. It was one long road from New Orleans to Grand Portage, Minnesota, near the Canadian border.

Honestly, the route today ain't much to look at. It's not particularly scenic. Like many highways, it goes through patches of desolation and clusters of commercial developments. But it is the fastest way to see many of the sights along the Blues Trail and to get a feel for the towns of the Mississippi Delta.

and dressers and shared bathrooms,. But there's Wi-Fi and the location is close to local blues sites. A historic tour of the building is included.

GETTING THERE

Clarksdale is about a 20-minute drive from Friars Point. Take Friars Point Road south for about 13 miles to get into the heart of Clarksdale. From Memphis it is a 1.5-hour drive (75 miles).

CLEVELAND

Thanks to Delta State University and a quaint, thriving downtown, Cleveland has sweet boutiques and plenty of restaurants and bars, plus a growing independent hotel scene.

✪ GRAMMY MUSEUM MISSISSIPPI

Opened in 2016, the **Grammy Museum Mississippi** (800 W. Sunflower Rd., 662/441-0100, www. grammymuseumms.org, 10am-5:30pm Tues.-Sat., 1pm-5:30pm Sun., adults $14, seniors $12, students and children 6 and over $8, children 4 and under free) is the institution's first outside Los Angeles. This says a lot about how seriously the music establishment takes preserving the blues and educating people about the role the

Mississippi Delta had in American music.

This 27,000-square-foot facility is spectacular. The building itself is designed to honor the architecture of the region, with a large front porch where people can hang out and listen to music, and incorporating building materials reflective of the types of materials used in the area, albeit on a much grander scale. The museum was purposefully located next to the campus of Delta State University, so that it can be an educational force was well as a tourism draw. The **Delta Center for Culture and Learning** (www. deltacenterdsu.com) is also nearby on campus and hosts educational programming.

The Grammy Museum has more than 12 different interactive exhibits, many designed for you to share with your fellow visitors. Plan to stay for several hours to listen to all the music, including in a 130-seat theater that often has concerts. The museum does an excellent job of linking the blues to other genres. There are exhibits where you can try to make your own music and poignant displays of artifacts from musicians from the region. It has a decent gift shop as well.

The Grammy Museum, by a function of its backers, is more professional

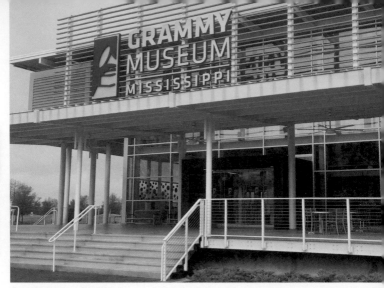
Grammy Museum Mississippi

than most of the other small, labor-of-love museums that dot U.S. 61. To be sure, there's a homegrown quality in those other venues that is lost here. But the professionalism doesn't give way to slickness; the character of the Delta and its music has been preserved. The museum has the feel of an important American institution, albeit in an out-of-the-way place.

FOOD

Pull in to ✪ **Airport Grocery** (3608 U.S. 61, 662/843-4817, 11am-10pm Mon.-Sat., 5pm-9pm Sun., $5-28). You'll find a friendly staff serving po'boys, barbecue, and burgers, plus fried and charcoal-grilled fish entrées, inside what was once a grocery store. Live blues music is played many nights.

Closer to downtown, **Hey Joe's** (118 E. Sunflower Rd., 662/843-5425, www.eatheyjoes.com, 11am-9pm Mon.-Sat., $6-12) serves gourmet burgers, wings, salads, and chili dogs in a casual but hipster environment.

Don't miss the signature dessert: the Moon Man, a deep-fried Moon Pie. This is a casual, kid-friendly spot for lunch, or a place to grab a beer and hear live music at night. If neither of these appeal, stroll down Cotton Row and Sharpe Avenue, where you'll find several charming options.

ACCOMMODATIONS

Hotel rooms can be at a premium in Cleveland, particularly when there's a football game at Delta State.

The 95-room **Cotton House** (215 Cotton Row, 662/843-7733, www.cottonhousecleveland.com, $189) is walking distance from the downtown district and the Grammy Museum. The hotel has retail space, **Bar Fontaine** (4pm-11pm daily), a dinner restaurant with a James Beard nominee as a chef, **Delta Meat Market**, a casual lunch place, and a rooftop bar.

The reliable **Holiday Inn Express & Suites** (808 N. Davis Ave., 662/843-9300, www.ihg.com/holidayinnexpress, $98-118) offers free breakfast and Wi-Fi and has an outdoor pool.

INFORMATION AND SERVICES

Bolivar Medical Center (901 MS-8 E., 662/846-0061, www.bolivarmedical. com) is centrally located near downtown Cleveland.

GETTING THERE

Cleveland is about 40 minutes south of Clarksdale. To get there, take U.S. 278 West/U.S. 61 South for about 33 miles.

INDIANOLA

Famed bluesman B. B. King was born in tiny Itta Bena, about 25 miles east of Indianola. The latter's impressive **B. B. King Museum and Delta Interpretive Center** (400 2nd St., 662/887-9539, www.bbkingmuseum. org, noon-5pm Sun.-Mon., 10am-5pm Tues.-Sat. Apr.-Oct., noon-5pm Sun., 10am-5pm Tues.-Sat. Nov.-Mar., adults $15, seniors $12, students and children 5-7 $10, children 5 and younger free) chronicles the legend's rise to fame. The galleries, located in an old cotton gin, cover the music of the Delta in the 1920s, Memphis in the 1950s, and beyond. There are high-tech recordings and videos, lots of artifacts, and a gift shop. The museum opened in 2008; when King died in 2015 he was buried here and a garden was planted in his honor.

GETTING THERE

Indianola is about 30 miles south of Cleveland. Take U.S. 278/U.S. 61 south for nearly 10 miles, then turn left onto MS-448 and follow it for 15 miles.

LELAND

U.S. 61 runs right through the Delta town of Leland, which has a history as both a hard-drinking music hub and a genteel Southern getaway. Today, it's home to five different Mississippi Blues Trail markers as well as other quirky stops. Each December, fully lighted Christmas trees and displays float on Deer Creek, the small waterway that runs through town. In the works is the **Leland Blues Project Murals** (www.highway61blues.com).

SIGHTS

The old Montgomery Hotel in the heart of downtown is home to the **Highway 61 Blues Museum** (307 N. Broad St., 662/686-7646, www. highway61blues.com, 10am-5pm Mon.-Sat., $7). This is a labor of love, jam-packed with blues artifacts and info compiled by local enthusiasts. This particular museum has more visual art, including paintings and photography by Delta artists, than most music museums. If you call ahead, they'll do their best to have some musicians show up to play while you peruse, an experience no blues fan should miss. As is the case at many homespun museums, you should allow plenty of time to have conversations with the enthusiastic staff.

When in Leland you must swing by the **Jim Henson Boyhood Home Museum** (415 SE Deer Creek Dr., 662/686-7383, www. birthplaceofthefrog.org, 10am-5pm Mon.-Thurs. late May-early Sept., 10am-4pm Mon.-Sat. early Sept.-late May, free, donations encouraged). Henson was born in the Delta, and his family donated many artifacts to this odd roadside museum chock-full of Muppets and memorabilia, such as a large Kermit the Frog sitting on a lily pad, straight out of *The Muppet Movie*. "The Rainbow Connection" plays on a loop. The tiny gift shop is well stocked.

The museum backs up to Deer Creek, so expect a Kermit-themed Christmas display on the water in December.

Opened in 2017, the **Mississippi Wildlife Heritage Museum** (302 N. Broad St., 662/686-7085, www.mswildlifeheritagemuseum.com, 10am-5pm Mon.-Fri., adults $10, seniors $7, free for kids 16 and under) displays artifacts relating to the region's agricultural past, as well as an 1897 dugout canoe and a collection of turkey calls, all inside a renovated hardware store downtown.

FOOD

For lunch, stop at **Leland Cafe** (117 E. 3rd St., 662/771-5022, 11am-6pm Mon.-Fri., $8-13) for specialties like catfish, brisket, and pulled pork. **Vito's Marketplace** (107 N. Main St., 662/686-8486, 10am-9pm Wed.-Fri. and Sun., 5pm-9pm Sat.) is famous for its popular salad dressing, sold in grocery stores throughout the South. Carbo-load at dinner here with Italian favorites such as lasagna and spaghetti. Opt for the cauliflower pizza crust. You can catch live music on the patio when the weather cooperates.

ACCOMMODATIONS

Leland has several serviceable motels, but for a more intimate experience, book a night at ✪ **The Thompson House** (111. N. Deer Creek Dr. W., 662/820-7829, www.thompsonhousebb.com, $125-185), a 1902 Queen Anne home converted into a B&B and event center. Rooms have lovely views of Deer Creek and the staff is devoted to helping guests see the best of the region. Your daily breakfast should be enjoyed here.

GETTING THERE

Leland is 15 miles west of Indianola on U.S. 82, a 20-minute drive.

Tupelo

With a population of more than 38,000, Tupelo isn't close to being Mississippi's biggest city (Jackson, Gulfport, Hattiesburg, and several others are larger). But thanks to some famous locals, including Elvis Presley himself, Tupelo is somewhere you can have big, unexpected fun.

Nestled in Mississippi Hill Country, Tupelo is home to rich American music history, as well as a modern live music scene. There are plenty of museums devoted to art and Civil War history, more than enough places to eat and drink, and easy access to the National Park Service's Natchez Trace Parkway.

Tupelo was the first city to gain electricity under President Franklin Roosevelt's Tennessee Valley Authority initiatives. Don't miss the lighted neon TVA arrow sign on your way to downtown at the intersection of Main and Gloster. This landmark has been part of the city since 1945.

SIGHTS

✪ ELVIS PRESLEY BIRTHPLACE

If there is one thing for which Tupelo is known, it is the **Elvis**

Tupelo

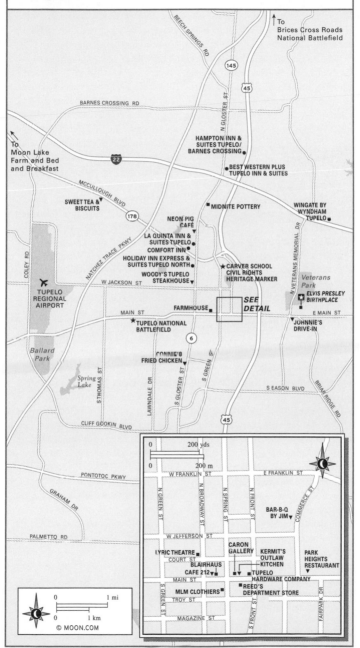

To
Brices Cross Roads
National Battlefield

145

45

BARNES CROSSING RD

To
Moon Lake
Farm and Bed
and Breakfast

22

BEECH SPRINGS RD

N GLOSTER ST

HAMPTON INN &
SUITES TUPELO/
BARNES CROSSING

BEST WESTERN PLUS
TUPELO INN & SUITES

MCCULLOUGH BLVD

SWEET TEA &
BISCUITS

178

MIDNITE POTTERY

WINGATE BY
WYNDHAM
TUPELO

NEON PIG
CAFÉ

LA QUINTA INN &
SUITES TUPELO
COMFORT INN

HOLIDAY INN EXPRESS &
SUITES TUPELO NORTH

WOODY'S TUPELO
STEAKHOUSE

Natchez Trace Pkwy

COLEY RD

TUPELO
REGIONAL
AIRPORT

CARVER SCHOOL
CIVIL RIGHTS
HERITAGE MARKER

W JACKSON ST

VETERANS MEMORIAL DR

Veterans
Park

ELVIS PRESLEY
BIRTHPLACE

MAIN ST

FARMHOUSE

SEE
DETAIL

E MAIN ST

Ballard
Park

TUPELO NATIONAL
BATTLEFIELD

6

JOHNNIE'S
DRIVE-IN

Spring
Lake

S THOMAS ST

LAWNDALE DR

S GLOSTER ST

S GREEN ST

CONNIE'S
FRIED CHICKEN

S EASON BLVD

BRIAR RIDGE RD

CLIFF GOOKIN BLVD

45

PONTOTOC PKWY

GRAHAM DR

PALMETTO RD

Detail

0   200 yds
0   200 m

W FRANKLIN ST   E FRANKLIN ST

COMMERCE ST

N GREEN ST

N BROADWAY ST

N SPRING ST

N FRONT ST

BAR-B-Q
BY JIM

W JEFFERSON ST

CARON
GALLERY

LYRIC THEATRE

KERMIT'S
OUTLAW
KITCHEN

PARK
HEIGHTS
RESTAURANT

COURT ST

BLAIRHAUS
CAFE 212

TUPELO
HARDWARE COMPANY

MAIN ST

S GREEN ST

MLM CLOTHIERS

REED'S
DEPARTMENT STORE

S FRONT ST

FAIRPARK DR

TROY ST

MAGAZINE ST

0   1 mi
0   1 km

© MOON.COM

Presley Birthplace (306 Elvis Presley Dr., 662/841-1245, www.elvispresleybirthplace.com, 9am-5pm Mon.-Sat., 1pm-5pm Sun., adults $18, seniors $14, children ages 7-12 $8, free for children under 7), which includes the house where Elvis was born, a museum, his childhood chapel, a gift shop, and much more. It's a physically compact site, accessible for fans of all ages.

the Elvis Presley Birthplace

Elvis Aaron Presley was born on January 8, 1935, in this two-room house that's been restored to its original condition. The family didn't live in the house long—hard financial times befell them. Elvis's talent was evident at a young age. When he was 11, his mother bought him a guitar at Tupelo Hardware Company. His pastor taught him to play, and the gospel music he learned in Tupelo influenced his entire career.

While Memphis's Graceland is better known, the Birthplace feels more immersive and more intimate. You can stop just to see the exterior of the small home and chapel. The **house tour** (adults $8, children $5) takes you inside the family home. True fans will find it worthwhile to take the **Grand Tour** (adults $18, seniors $14, children

$8), which provides entry to the chapel and museum, which is full of artifacts that celebrate his life and music. You'll learn about how blues and gospel influenced Elvis's signature sound.

Based at Elvis's mansion in Memphis, **Graceland Excursions** (901/332-3322 or 800/238-2000, www.graceland.com or www.elvis.com) offers motorcoach tours of historic music-centric regions including Tupelo (adults $99, children 5-12 $79) and the Mississippi Delta (adults $119, children $89), an option if you don't want to DIY. Tupelo stops include the Elvis Presley Birthplace, Tupelo Hardware Company, and Johnnie's Drive-In.

BRICES CROSS ROADS NATIONAL BATTLEFIELD

The **Brices Cross Roads National Battlefield** (U.S. 45 and MS-370, Baldwyn, 662/365-3969, www.nps.gov/brcr, 9am-5pm Tues.-Sat., free) marks the site where in June 1864 a scrappy Confederate army, led by Major General Nathan Bedford Forrest, defeated a larger Union force. Some counts suggest that as many as five times more Union troops died here than Confederate soldiers. This battle, also referred to as the Battle of Guntown or Tishomingo Creek, allowed the Confederates to temporarily secure supply lines between Nashville and Chattanooga, Tennessee.

History buffs should plan to spend at least 90 minutes at this collection of sites about 20 miles north of Tupelo proper. These sites are close together, so it's an easy walk to see it all. The best-known site is a one-acre section of the battlefield, which includes an imposing concrete monument topped by an eagle. The **monument,** at the corner of the park near MS-370, honors those who lost their lives in the battle. It's surrounded by cannons and foliage. You can also pay your respects at the 96 Confederate graves at **Bethany A. R. P. Church Cemetery,** visit the church (which became a field hospital after the battle), and walk interpretive trails.

Nearby, in the town of Baldwyn, is the **Final Stands Interpretive Center** (607 Grisham St., Baldwyn, 662/365-3969, www.finalstands.com, 9am-5pm Tues.-Sat., adults $5, children 12 and under $2). This center has a 4,000-square-foot building with artifacts, museum-style exhibits, a bookstore, and two short films for those who want to immerse themselves in the battle.

To get to Brices Cross Roads from Tupelo, take U.S. 45 north for nearly 10 miles, exiting at MS-348. Go west for less than a mile, then turn right (north) onto County Road 833. Go five miles and continue straight when CR 833 becomes MS-370. The entrance will be on your right.

TUPELO NATIONAL BATTLEFIELD
For two days in July 1864, 20,000 Confederate and Union soldiers fought at the site of **Tupelo National Battlefield** (2083 Main St., www. nps.gov/tupe, dawn-dusk daily, free). Today the battlefield resembles a small city park. It contains a small statue with an eagle atop it next to two cannons and an American flag. It can be tricky to find parking right at the battlefield site, but there is plenty of street parking on surrounding blocks. The site is listed in the National Register of Historic Places.

Tupelo National Battlefield

CARVER SCHOOL CIVIL RIGHTS HERITAGE MARKER
Built in 1939, Carver Elementary School was an important part of the Tupelo civil rights movement, both as a school for African American students as well as a meeting place for the black community. The **Carver School Civil Rights Heritage Marker** (1045 N. Green St.), standing in front of what is still an elementary school today, acknowledges this history.

OREN DUNN CITY MUSEUM
Housed in a converted dairy barn inside Ballard Park, the **Oren Dunn City Museum** (689 Rutherford Rd., 662/841-6438, www.tupeloms.gov, 9am-5pm Mon.-Fri., free) tells the story of Tupelo, Mississippi Hill Country, and Chickasaw cultural history. This is a great place to take the kids for an hour or two, thanks to its playgrounds, picnic areas, and a lakeside walking trail. The museum hosts the annual Dudie Burger Festival and the Dogtrot Rockabilly Festival.

Just west of Tupelo, the Natchez Trace Parkway is a 444-mile ribbon of green connecting three states and 10,000 years of history. As you walk in the sunken footsteps of the Native Americans, Kaintuck boatmen, Confederate soldiers, and Daughters of the American Revolution, it's impossible not to feel connected to their journeys.

It's likely that the Choctaw and Chickasaw people made the first footpaths through the region. Early white settlers quickly identified the importance of a land route from Natchez to Nashville. One historian characterized the diverse array of people who used the Trace as "robbers, rugged pioneers, fashionable ladies, shysters, politicians, soldiers, scientists, and men of destiny, such as Aaron Burr, Andrew Jackson, and Meriwether Lewis."

Natchez Trace Parkway Headquarters and Visitors Center

Today. the parkway follows the general path of the old, sunken, unpaved Natchez Trace. It's great for walks, hikes, and photography. The **Natchez Trace Parkway Headquarters and Visitor Center** is just outside of Tupelo, near milepost 266. It's worth a quick detour while in town. The **National Park Service** (800/305-7417, http://nps.gov/natr) publishes a foldout map, available in the headquarters gift shop. For more information on traveling on the Trace, see *Moon Nashville to New Orleans Road Trip.*

ENTERTAINMENT AND EVENTS

An art deco-style building near downtown, the historic **Lyric Theatre** (201 N. Broadway St., 662/844-1935, www.tct.ms) is home to many of Tupelo's performing arts productions by the Tupelo Community Theatre. TCT also operates **TCT Off Broadway** (213 E. Franklin St.), an 80-seat cabaret space. Ticket prices and showtimes vary by performance.

Folks in Mississippi love a festival. The Dudie Burger, named for the Dudie Diner, was a Tupelo mainstay, a burger made with meat, flour, and water. The diner is now part of the Oren Dunn City Museum, which brings the burger back for one day a year at the **Dudie Burger Festival** (662/841-6438) each May. May also brings people to downtown Tupelo for the two-day **GumTree Festival** (www.gumtreefestival.com), which includes a juried visual arts exhibition and singer-songwriter contest.

The **Tupelo Elvis Festival** (www.tupeloelvisfestival.com) honors hometown king Elvis Presley with live music for four days in early June.

SHOPPING

Shopping in downtown Tupelo is a browser's dream, with lots of small boutiques with one-of-a-kind wares. Find linens, furniture, antiques, and art at **FarmHouse** (530 W. Main St., 662/269-2934, www.farmhousetupelo.com, 10am-5:30pm Mon.-Sat., 1pm-5pm Sun.).

Even if you are not a shopper, you must stop at the historic **Tupelo**

Hardware Company (114 W. Main St., 662/842-4637, www.tupelohardware. com, 7am-5:30pm Mon.-Fri., 7am-noon Sat.). Open since 1926, this is a traditional hardware store, but it is where Elvis Presley's mother, Gladys, bought him his first guitar. He wanted a .22-caliber rifle for his birthday, but she didn't want him to have a gun, so she bought the guitar instead and history was born. The store has a plaque out front.

Caron Gallery (126 W. Main St., 662/205-0351, www.thecarongallery. com, 10am-5pm Mon.-Fri., 10am-4pm Sat.) represents more than 50 artists from the state of Mississippi. Interior design firm Blair Haus (208 W. Main St., 662/269-2513, www.blairhaus.com, 10am-5pm Tues.-Fri., 11am-4pm Sat.) has a small storefront space that sells furniture, linens, and artwork.

LM Clothiers (108 M. Spring St., 662/842-4165, www.mlmclothiers. com, 9am-6pm Mon.-Fri., 10am-5pm Sat.) claims to be the oldest men's clothing store in Mississippi.

First opened in 1905 as a dry goods general store, Reed's Department Store (131 W. Main St., 662/842-6453, www.reedsms.com, 9:30am-5:30pm Mon.-Sat.) is now a favorite Southern department store with clothing for men, women, and children.

Not downtown, but worth the drive,

is Midnite Pottery (2004 N. Gloster St., 662/842-8058, 10am-5pm Mon.-Sat.), a pottery studio with a creative local take on ceramics. Come for dishes, platters, candles, and jewelry.

FOOD

✪ Connie's Fried Chicken (821 M. Gloster St., 662/842-7260, 6am-8pm Mon.-Sat., 7am-1pm Sun., $8) is sometimes referred to as the "Café Du Monde of Tupelo," a reference to New Orleans's famous beignets. Connie's is a chicken shack, sure, but one that also sells delicious blueberry doughnuts, a Tupelo favorite. The doughnuts are light and sweet and are also featured as an ingredient in other local desserts. The fried chicken is tasty, too, and the biscuits are flaky, but the reason to come to Connie's is the doughnuts. Go ahead, get a dozen to go.

When in Tupelo, you must eat somewhere Elvis ate. And that somewhere should be ✪ Johnnie's Drive-In (908 E. Main St., 662/842-6748, 7am-9pm Mon.-Sat.). The King loved the dough burgers—hamburgers with flour added to stretch the meat farther in lean times. Fried green beans, fried chicken, eggs, and biscuits round out the no-frills menu. If it isn't crowded, you may be able to sit in Elvis's favorite booth, but they also have car service if you don't want to go inside.

Woody's Tupelo Steakhouse (619 N. Gloster St., 662/840-0460, www. woodyssteak.com, 4:30pm-8:30pm Mon., 4:30pm-9pm Tues.-Thurs., 4:30pm-9:30pm Fri.-Sat., $10-30) isn't your run-of-the-mill steak house thanks to its wild game menu options such as quail and alligator. Locals like the burgers, po'boys, and catfish, and the karaoke lounge on Thursday nights.

Johnnie's Drive-In

Since 1982 **Park Heights Restaurant** (335 E. Main St., 662/842-5665, www.parkheightstupelo.com, lunch 11am-2pm Mon.-Fri., dinner 5:30pm-9:30pm Mon.-Sat., $18-30) has been a downtown mainstay, with global, contemporary twists on Southern classics. Park Heights is a good choice for quality seafood.

Blue Canoe

Locals are passionate about ✪ **Blue Canoe** (2006 N. Gloster St., 662/269-2642, www.bluecanoebar.com, 3pm-midnight Mon.-Thurs., 3pm-1am Fri., 2pm-1am Sat., $8-13), a bar and restaurant with live music and a better-than-bar-food menu. There are two things you shouldn't skip: the fries with "crack dip" (an addictive sausage and cheese sauce) and the bread pudding, made with blueberry doughnuts from Connie's Fried Chicken. This is a great place to try local beers on tap or watch a football game.

The farm-to-table menu at ✪ **Kermit's Outlaw Kitchen** (124 W. Main St., 662/620-6622, www.kermitsoutlawkitchen.com, lunch 11am-2pm Mon.-Sat., dinner 5pm-10pm Thurs.-Sat., $13-28) changes weekly, but it always features fresh, local, and delicious ingredients. Don't

miss the Vegetable Art Project, a vegetarian entrée made with local seasonal veggies. Owned by the same folks, **Neon Pig Café** (1203 N. Gloster St., 662/296-2533, www.tupelo.eatneonpig.com, 11am-9pm Mon.-Fri., 11am-10pm Sat., 11am-2pm Sun., $7-12) is a two-room homage to all things pork. Order tacos, sandwiches, or burgers for takeout or to eat in, or avail yourself of the butcher shop. This is a popular spot; lines can be long at night.

A casual coffee shop, **Cafe 212** (212 W. Main St., 662/844-6323, www.cafe212tupelo.com, 7:30am-2pm Mon.-Fri., $5-7) serves coffee all day and lunch 11am-2pm. In addition to salads, grilled sandwiches, and cold sandwiches, there's a Blue Suede Grill inspired by Elvis: a grilled sandwich with bananas, peanut butter, and honey. **Strange Brew** (220 N. Gloster St., 662/ 350-0215, http://strangebrewcoffeehouse.com, 6am-10pm Sun.-Thurs., 6am-midnight Fri.-Sat.) is another good choice for a quick cup of joe.

When in the South you don't want to miss the opportunity for a good pimento cheese sandwich. Order one at **Sweet Tea & Biscuits Café** (2025 McCullough Blvd., 662/322-7322, www.sweetteaandb.com, 11am-2pm Tues.-Sat., $8-9.50). The BLT made with fried green tomatoes is another Southern favorite.

If you can't resist the siren call of barbecue, **Bar-B-Q by Jim** (203 Commerce St., 662/840-8800, 10:30am-6pm Mon.-Wed., 10:30am-7:30pm Thurs.-Sat., $7-18) is a traditional mainstay. The smoked chicken salad is a modern twist on the classic dish.

ACCOMMODATIONS

Tupelo has many chain hotels, totaling more than 1,900 rooms, many of which are affordable and well located. There are also several options from **Airbnb** (www.airbnb).

The ✪ **Moon Lake Farm B&B** (3130 Endville Rd., 662/420-1423, www.moonlakefarm.com, $129-149) has three lakeside guest rooms, all with their own entrances and decks offering great views of the property. You can fish on-site and go horseback riding; all this rural serenity is just 12 miles from downtown Tupelo.

Hampton Inn & Suites Tupelo/ Barnes Crossing (1116 Carter Cove, 662/821-0317, www.hamptoninn.com, $105-149) is close to the mall. Choose from standard rooms or suites with kitchens. Take advantage of the outdoor pool, free hot breakfast, free Wi-Fi, and fitness center. East of the mall is the **Wingate by Wyndham** (186 Stone Creek Blvd., 662/680-8887, www.wyndhamhotels.com, $84-140), with a fitness center, whirlpool, business center, and free Wi-Fi and breakfast buffet. Also nearby is the **Holiday Inn Express & Suites Tupelo** (1612 McClure Cove, 662/620-8184, www. ihg.com, $111-140), with a free breakfast buffet and indoor pool. **Fairfield Inn & Suites Tupelo** (3070 Tom Watson Dr., 662/680-6798, www. marriott.com, $108-164) includes evening welcome receptions with free beer and wine. **Best Western Plus Tupelo Inn & Suites** (3158 N. Gloster St., 662/847-0300, www.bestwestern. com, $93-168) offers a picnic area with grills.

Several hotels dot Gloster Street: **Holiday Inn Hotel & Suites Tupelo North** (923 N. Gloster, 662/269-0096, www.ihg.com, $107-165), which has an indoor pool, an on-site restaurant and bar, and free Wi-Fi. Rooms at **LaQuinta Inn & Suites Tupelo** (1013 Gloster St., 662/847-8000, www. laquintatupeloms.com, $80-99) are pet friendly and have both a microwave and a fridge. Nearby is the affordable **Comfort Inn** (1532 McCullough Blvd., 662/269-1508, www.choicehotels.com, $79-99), with an outdoor pool and a fitness center.

INFORMATION AND SERVICES

You can't miss the **Natchez Trace Parkway Headquarters and Visitor Center** (2680 Natchez Trace Pkwy., 800/305-7417, 8am-5pm daily) as you drive by (near milepost 266). The headquarters has an interpretive center, a gift shop with some snacks, bathrooms, ample parking, picnic areas, and access to hiking trails. This is a great place to get questions answered from knowledgeable rangers. For information about the city's attractions, stop by the **Tupelo Convention & Visitors Bureau** (399 E. Main St., 662/841-6521, www.tupelo.net, 8am-5pm Mon.-Fri.).

TRANSPORTATION

Tupelo is 115 miles southeast of Memphis on I-22. If you aren't interested in a road trip, **Tupelo Regional Airport** (2763 W. Jackson St.,www. flytupelo.com) has nonstop service from Nashville.

The **Rock Region Metro** (http:// rrmetro.org) operates buses and streetcars in Little Rock. An adult one-way fare is $1.35; a day pass is $3.75.

Tupelo Transit operates a three-line bus system (http://www.tupeloms. gov/tupelo-transit). It runs Mondays-Fridays. Fares are $2, including a transfer to another line.

Oxford

The city of Oxford is unlike anywhere else in the state of Mississippi. Founded in May 1837, it was built on land that had once belonged to the Chickasaw Nation. It was named after Oxford, England, aspiring to be a university town. By 1841 the Mississippi legislature indeed voted to make Oxford the home of the University of Mississippi, the state's first, and the city's fate as an intellectual hub was sealed. Today, Ole Miss, as it is called, is a major public university.

Life hasn't always been easy in Oxford. In 1864 the city was nearly destroyed when Union troops set fire to the town. It was rebuilt, and in 1962 conflict came again, when James Meredith entered the University of Mississippi as its first African American student amid protests by more than 2,000 people.

Like many college towns, today Oxford is known for its rich intellectual and cultural life, having been home to authors ranging from William Faulkner to John Grisham, plus a tradition of art and music.

Oxford is a small, walkable town, but if you are not used to the heat and humidity of a Mississippi summer, you may find walking to be a sweaty experience.

SIGHTS

✪ UNIVERSITY OF MISSISSIPPI

First things first: No one calls the **University of Mississippi** (123 University Circle, 662/915-7211, www.olemiss.edu) by its proper name. It's "Ole Miss." Founded in 1848, the school today has more than 24,000

students. The city itself has a population of 23,000, so it is easy to see how the school dominates this area.

Wander through the scenic backdrop of the Ole Miss campus, centered around the **Lyceum.** Looking closer at the building, its physical and historic imperfections become more apparent. Bullet holes above the doorway are a sign of the violence that broke out in 1962 when James Meredith tried to integrate the then-whites-only school. Behind the building is a **civil rights monument** with Meredith's figure.

Ventress Hall, built in 1889, was the first major building erected on campus after the Civil War. It is said that author William Faulkner helped paint and renovate this building as a young man. **The Grove** is the open space where tailgating becomes a pastime before football games. This is also where graduation is held.

The **University Museum** (University Ave. and 5th St., 662/915-7073, www.museum.olemiss.edu, 10am-6pm Tues.-Sat., free) has an impressive collection and exhibition space. While the museum is free, there is a fee for special exhibits (adults $5, seniors $4, children $3). Guided tours are available by request. Past exhibitions have included Greek and Roman antiquities and the work of photographer William Eggleston. It's possible to get here via the Bailey's Woods Trail from Rowan Oak. The museum operates Rowan Oak and the Walton-Young Historic House, which is closed for renovations.

The **J. D. Williams Library** (1 Library Loop, 662/915-7092, generally 7am-10pm Mon.-Thurs., 7am-6pm

the Lyceum on the University of Mississippi campus

Fri., 10am-6pm Sat., noon-9pm Sun.) has an impressive archive, including William Faulkner collections, Civil War and civil rights materials, and comprehensive blues music materials. It's an excellent place to pass a few hours.

Confederate soldiers who died after the Battle of Shiloh in 1862 are buried at **Confederate Cemetery** (Hill Dr. and Manning Way). At one time the cemetery had individual markers, but lore suggests a groundskeeper removed them to mow and forgot where they belonged. The cemetery is on campus, south of the Tad Smith Coliseum in a walled-in lawn area.

On weekdays, you'll need a visitor parking pass ($3 daily) to park on campus. Order one ahead of time online (662/915-7235, www.olemiss.edu/parking) or purchase one on-site at the Lyceum Circle welcome booth. There are a few metered spots on campus that don't require a permit (exact change only).

Oh, and if you hear anyone say,

"Hotty Toddy," just say "Hotty Toddy" right back. It's the Ole Miss greeting, school cheer, and football game chant.

THE SQUARE

Nothing else fully encapsulates Oxford's charms as does **The Square** (Jackson Ave. and Courthouse Sq., http://visitoxfordms.com), its historic town square and city center. Three different bookstores (technically outposts of the same store) bring author readings, live music, and discussions to the area. Live music venues, bars, and restaurants attract faculty and students from Ole Miss, as well as other locals and tourists. There are plenty of shops, too, of the higher-end and university-focused sort. You could easily spend a weekend within walking distance of The Square.

L. Q. C. LAMAR HOUSE

A National Historic Landmark, the **L. Q. C. Lamar House Museum** (616 N. 14th St., 662/513-6071, www.

lqclamarhouse.com, 1pm-4pm Fri.-Sun., free) is dedicated to preserving the legacy of Lucius Quintus Cincinnatus Lamar II. Lamar was a senator and U.S. secretary of the interior (under President Grover Cleveland) and was included in President John F. Kennedy's Pulitzer Prize-winning book, *Profiles in Courage,* for his work in trying to reunite the North and the South after the Civil War.

Housed in Lamar's former home, the museum is a labor of love. It is chock-full of information—more than the average history buff can read. The building itself has been restored, and docents can explain some of the decisions that were made in the restoration process.

✪ ROWAN OAK

Even those who don't think of themselves as fans of the great Southern writer William Faulkner (1897-1962) will be charmed by Rowan Oak (916 Old Taylor Rd., 662/234-3284, www.rowanoak.com, grounds dawn-dusk daily, house 10am-4pm Tues.-Sat., 1pm-4pm Sun. Aug.-May, 10am-6pm Mon.-Sat., 1pm-6pm Sun. June-July; grounds free, house $5 cash only), his former family home. The Greek Revival-style house, sitting on 29 acres, offers insight about the Nobel and Pulitzer Prize winner, as well as his creative process. Rowan Oak feels like Faulkner is just out for a walk, with his outline for *A Fable* scrawled on the walls to help him focus and numbers scribbled next to the phone in the 1844 building. Faulkner restored much of the home himself.

The grounds are said to be the inspiration for Yoknapatawpha County, the fictional setting for all but three of Faulkner's works. The grounds connect to the University of Mississippi campus through the Bailey's Woods Trail (www.museum.olemiss.edu/baileys-woods-trail). It takes about 20 minutes to walk the length of this National Recreational Trail, which comes out at the University Museum. The trail is about two-thirds of a mile long and is well maintained. Four footbridges span steep areas in the woods.

If you want more than a self-guided look around, call ahead to schedule a tour. Note that the entrance to the home is easy to miss when rounding the bend on Old Taylor Road. From town, drive slowly after passing 10th Street, then turn right.

North of University Avenue and up a few blocks is Saint Peter's Cemetery (Jefferson Ave. and N. 16th St.), where you can see William Faulkner's tombstone. The large monument is close to the sidewalk and often covered with whiskey bottles that fans leave for their favorite author.

CEDAR OAK

Many of Oxford's antebellum structures were lost to fires set by the Union troops during the Civil War. Cedar Oaks (61 Murray St., 662/801-1427, www.cedaroaks.org, 11am-4pm Fri., 1pm-4pm Sun., free) survived, not because the armies spared it, but because Molly Turner Orr, the sister of William Turner, the man who built the house, organized a group of people to fight the fire. In the mid-1900s Cedar Oak was moved 2.2 miles from its original location.

Docent-led tours of the Greek Revival structure are scheduled on Fridays and Sundays, although you may be able to make an appointment for another day by calling in advance.

Burns-Belfry Museum

BURNS-BELFRY MUSEUM

Burns Methodist Episcopal Church was a church organized by freed African Americans. This beautiful 1910 brick building is now home to the Burns-Belfry Museum (710 E. Jackson Ave., 662/281-9963, www. burns-belfry.com, noon-3pm Wed.-Fri., 1pm-4pm Sun., free), a multicultural center that invites discussions of civil rights, slavery, and more. The museum exhibits are professional and thought-provoking. While the museum is free, donations are accepted to fund expansion and educational programs.

ENTERTAINMENT AND EVENTS

PERFORMING ARTS

Built in the 1800s as a livery stable for William Faulkner's family, The Lyric (1006 Van Buren Ave., 662/234-5333, www.thelyricoxford.com, box office noon-5pm Wed.-Fri.) is now the place to see concerts, film festivals, and other live events in Oxford.

People come to Proud Larry's (211 M. Lamar Blvd., 662/236-0050, www. proudlarrys.com, 11am-midnight Mon.-Wed. and Sat., 11am-1am Thurs.-Fri., 11am-2pm Sun.) for the impressive lineup of live musical acts. It doubles as a restaurant.

The Thacker Mountain Radio Hour (www.thackermountain.com, 6pm Thurs., fall and spring, free) is a lively, smart live radio show with author readings and music, broadcast from Off Square Books (129 Courthouse Sq.) and occasionally from the Lyric Theatre (1006 Van Buren Ave.). Arrive early if you want a good seat. The show is rebroadcast every Saturday at 7pm on Mississippi Public Radio. It's produced only in the fall and spring.

FESTIVALS AND EVENTS

Held over a week in late July at Ole Miss, the Faulkner and Yoknapatawpha Conference (www. outreach.olemiss.edu/events/faulkner) discusses the work of Oxford's favorite son. A celebration of all things related to the written word, the **Oxford Conference for the Book** (www.oxfordconferenceforthebook.com) is held for three days in March each year at Ole Miss.

The **Double Decker Festival** (Historic Courthouse Sq., 662/232-2477, www.doubledeckerfestival.com) started as a modest event on a double-decker bus imported from England. Now it's a two-day fest of music, arts, and food each April.

SHOPPING

Oxford's historic courthouse square, aka **The Square** (Jackson Ave. and Courthouse Sq.), is the hub of downtown and the place to start shopping.

Square Books (160 Courthouse Sq., 662/236-2262, www.squarebooks.com, 9am-9pm Mon.-Sat., 9am-6pm Sun.) actually has three locations on The Square. Aside from the main outpost, there's **Square Books Jr.** (111 Courthouse Sq., 662/236-2207, 9am-7pm Mon.-Sat., noon-5pm Sun.), just for kids, and **Off Square Books** (129 Courthouse Sq., 662/236-2828, 9am-8pm Mon.-Sat., noon-5pm Sun.), the company's "lifestyle and leisure" location. Off Square is also home of the Thursday night **Thacker Mountain Radio Hour** (http://thackermountain.com).

Amy Head Cosmetics (301 M. Lamar Blvd., 662/513-0711, www.amyheadcosmetics.com, 10am-5:30pm Mon.-Fri., 10am-5pm Sat.) sells a boutique makeup line.

Belles and Beaus (1005 Van Buren Ave., 662/236-6880, www.bellesandbeausoxford.com, 9:30am-6pm Mon.-Sat.) is the place for kids' clothing. **Lulu's Shoes and Accessories** (265 N. Lamar Blvd., 662/234-4111, www.lulusoxford.com,

10am-6pm Mon.-Sat., 11am-3pm Sun.) is a go-to for women's clothing, jewelry, shoes, and accessories. **My Favorite Shoes** (138 Courthouse Sq., 662/234-0059, 10am-5:30pm Mon.-Thurs., 10am-6pm Fri.-Sat.) and **Nella's Clothing** (103 Courthouse Sq., 662/281-8711, 10am-5:30pm Mon.-Sat.) are more good options for women.

Looking for something one of a kind? **Mississippi Madness** (141 Courthouse Sq., 662/234-5280, 10am-5:30pm Mon.-Sat.) has gifts and home decor from Mississippi artists. The motto of **Neilson's** (119 Courthouse Sq., 662/234-1161, www.neilsonsdepartmentstore.com, 9am-5:30pm Mon.-Sat.) is "Where trends meet tradition." This Southern department store was established in 1839, so it knows about tradition.

The End of All Music (103A Courthouse Sq., 662/281-1909, www.theendofallmusic.com, noon-6pm Mon., 10am-7pm Tues., 10am-9pm Wed.-Sat., noon-6pm Sun.) is a few miles from The Square, but it's worth the drive if you are an indie record shop fan. It stocks country, rock, jazz, and anything else you want.

FOOD

THE SQUARE

Once a tiny outpost in an alley next to the Lyric Theatre, ✪ **Oxford Canteen** (766 N. Lamar Blvd., 662/234-5345, www.oxfordcanteen.com, 8am-8pm Tues.-Sat., 10am-noon Sun., $7-9) has a loyal local following. Brisket grilled cheese, breakfast tacos, and other treats made with sustainable ingredients are part of chef Corbin Evan's signature menu. This is the only restaurant in Mississippi to serve High Walk coffee from New Orleans.

Chef John Currence is the man

largely responsible for Oxford's culinary renaissance. ✪ **City Grocery** (152 Courthouse Sq., 662/232-8080, www.citygroceryonline.com, 11:30am-2:30pm and 6pm-10pm Mon.-Thurs., 11:30am-2:30pm and 6pm-10:30pm Fri.-Sat., 11am-2:30pm Sun., $10-37) was his first Oxford restaurant, one that combines fine dining with traditional Southern ingredients in an old livery stable. There's a casual bar menu upstairs and a more traditional fine-dining experience downstairs. City Grocery is so much a part of the city fabric that some locals have standing reservations and their own table. Another John Currence restaurant, **Bouré** (110 Courthouse Sq., 662/234-1968, www.citygroceryonline.com, 11am-10pm Mon.-Thurs., 11am-10:30pm Fri.-Sat., $11-32), serves Creole-inspired dishes.

Expect a worthwhile wait at ✪ **Bottletree Bakery** (923 Van Buren Ave., 662/236-5000, 7am-2:30pm Tues.-Fri., 8am-2pm Sat.-Sun., $6-8), a funky diner-turned-bakery with freshly made pastries and sandwiches.

Football legend Eli Manning reportedly counts **Ajax Diner** (118 Courthouse Sq., 662/232-8880, www.ajaxdiner.net, 11:30am-10pm, $8-15) as a favorite. Both the lunch and dinner menus highlight soul food, such as turnip green dip, po'boys, and fried catfish.

Brunch fans should make reservations at **McEwen's Oxford** (1110 Van Buren Ave., 662/234-7003, www.mcewensoxford.com, 11am-2pm and 5pm-9pm Tues.-Thurs., 11am-2pm and 5pm-10pm Fri., 5pm-10pm Sat., 10:30am-2pm Sun., $23-35). This is also the place to go for fancy cocktails.

A sleek, modern pizza parlor, **Saint Leo** (1101 Jackson Ave. E., 662/380-5141, www.eatsaintleo.com,

11am-midnight Mon. and Wed., 11am-midnight Thurs.-Sat., 11am-9pm Sun., $13-20) is a sophisticated favorite of locals looking for alternatives to Southern food. They make some of their cheeses (ricotta and mozzarella) and cure some of their meats (pork belly) in-house.

NORTH LAMAR

The food served at chef John Currence's morning spot, **Big Bad Breakfast** (719 N. Lamar Blvd., 662/236-2666, www.citygroceryonline.com, 7am-1:30pm Mon.-Fri., 8am-3pm Sat.-Sun., $7-13), features ingredients such as house-cured Tabasco-and-brown sugar bacon. Also from John Currence's City Grocery group, **Snackbar** (721 N. Lamar Blvd., 662/236-6363, www.citygroceryonline.com, 5:30pm-10pm Mon.-Thurs., 5:30pm-10:30pm Fri.-Sat., $12-27) is a trendy eatery with a raw bar, charcuterie, and small plates.

Tired of grits and fried chicken? **Jinsei Sushi** (713 Lamar Blvd., 662/234-0109, www.jinseioxford.com, 5pm-10pm daily, $15-20) is a sleek sushi bar with traditional sashimi and *nigiri*, plus contemporary maki and hot dishes, including a wagyu steak that you sear yourself on a hot rock.

ACCOMMODATIONS

If you want a hotel room the weekend of a big football game or other event at Ole Miss, book as far ahead as possible.

Inn at Ole Miss Hotel & Conference Center (120 Alumni Dr., 662/234-2331, www.theinnatolemiss.com, $109-135) has 146 rooms, with standards in the original Alumni House building and deluxe rooms in an addition. Deluxe rooms are a little bigger and have sleeper sofas. The hotel offers all the standard amenities, such free Wi-Fi and a fitness center (with an outdoor pool), plus a shuttle to downtown Oxford. Rates include breakfast.

A cute and quirky boutique hotel located on The Square, **Graduate Oxford** (400 N. Lamar Blvd., 662/234-3031, www.graduateoxford.com, $119-175) is a favorite of locals as well as visitors, thanks to the rooftop bar The Coop and the lobby lounge decorated with vintage books. Pets are welcome in this funky hotel.

There are several decent chain hotels in Oxford. **Courtyard by Marriott** (305 Jackson Ave. E., 662/638-6014, www.marriott.com, $140-190) has the standard amenities plus the Green Roof Lounge, which serves dinner and cocktails. **The Hampton Inn Oxford/Convention Center** (103 Ed Perry Blvd., 662/234-5565, www.hamptoninn.com, $93-169) is a nonsmoking hotel with a fitness center, pool, and free Wi-Fi. **Holiday Inn Express & Suites Oxford** (112 Heritage Dr., 662/236-2500, www.holidayinn.com/oxford, $99-115) touts a business center, free breakfast bar, fitness center, and free Wi-Fi. You'll feel more at home at **Marriott TownePlace Suites** (105 Ed Perry Blvd., 662/238-3522, www.marriott.com, $123-129), where rooms have pullout sofa beds and fully equipped kitchens.

Walking distance to downtown, ○ **The Z Bed & Breakfast** (1405 Pierce Ave., 832/259-0088, www.thez-oxford.com, $119-209) is a quirky, homey B&B with three rooms, each tastefully and uniquely decorated. Prices include full homemade breakfast plus wine and cookies nightly. There are two bikes available for your use, plus the backyard has a fire pit and grill. The owners have two other properties in town, The Z Shanty and The White House, which are appropriate for larger parties and family reunions.

Blue Creek Cabin (535 MS-30, East Oxford, 662/238-2897, www.bluecreekcabin.com, $138 s/d, $69 for each additional guest) is a good option for those not traveling with young kids (no children under the age of 10 are allowed) and who want something a little different. This is a two-bedroom 1800s log cabin with shared bathroom and kitchenette.

Popular for weddings, the seven-room **Castle Hill** (120 Castle Hill Dr., 662/234-3735, www.castlehilloxford.com, $99-225) has a ballroom, pool, dining rooms, and a courtyard.

A Victorian-style home converted into a B&B, with a horse pasture to boot, **Oak Hill Stables** (670 County Rd. 101, 662/234-8488, www.oakhillstablesbedandbreakfast.com, $100-200) isn't your average hotel. There are also guest rooms available in a converted barn.

Ravine (53 County Rd. 321, 662/234-4555, www.oxfordravine.com/inn, $135-195) is also a log cabin-style B&B with rooms with kitchenettes. Amenities include Wi-Fi, breakfast, and a pool. There's a 70-seat restaurant on the premises.

The Barn Loft at Willowdale Farm (28 County Rd. 225, 662/801-8600, www.thefarmatwillowdale.com, $78-156) is good if you want more than just a bedroom. Rent out the loft, the upper level of a barn that's been fashioned into a living space with a porch, living room, kitchen, washer and dryer, two bedrooms, a sleeper sofa, and a bathroom.

INFORMATION AND SERVICES

Your first stop in town should be the charming **Visit Oxford Visitor's Center** (1013 Jackson Ave. E., 662/232-2477, www.visitoxfordms.com, 8am-5pm Mon.-Fri., 10am-4pm Sat., 1pm-4pm Sun.). The office is filled with maps, information, and Southern hospitality.

Get bicycles serviced and find parts at **Oxford Bicycle Company** (407 Jackson Ave. E., 662/236-6507, www.oxfordbike.com, 10am-6pm Mon.-Fri., 10am-4pm Sat.).

Baptist Memorial Hospital (1100 Belk Blvd., 662/636-1000, www.baptistonline.org) is a full-service hospital.

GETTING THERE

Oxford is 85 miles southeast of Memphis on I-55.

Little Rock

Little Rock is the capital of the state of Arkansas and its largest city. In recent years, it's a city that has come into its own. It's a city that acknowledges and remembers its past, from Native American roots to civil rights struggles. It is a city with a deep appreciation of the groundbreaking women who thrived here. It is a city of Southern traditions and modern food, of makers and outdoorsmen, of politicians and entrepreneurs.

And yes, there really is a "Little Rock." On the banks of the Arkansas River in 1722, French explorer Jean-Baptiste Bénard de La Harpe saw this rocky outcropping that made it possible to ford the river. The spot was near an existing Quapaw Indian settlement, and eventually became the site for the railroad bridge that allowed trains to cross the river. It took another century after Harpe's visit for the city to be incorporated.

Today, you can see where it all started in the River Market District, which is central to Little Rock's downtown. It includes a sculpture garden, farmers market, shops, restaurants, and access to pathways for scenic walks or bike rides. The paved paths are generally flat in the area near the river downtown and are accessible to all. At night, the bridges are illuminated with differently colored lights (purple for Mardi Gras, green for St. Patrick's Day, and maybe even a specialty color for a wedding).

SIGHTS

If you want someone else to help you see the sights, book a 75-minute Segway tour with **404 Tour Co.** (River Market area and Clinton Presidential Park, 501/404-0404, 10am-4pm Tues.-Sat., by appointment Sun.-Mon., 75-minute tours $60, reservations recommended).

TOP EXPERIENCE

✪ LITTLE ROCK CENTRAL HIGH SCHOOL NATIONAL HISTORIC SITE

In 1957, nine African American students enrolled in Little Rock's all-white Central High School, testing the *Brown v. Board of Education*

Little Rock

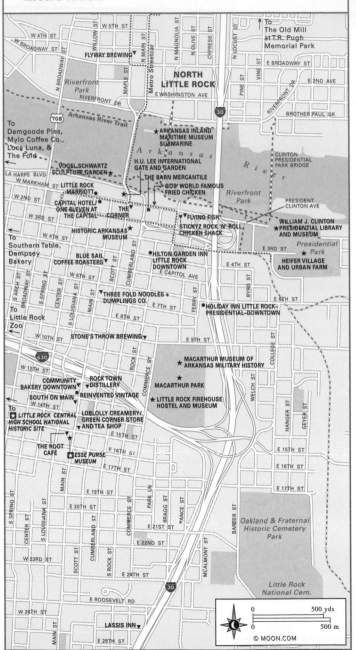

NORTH LITTLE ROCK

To The Old Mill at T.R. Pugh Memorial Park

Riverfront Park

Metro Streetcar

Arkansas River Trail

Arkansas River

To Damgoode Pies, Mylo Coffee Co., Loca Luna, & The Fold

FLYWAY BREWING

VOGEL SCHWARTZ SCULPTURE GARDEN

★ ARKANSAS INLAND MARITIME MUSEUM SUBMARINE

H.U. LEE INTERNATIONAL GATE AND GARDEN

THE BARN MERCANTILE

609' WORLD FAMOUS FRIED CHICKEN

LITTLE ROCK MARRIOTT

CAPITAL HOTEL • ONE ELEVEN AT THE CAPITAL

THE CORNER

FLYING FISH

STICKYZ ROCK 'N' ROLL CHICKEN SHACK

CLINTON PRESIDENTIAL PARK BRIDGE

Clinton Presidential Park

Riverfront Park

PRESIDENT CLINTON AVE

WILLIAM J. CLINTON PRESIDENTIAL LIBRARY AND MUSEUM

Presidential Park

HEIFER VILLAGE AND URBAN FARM

To Southern Table, Dempsey Bakery

HISTORIC ARKANSAS MUSEUM

BLUE SAIL COFFEE ROASTERS

HILTON GARDEN INN LITTLE ROCK DOWNTOWN

THREE FOLD NOODLES + DUMPLINGS CO.

HOLIDAY INN LITTLE ROCK PRESIDENTIAL–DOWNTOWN

To Little Rock Zoo

STONE'S THROW BREWING

MACARTHUR MUSEUM OF ARKANSAS MILITARY HISTORY

MACARTHUR PARK

LITTLE ROCK FIREHOUSE HOSTEL AND MUSEUM

COMMUNITY BAKERY DOWNTOWN

ROCK TOWN DISTILLERY

REINVENTED VINTAGE

SOUTH ON MAIN

To LITTLE ROCK CENTRAL HIGH SCHOOL NATIONAL HISTORIC SITE

LOBLOLLY CREAMERY, GREEN CORNER STORE AND TEA SHOP

THE ROOT CAFE

ESSE PURSE MUSEUM

Oakland & Fraternal Historic Cemetery Park

Little Rock National Cem.

LASSIS INN

0   500 yds
0   500 m

© MOON.COM

Supreme Court ruling that found school segregation unconstitutional. The school became a flash point in the struggle for civil rights. The Arkansas National Guard was ordered not to allow the students to enter, while federal troops were ordered to protect them. The students, who came to be known as the Little Rock Nine, faced years of violence and protests. President Barack Obama invited them to his inauguration in 2009, citing their bravery as one of his personal inspirations.

You can learn this detailed history at the **Little Rock Central High School National Historic Site** (2120 W. Daisy L. Gatson Bates Dr., 501/374-1957, www.nps.gov/chsc, 9am-4:30pm daily, free, call ahead for guided tour reservations), a site managed by the National Park Service. Start your visit across the street from the school, at the National Park Visitor Center, which includes historical video and photographs. While many of the images are disturbing, they are presented in a way that is appropriate for visitors of all ages. The school itself is still a public school, with 2,500 students in attendance, so you can only enter the building with a guide, reserved in advance.

Little Rock Central High School National Historic Site

Several of the guides here are Little Rock natives with firsthand memories of this tumultuous time. Allow several hours to fully experience the tour, which includes the several-block radius around the school. The exterior of the school is open to the public for photographs and reflection without scheduling a tour.

Tours include the restored Mobil gas station, to the south across Daisy L. Gatson Bates Drive/14th Street, which had the only public telephone at the time. This was where national news media used to file reports on the conflict. Other nearby landmarks include a memorial to the Little Rock Nine across Park Street east of the school, and a bus bench at 13th and Park Streets, where one student sought refuge from the violent crowds.

There's a powerful sculpture memorial to the Little Rock Nine, titled *Testaments,* on the lovely grounds of the **Arkansas State Capitol** (500 Woodlane Ave., 501/682-5080).

CLINTON LIBRARY

Opened in 2004 to honor Little Rock's favorite son, the **William J. Clinton Presidential Library and Museum** (1200 President Clinton Ave., 501/374-4242, www.clintonlibrary.gov, 9am-5pm Mon.-Sat., 1pm-5pm Sun., adults $10, children 6 and over $6, children 5 and under free, seniors $8) is a stunning architectural gem, an impressive park, and a mammoth museum. It would take even the hardest-core fan of the Clinton administration decades to look through the official archives here: There are reportedly more than 80 million pages of paper, 2 million photographs, and more than 90,000 artifacts.

Even if you're not a serious historian, the library is an inviting,

William J. Clinton Presidential Library and Museum

intellectually stimulating place. The bright open spaces have chronological displays from the president's two terms in office, as well as artifacts from Hillary Clinton. An exact replica of the Oval Office—down to the last inch—allows you to mimic the experience of sitting behind the big desk. You cannot take your own photos in the Oval Office, but you can do so in the rest of the museum, which also has changing temporary exhibits. The building also houses the offices of the Clinton Foundation, the University of Arkansas Clinton School of Public Service, a restaurant, and a gift shop.

True Clinton history buffs should get a list of sights from the Little Rock Convention and Visitors Bureau, (www.littlerock.com), which include the Clintons' **former homes** (5419 L St. and 816 Midland St.) and the **Hillary Rodham Clinton Children's Library** (4800 W. 10th St.). You can also drive by **Clinton/ Gore Campaign Headquarters** (112 W. 3rd St.).

HISTORIC ARKANSAS MUSEUM

Days gone by are open for discovery at the **Historic Arkansas Museum** (200 E. 3rd St., 501/324-9351, www. historicarkansas.org, museum open 9am-5pm Mon.-Sat., 1pm-5pm Sun., grounds 10am-4pm Mon.-Sat., 1pm-5pm Sun., free admission to the museum center, grounds admission adults $2.50, children $1, seniors $1.50). Explore the oldest home in Little Rock, historical gardens, and exhibits about the Native American communities that once thrived in this part of Arkansas.

✪ ESSE PURSE MUSEUM

Judging the **ESSE Purse Museum** (1510 Main St., 501/916-9022, www. essepursemuseum.com, 11am-4pm Tues.-Sat., 11am-3pm Sun., adults $10, children under 6 free, seniors $8) by its name alone is to underestimate what is on display here. Yes, it is a purse museum, only of three in the world and the only one in the United States. But

JOHNNY CASH BOYHOOD HOME

While Elvis Presley (1935-1977) was growing up in Tupelo, Johnny Cash (1932-2003) was spending his childhood in Dyess, Arkansas. The town is an easy detour between Memphis and Little Rock. While Cash today is thought of as a country music icon, he played gospel, rockabilly, and more, and had a transformative effect on modern music. Cash moved to Memphis in 1954, signing with Sun Records the next year, leading to hits like "I Walk the Line" and "Ring of Fire." Even as he became musical royalty, he remembered his hardscrabble roots in Dyess and often sang about those living in poverty.

Johnny Cash Boyhood Home

Created in 1934 as part of President Franklin D. Roosevelt's New Deal, **Historic Dyess Colony** (110 Center Dr., Dyess, Arkansas, 870/764-CASH (2274), http://dyesscash. astate.edu, tours 9am-3pm Mon-Sat., $10 adults, $8 seniors and groups, $5 students, free for children, Arkansas State University students, and Dyess residents) was a community planned to encourage economic recovery from the Great Depression. Almost 500 families moved here for a chance at a better life, working the land to grow soybeans and cotton. One of those families was that of Ray and Carrie Cash, who had five children, one who grew up to be the Man in Black. Cash lived here until he graduated from high school. His song "Five Feet High and Rising" refers to the 1937 floods in Dyess.

In 1976, the colony was listed in the National Register of Historic Places. Between 2009 and 2012, Arkansas State University began drawing visitors to the **Johnny Cash Boyhood Home.** The former home of the megastar has been restored to the 1940s period, with input from Cash's siblings, Joanne Cash Yates and Tommy Cash. Artifacts include a piano adorned with sheet music and family photos, period furniture, and a pantry filled with canned goods. Even if your primary interest is Johnny Cash, don't skip the Dyess museum exhibits, which offer insight into history, economic development—and yes, country music.

From Memphis, Dyess is a 45-mile drive. Take exit 41 off I-55 North. (GPS systems will guide you to the wrong exit, one that requires driving on dirt roads and through fields.) Check in at the gift shop and buy a ticket; you'll be transported to the Cash home by bus. While Dyess Colony was once a thriving community, it is now a remote tourist site. There's a small convenience store and gas station, and a gift shop, but there are no hotels, restaurants, or other amenities.

this little museum is really about women's experiences. Purses are arranged chronologically, with items that would have been in women's purses during that decade. Makeup changed, fashion changed, and women's lives changed as they gained more freedom, worked outside the home, and pushed against the restrictions of society. A fun exhibit allows you to weigh the contents of your purse and write about what you carry. The gift shop, of course, is spectacular, with purses of all shapes, sizes, colors, and price points.

HEIFER VILLAGE AND URBAN FARM

Tucked away a few blocks from the William J. Clinton Presidential Library is the unexpected gem of the **Heifer**

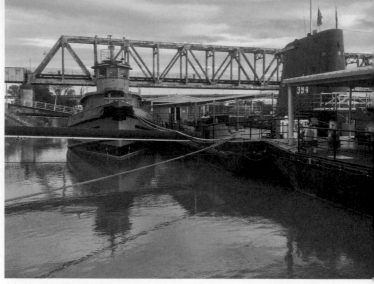

Arkansas Inland Maritime Museum

Village and Urban Farm (1 World Ave., 855/343-4337, www.heifer.org, 9am-5pm Mon.-Sat., free self-guided tours and exhibits). Heifer's mission is to help farmers—both in rural communities in the United States and overseas—develop sustainable methods for feeding their families. The impressive Little Rock headquarters has interactive, kid-friendly exhibits on water, farming, animals, and more. The urban farm shows many of these strategies in action, and is home to livestock, chickens, and other animals. Check the schedule for special events.

ARKANSAS INLAND MARITIME MUSEUM SUBMARINE

Climb down a 14-foot ladder into the **Arkansas Inland Maritime Museum Submarine** (120 Riverfront Park Dr., 501/371-8320, www.aimmuseum. org, summer 10am-6pm Wed.-Sat., 1pm-6pm Sun., call ahead for hours by season, adults $7.50, children and seniors $5). Inside, you get to tour

the USS *Razorback,* which served in Tokyo Bay during World War II. The sub is 90 percent operational, so you can see (and hear) what it is was like to work underwater. This tour is not for those who cannot climb a ladder or are claustrophobic, although there are plenty of museum-style exhibits at land level. It's in North Little Rock, across the Main Street bridge over the Arkansas River, just a five-minute drive from downtown.

OLD STATE HOUSE MUSEUM

The **Old State House Museum** (300 W. Markham, 501/324-9684, www. oldstatehouse.com, 9am-5pm Mon.-Sat., 1pm-5pm Sun., free) is inside the former state capitol building. The structure, built between 1833 and 1843, is a big, beautiful building in and of itself, set on genteel grounds. Exhibits give fascinating insight into Arkansas' history, with everything from first ladies' ball gowns to rodeo queen costumes. Bill Clinton announced his run for presidential office here in 1991 and made his acceptance speeches here in 1992 and 1996. The gift shop is stocked with works by Arkansas artists.

MACARTHUR PARK SIGHTS

Several sights are located in scenic MacArthur Park. The MacArthur Museum of Arkansas Military History (503 E. 9th St., 501/376-4602, 9am-4pm Mon.-Sat., 1pm-4pm Sun., free) features weapons, uniforms, documents, and historical photographs. It's located inside the Tower Building of the Little Rock Arsenal, which was also the birthplace of General Douglas MacArthur (he was born in the onetime barracks to a military family). On the other side of the park, the Little Rock Firehouse Hostel and Museum (1201 Commerce St., 501/476-0294, www.firehousehostel.org, tours by appointment, 9am-6pm) houses a surprisingly robust collection in a 1917 fire station (that also serves as a hostel). A third gem is the Arkansas Arts Center (501 E. 9th St., 501/372-4000, www.arkansasartscenter.org, 10am-5pm Tues.-Sat., 11am-5pm Sun., free museum admission, special exhibitions may require tickets), a museum that also hosts performing arts and lectures.

RECREATION

They call Arkansas "the Natural State," and its natural beauty is evident along downtown Little Rock's riverwalk and in the city's many lush, green parks.

At The Old Mill at T.R. Pugh Memorial Park (3800 Lakeshore Dr., 501/791-8538, 8am-10pm daily April-Oct., 8am-7pm Nov.-March, free, tours available through the North Little Rock Convention and Visitors Bureau, 501/758-1424) you'll find a reproduction of a water-powered gristmill, albeit one with a history. Built in 1933 but intended to look like it was from the 1800s, it is the mill in the opening sequences of the film *Gone With the Wind*. Pugh Park is also home to many sculptures by Mexican artist Dionicio Rodríguez. Known for *faux bois*, concrete works that look like wood, Rodríguez designed bridges and sculptures through the park. His work can also be seen in Lakewood Park in North Little Rock and at the Crystal Shrine Grotto in Memphis.

The Old Mill at T.R. Pugh Memorial Park

H. U. Lee was the founder of the American Taekwondo Association. The H. U. Lee International Gate and Garden (101 E. Markham St., 501/376-4781) honors him by helping the fine folk of Little Rock learn more about South Korea and the martial arts. It's right downtown, at the base of the Main Street bridge.

Little Rock's oldest park, MacArthur Park (601 E. Commerce St., 501/371-4770, www.macarthurparklr.com, 6am-10pm) is home to several museums, a dog park where pups can run unleashed, a performing arts center, a veterans memorial, a small lake, a hostel, playground, and much more.

Downtown, along the banks of the Arkansas River, the **Vogel Schwartz Sculpture Garden** (Arkansas River Trail, 501/539-0913, www.sculptureattherivermarket.com, free) features works of art interspersed with rock outcroppings and native plants. It's located between the Little Rock Marriott Hotel and River Market.

ART AND CULTURE

For more than four decades **Ballet Arkansas** (520 Main St., 501/223-5150, www.balletarkansas.org, $10-99) has been producing performances such as the *Nutcracker, Dracula, Mary Poppins*, and *The Ugly Duckling*. Venues change based on show.

As one of only two theater companies in the state working with equity actors, **Arkansas Repertory Theater** (601 Main St., 501/378-0405, www.therep.org) is a respected institution on the Little Rock arts scene. Annual

events include the summer cabaret, a holiday show, and free play days.

FESTIVALS AND EVENTS

If there is one claim to fame on which Little Rock residents agree, it is that cheese dip was invented in North Little Rock in 1935. To celebrate this spicy melted cheese served with chips, they host the **World Cheese Dip Festival** (Clinton Presidential Center, 1200 President Clinton Ave., www.cheesedip.net, $10-15) each October. Contestants prepare their favorite recipes—with meats, vegetables, and even vegan cheeses—and attendees vote for their favorites. Hot tip: Bring an empty muffin tin…the small samples of dip fit perfectly in the tray, so you can carry them with one hand and chips with the other.

Also in October is the **Arkansas Cornbread Festival** (M. Main St.,

the Arkansas Cornbread Festival

www.arkansascornbreadfestival.com, $8-10), a taste test of different recipes and side dishes. A cash bar with beer from local breweries is also available. Held in the fun SoMa neighborhood, the nonprofit festival is a celebration of this Southern staple.

SHOPPING

Little Rock is a boutique lover's paradise with several areas worth visiting.

Hip **SoMa** (M. Main St. from 12th to 17th Sts.) is a walkable stretch of Main Street just east of downtown. Over the past decade it has been revitalized and now buzzes with activity from shops, restaurants, the **Bernice Sculpture Garden** (often home to small craft markets), music venues, and lots of murals.

More than 15 on-site food vendors, art galleries, and recreation rentals make up **River Market** (400 President Clinton Ave., 501/375-3552, market hall hours 7am-6pm Mon.-Sat., individual vendor hours may vary), along the Arkansas River downtown. In addition to the eating and shopping, there is an art walk the second Friday of each month, movies in the park, and jazz in the park. The adjacent **River Market Farmers Market** (400 President Clinton Ave. 501/375-3552, 7am-3pm Sat. May-Sept., free admission and free on-site parking) is a draw in the warm-weather months.

On the charming streets of **Hillcrest** and **The Heights,** said to be Little Rock's oldest neighborhoods, you'll find children's clothing stores, running shops, home décor boutiques, and more. Kavanaugh Boulevard and Van Buren Street in particular are worth browsing.

After you've seen the exhibit at the **ESSE Purse Museum** (1510 Main St., 501/916-9022, www.

essepursemuseum.com, 11am-4pm Tues.-Sat., 11am-3pm Sun., adults $10, seniors $8, children under 6 free), you may also want to browse the connected gift shop, with multiple little rooms displaying everything from bags to impulse-buy sunglass holders to serious works of art in leather. Many of these designs are handbags that are hard to find elsewhere.

The focus of the charming **Green Corner Store and Tea Shop** (1423 Main St., 501/374-1111, www. thegreencornerstore.com, 10am-6pm Tues.-Fri., 10am-5pm Sat.-Sun.) is on environmentally friendly products, from cleaning supplies to makeup to leather- and plastic-free bags and containers. You'll likely want to sit awhile at the welcoming tea shop.

Jam-packed with goods, **The Barn Mercantile** (301A President Clinton Ave., 501/615-5287, 11am-6pm Mon. and Thurs.-Fri., 11am-4pm Tues.-Wed., 10am-7pm Sat., 1pm-5pm Sun.) is the place to look for souvenirs and mementos. The emphasis is on jewelry, art, and Arkansas crafts.

Annabelle Rector gives old furniture and home décor a makeover at her appropriately named SoMa shop, **Reinvented Vintage** (1222 M. Main St., 501/350-4769, www.reinvented-vintage.com, 11am-6pm Tues.-Sat.). Not only can you search for great finds, you can bring her your old stuff and have her update it for you.

NIGHTLIFE

Located right downtown in River Market, **Stickyz Rock 'n' Roll Chicken Shack** (107 River Market Ave., 501/372-7707, www.stickyz.com, 11am-midnight Sun.-Mon., 11am-2am Tues.-Fri., 11am-1am Sat., menu $4-14, cover for bands varies) offers exactly what its name suggests:

a live music venue that serves gourmet chicken fingers (and sandwiches, salads, and other dishes) and, of course, beer.

Rock Town Distillery (1201 Main St., 501/907-5244, www.rocktowndistillery.com, tasting room 11am-10pm Sun. and Tues.-Thurs., 11am-midnight Fri.-Sat., distillery tours 2pm, 4pm, and 7pm Tues.-Sun., $10-15) was the first legal distillery to open its doors in the state of Arkansas since Prohibition. Its craft-distilled spirits are sold around town, but this facility's casual vibe and overview of the distilling process make it worth a visit. Come to drink, hang out, or take a distillery tour.

North Little Rock's **Flyway Brewing** (314 Maple St., 501/812-3192, www.flywaybrewing.com, 4pm-9pm Mon.-Thurs., 11am-10pm Fri.-Sat., 10am-9pm Sun.) is a friendly taproom with a rotating tap list of 12 beers.

The soft pretzels are a topic of near-obsession in town.

Fourteen different local beers and ciders are available for your drinking pleasure at **Stone's Throw Brewing** (402 E. 9th St., 501/244-9154, www.stonesthrowbeer.com, 4pm-9pm Tues.-Thurs., 4pm-10pm Fri., noon-10pm Sat., 11am-9pm Sun.). Food from Aphrosense food truck, board games, and soft drinks make this a friendly place to hang out in the MacArthur Park neighborhood.

FOOD

Much of the food in Little Rock is Southern cooking. Not that there's anything wrong with that.

More than a restaurant or a live music venue, ✪ **South on Main** (1304 M. Main St., 501/244-9660, www.southonmain.com, lunch 11am-2:30pm Mon.-Fri., dinner 5pm-10pm Tues.-Sat., brunch 10am-2pm

Rock Town Distillery

Sat., $3-25) is a cultural experience. Operated by the folks who bring you *Oxford American* magazine, this venue hosts bands, literary readings, and other events while serving Southern food from chef Matthew Bell. South of Main is considered a neighborhood gathering place and one of the corner-stones that helped revitalize SoMa.

The idea at ✪ **The Root Cafe** (1500 Main St., 501/414-0423, www.therootcafe.com, 7am-2:30pm Tues., 7am-2:30 and 5pm-9pm Wed.-Fri., 8am-3:30pm and 5pm-9pm Sat., 9am-2pm Sun., $3-15) is to build community through food. This laid-back SoMa restaurant serves exceptional breakfast, lunch, and dinner made with ingredients grown and raised in Arkansas. This is the kind of place where you walk in a stranger and walk out thinking you might move to Little Rock. The doughnut muffins are a miracle of baking: They look like a standard muffin, but somehow taste like a deep-fried cinnamon doughnut.

The Capital Hotel is Little Rock's most refined hotel, and its restaurant, **One Eleven at The Capital** (111 W. Markham St., 501/370-7011, http://capitalhotel.com/dining, 6:30am-10am Mon., 6:30am-9pm Tues.-Sat., 6:30am-2pm Sun., $25-125), lives up

cocktail at One Eleven at The Capital

to that standard, with a multicourse experience designed by a James Beard Award-winning chef. Expect seasonal dishes prepared with a French flair and impeccable service. Across the lobby the **Capital Bar and Grill** has a more casual vibe—wood paneling and an extensive bar—but is just as delicious.

If you want fancy, **Lassis Inn** (518 E. 27th St., 501/372-8714, 11am-6pm

Lassis Inn

Tues.-Thurs., 11am-6:30pm Fri.-Sat., $6 12) ain't it. If you want fried catfish, fish ribs, hush puppies, and Little Rock stories in a cozy shack where everyone is welcome, then head to the south side of town for this feast. Everything is fried to order—and the stories are long—so be prepared to sit and listen for a while.

It has moved locations over the years, but in one way or another, **Community Bakery Downtown** (1200 Main St., 501/375-7105, www.communitybakery.com, 6am-8pm Mon.-Thurs., 6am-9pm Fri.-Sat., 7am-8pm Sun., $4.25-7.75) has been part of Little Rock diets since 1947. Come for a meal or just a sweet to go. There's a second location in West Little Rock (270 M. Shackleford Rd., 501/224-1656).

Little Rock's gluten-free bakery, **Dempsey Bakery** (323 M. Cross St.,

501/375-2257, www.dempseybakery. com, 10am-5pm Tues.-Fri., 9am-1pm Sat., $4.50-11.50) is housed in a 1940 building downtown. In addition to the GF breads, Dempsey Bakery serves coffee and a lovely lunch of sandwiches and salads.

If you only have time for one breakfast in Little Rock, it ought to be at @ **The Corner** (201 E. Markham St., 501/400-8458, www.thecornerlr.com, 7am-2pm Tues.-Fri., 8:30am-2pm Sat., 10am-2pm Sun., $8-14). The vibe is retro, with an old diner aesthetic, but the food is modern, with lots of vegetarian dishes and ingredients from more than 100 local farms.

An outpost of the Memphis joint **Flying Fish** (511 President Clinton Ave., 501/375-3474, www. flyingfishinthe.net, 11am-10pm Sun.-Thurs., 11am-11pm Fri.-Sat., $3.50-31) has affordable, family-friendly fried fish, po'boys, and gumbo. Another familiar chain, **Gus' World Famous Fried Chicken** (300 President Clinton Ave., 501/372-2211, www. gusfriedchicken.com, 11am-9pm Sun.-Thurs., 11am-10pm Fri.-Sat., $6-28), also has an outpost in Little Rock.

Local hangout **Loca Luna: Bold Bistro** (3519 Old Cantrell Rd., 501/663-4666, www.localuna.com, lunch 11am-2pm Mon.-Fri., dinner 5:30pm-9pm Sun.-Thurs., 5:30pm-10pm Fri.-Sat., brunch 9am-2pm Sat., 10am-2pm Sun., $3.50-30) is a raucous restaurant where the Bloody Marys flow freely at brunch. This Riverdale neighborhood restaurant is also a great place for a night out. Pizza, crawfish, and cheese dip are among the favorite dishes.

The Fold: Botanas & Bar (3501 Old Cantrell Rd., 501/916-9706, www. thefoldlr.com, 11am-10pm Tues.-Thurs. and Sun., 11am-11pm Fri.-Sat.,

$3-16) is destined for Instagram greatness. The beautifully designed space, a converted filling station in the Riverdale neighborhood, is worth a pic. Come for the cocktails, the delicious tacos, and the pet-friendly patio.

Finding something completely different at **Three Fold Noodles + Dumplings Co.** (611 M. Main St., 501/372-1739, www.eat3fold.com, 11am-9pm Mon.-Sat., $6.50-13). This sleek, minimalist fast-casual spot serves noodles and dumplings made to order.

Three Fold Noodles + Dumplings Co.

If you need a pizza fix, **Damgoode Pies** (2701 Kavanaugh Blvd., 501/664-2239, 11am-10pm Sun.-Thurs., 11am-11pm Fri.-Sat., $3-35) is the place to stop for a slice—or a whole pie. There are additional locations in the Museum of Discovery downtown and at 6706 Cantrell Road.

Loblolly Creamery (1423 M. Main St., 501/503-5164, www. loblollycreamery.com, 11am-9pm Tues.-Sat., 11am-6pm Sun.-Mon., $3-10) is mecca for those with a sweet tooth. Small-batch ice creams are made with local ingredients, such as Rock Town bourbon. You can find the ice cream in lots of restaurants and shops around town, but this SoMa

Capital Hotel

creamery is charming and worth a visit.

Get properly caffeinated downtown at **Blue Sail Coffee Roasters** (417 Main St., 501/753-6622, www.bluesail.coffee, 7am-5pm Mon.-Sat., $2-6). If you are in Hillcrest, **Mylo Coffee Co.** (2715 Kavanaugh Blvd., 501/747-1880, www.mylocoffee.com, 7am-9pm Mon.-Sat., 7am-7pm Sun., $3-10) is your best bet.

ACCOMMODATIONS

Little Rock is the state capital, the largest city in the state, and home to lots of conventions, so there are plenty of places to stay.

✪ **Capital Hotel** (111 W. Markham St., 501/374-7474, www.capitalhotel.com, $186-682) is a place to splurge. For more than 140 years, it has been thought of as Little Rock's "front porch." From the impeccable service to the jaw-dropping lobby to chocolate toffee on the pillow each night, this is the kind of hotel where you'll be tempted to stay permanently. Because

this is an older building, there are some quirks—the gym is in the building across the street, for example—but they don't detract from the luxury experience. Even if you don't stay here, stop by to listen to jazz in the lobby.

Staying in a hostel is not for everyone, but **Little Rock Firehouse Hostel and Museum** (1201 Commerce St., 501/476-0294, www.firehousehostel.org, $31-43) might convince you to give it a try. This converted historical firehouse in MacArthur Park is a comfortable place to stay, with exceptional communal rooms, including a kitchen. No outside bedding (i.e., sleeping bags) is permitted. In addition to the men's and women's dorm-style accommodations, there are a few private rooms for families. Even if you don't stay here, it is worth stopping for a tour of the museum (make an appointment).

Solid chain hotels downtown include the **Little Rock Marriott** (3 Statehouse Plaza, 501/906-4000, www.marriott.com, $93-205), **Hilton Garden Inn Little Rock Downtown**

(322 Rock St., 501/244-0044, www. hiltongardeninn3.hilton.com, $99-304), and the **Holiday Inn Little Rock-Presidential-Downtown** (600 Interstate 30, 501/375-2100, www. ihg.com/holidayinn, $83-170), which has a surprising, almost museum-like collection of President Clinton memorabilia.

INFORMATION AND SERVICES

The **Little Rock Convention and Visitors Bureau** has a number of visitors centers around town, including in the Statehouse Convention Center (101 E. Markham St. 501/370-3250), in Curran Hall (615 E. Capitol Ave., 501/371-0076), and at the airport (1 Airport Rd., 501/537-1751, 7:30am-10pm daily), as well as a wealth of information on its website (www. littlerock.com).

As the state capital, Little Rock has plenty of hospitals and urgent care facilities for medical emergencies.

TRANSPORTATION

Little Rock is 135 miles west of Memphis on I-40. Nonstop flights from major cities including Los Angeles, Las Vegas, Houston, Chicago,

Washington DC, and Atlanta arrive at **The Bill and Hillary Clinton National Airport** (1 Airport Rd., www. clintonairport.com). Airlines that serve the airport include American, Southwest, and United.

While a car is useful, particularly to get to outer neighborhoods Hillcrest, The Heights, and North Little Rock, you can easily explore many of the sights on foot, by bicycle, or by using the **METRO Streetcar** (http://rrmetro.org, adults $1, seniors and children 5-11 $0.50, children 4 and under free, exact change recommended for onboard payments). There are 15 stops on two different lines. The Blue Line loops through the Argenta District and travels south across the Arkansas River to the River Market District. The Green Line streetcar loops around the River Market District and extends east to the Clinton Presidential Park (only until 5:45pm, daily). Smartphone users can download an app or text numbers at each stop to track arrival times. Purchase passes at **Rock Region METRO Administration Office** (901 Maple St., 8am-4:30pm Mon.-Fri.) or **River Cities Travel Center** (310 E. Capitol Ave., 7am-6pm Mon.-Fri.) or online.

Hot Springs

Thanks to the natural thermal springs flowing in its mountains, Hot Springs has been a destination as far back as history can document. Native Americans are said to have called this scenic area "the Valley of the Vapors," due to the mist that rises from the 143°F (62°C) waters. Some research suggests this was a

neutral territory where members of different tribes could soak together in peace. Explorer Hernando de Soto is thought to be the first European to visit Hot Springs in 1541, and a white settlement soon followed. In 1832, President Andrew Jackson named Hot Springs the country's first federal reservation. That means Hot Springs

Reservation was essentially America's first national park, a full four decades before Yellowstone achieved that official designation. Hot Springs become a national park in 1921.

As Western medicine took its hold on American's health, the purported healing powers of the hot springs fell out of favor and the bathhouse industry experienced a steep decline. Eventually all the bathhouses on Bathhouse Row closed and their magnificent buildings fell into disrepair. But advocates continued to believe in the therapeutic properties of these waters, the beauty of these mountains, and the significance of the city's architecture and history.

There is some hiking and camping available in Hot Springs National Park—and one amazing observation tower—but this is not your traditional roughin' it experience. It's a family-friendly destination for breathing mountain air, soaking in thermal waters, drinking mineral water out of the tap, and appreciating the layers of history. And don't forget to browse some kitschy souvenir shops before dinner.

Peak season is Memorial Day through Labor Day. Spring brings blooming wildflowers and fall means the turning of leaves. Crowds are smaller during these shoulder seasons, but some businesses may close early. During the off-season, plan to visit the spas and downtown businesses between noon and 5pm.

SIGHTS

The *raison d'etre* of a road trip to Hot Springs is to visit 5,500-acre **Hot Springs National Park** (101 Reserve St., 501/620-6715, www.nps.gov/hosp, visitors center 9am-5pm daily, free park admission). While there are lush mountains, bright wildflowers, and expansive overlooks, the park is less

natural thermal pool at Hot Springs

Hot Springs National Park

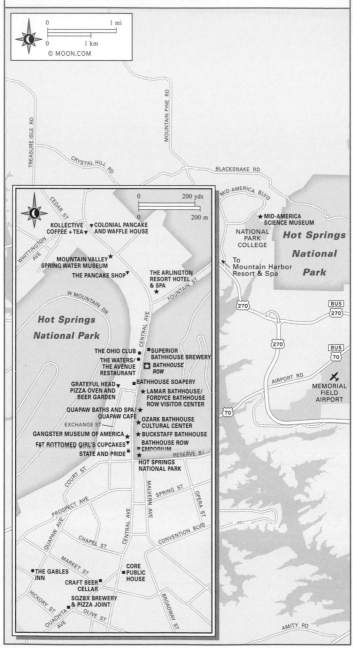

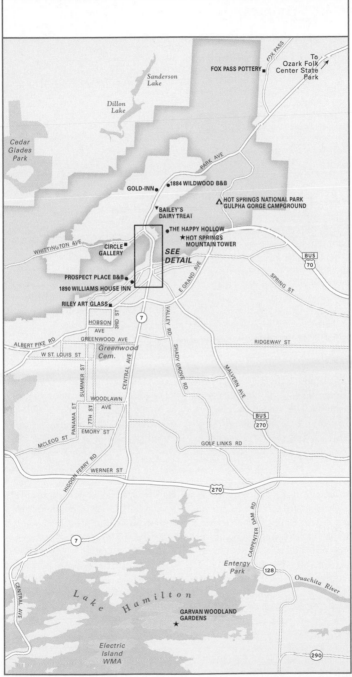

TALL TALES AND FAMOUS FIRSTS

Hot Springs was named the country's first federal reservation—a forerunner to the national park designation—which means Hot Springs Reservation is America's first national park, at least from a certain point of view. It is notable for both groundbreaking history and tall tales.

For decades this region of Arkansas was considered the wild frontier, with skirmishes like those associated with the American West. In the late 1880s Victorian-style homes and bathhouses were built in the town of Hot Springs, and the Chicago White Stockings (now the Chicago Cubs) started something which was new at the time: baseball spring training.

After the National Park Service was established in 1916, Hot Springs Reservation became Hot Springs National Park in 1921. Significant bathhouse buildings, each with its own architectural style and target customer base, were constructed, at considerable expense to independent business owners. Eight of these early 20th-century buildings remain today. (Note: While the term "bathhouse" may have sexual connotations in some communities, the Hot Springs bathhouses were primarily for good, clean—pun-intended—fun.) Soon Al Capone, Bugsy Siegel, and other gangsters of the 1930s discovered Hot Springs, lured by illegal gambling and the fact that they could hide away in the Ouachita Mountains.

about wildlife and scenic vistas and more about thermal waters, history, and great architecture.

About 700,000 gallons per day of thermal water is collected on Hot Springs Mountain by the National Park Service to be used in what is called America's first resort. Because Hot Springs Mountain has no volcanic component, the water from the geothermal springs has no sulfur, and therefore no taste and no smell. This is great drinking water—whether or not you believe it has healing or therapeutic powers. Because the water is owned by the national park, it is owned by the people of the United States. You are encouraged to buy a commemorative glass jug or use your own bottles to fill up at taps throughout the park, primarily along Central Avenue, as well as on Whittington Avenue and Fountain Street. Some taps have both hot and cold spigots. A fountain map—complete with chemical analysis of the water at each stop—is available from park rangers in the Fordyce Bathhouse Row Visitor Center. (Note that Reserve Street is the address for

the park office itself, and is listed on many of the park maps and brochures. This is not the address for Bathhouse Row, which runs downtown on the east side of Central Avenue.)

TOP EXPERIENCE

❂ BATHHOUSE ROW

Eight of the historic Bathhouse Row buildings remain, and are still referred to by their original names. You can see these buildings by strolling up the Grand Promenade, which was designated a National Historic Landmark District in 1987. Some of these large 20th-century buildings replaced older 19th-century Victorian bathhouses, and some of that style remains in town away from Central Avenue. Architecture fans will enjoy the different styles that individual owners used in their creations.

Between 1915 and 1962, **Fordyce Bathhouse Row Visitor Center** (369 Central Ave., 501/620-6715, 9am-5pm daily, free) was one of the gems of **Bathhouse Row.** Of these original buildings, it was the most

Bathhouse Row

opulent, with stained glass windows and indoor fountains to accentuate its Renaissance Revival architectural design. In its heyday, it had a gym, men's and women's treatment areas, and even a bowling alley. It also had a place to see the natural spring happily gurgling. Fordyce reopened in 1989 as the visitors center. This is the best place to go to get a full understanding of what Hot Springs was like when bathhouses were the country's favorite form of medical treatment and recreation. A nine-minute movie and several floors of artifacts on display paint a complete picture. The artifacts are displayed in the preserved bathhouse rooms, contributing to the sense of discovery. Park rangers are available to answer questions.

Built in 1922, the **Ozark Bathhouse Cultural Center** (491 Central Ave., 501/623-2824, www.hotsprings.org, noon-5pm Fri.-Sat., free) is one of the eight original Bathhouse Row buildings, closed in 1977 for restoration and reopened to the public in 2014. It now

is an events space for the National Park Service and other community groups. Volunteer groups are working to extend hours for public tours.

While the bathhouse buildings are owned by the National Park Service, the restoration and renovation of such historic building can be costly, so the NPS looks for long-term tenants who can operate these landmarks in a way that is consistent with Hot Springs's history. The Friends of Hot Springs National Park (http://friendsofhotspringsnationalpark.org) is a nonprofit organization that helps raise money for restoration efforts and recruits volunteers to work on these projects. Architecture fans will enjoy the different styles that individual owners used in their creations.

HOT SPRINGS MOUNTAIN TOWER

The 360-degree panorama from the **Hot Springs Mountain Tower** (401 Hot Springs Mountain Dr., 501/881-4020, www.hotspringstower.com,

BATH HOUSE ROW'S ORIGINAL EIGHT

- **Buckstaff:** Built in 1912, this stucco neoclassical building has been restored to its original intent: It is an operating bathhouse, with soaking areas for men and women, as well as traditional salon services.

- **Fordyce:** Built in 1915, this Renaissance Revival bathhouse was the most opulent of the eight. Today it offers the most complete look at Hot Springs's history as the **Fordyce Bathhouse Row Visitor Center** for the park service.

- **Hale:** The first Hale bathhouse, built in 1841, was replaced in 1892 with a building that has gone through several renovations. Today, it has been restored for use as a hotel and restaurant.

- **Lamar:** The two-story 1923 building, with its big windows and long sunporch, is home to the **Bathhouse Row Emporium** gift shop.

- **Maurice:** The elegant 1912 Maurice bathhouse was built of concrete, steel, and ceramic.

- **Ozark:** Opened in 1922, this Spanish Colonial Revival building had 27 soaking tubs. The two-story building is now an event space for the park service.

- **Quapaw:** This 1922 Spanish Colonial Revival building was built on the site of two previous bathhouses. Its glistening dome is a landmark on Central Avenue. Today, it houses the **Quapaw Baths and Spa.**

- **Superior:** An 1880s Victorian-style bathhouse was replaced in 1916 by the Classical Revival Superior. The restored two-story building houses the **Superior Bathhouse Brewery.**

hours vary seasonally 9am-5pm Nov.-Feb., 9am-6:30pm Mar., 9am-7pm April, 9am-8pm May, 9am-9pm Memorial Day-Labor Day, 9am-6:30pm Sept.-Oct., adults $8, children $4.50, seniors $7), is beautiful year-round, but particularly in fall and spring when there is color on the trees. You can hike there or drive to its parking lot. Take the elevator up 216 feet (66 m) for views of Hot Springs, the Ouachita Mountains, and the surrounding lakes. The gift shop is stocked with all kinds of themed souvenirs.

GARVAN WOODLAND GARDENS

When you've had enough soaking in the waters, your first outing away from downtown ought to be to

Garvan Woodland Gardens (500 Arkridge Rd., 501/262-9300, www.garvangardens.org, 9am-6pm daily, $15 adults, $5 kids). This natural paradise on the Ouachita River and Lake Hamilton is owned by the University of Arkansas. Its 210 acres have manicured horticultural displays as well as forests of Southern pines and rocky shores. Unlike some botanic gardens, leashed dogs are welcome ($5 per dog).

The stunner here, and the reason for driving the six miles from downtown Hot Springs even if you are not a botanic garden type of person, is **Anthony Chapel,** a glass and wood sanctuary designed by Faye Jones and Maurice Jennings. Jones was an apprentice of Frank Lloyd Wright and you can see Wright's belief that buildings ought to integrate with nature

Mid-America Science Museum

taken to the next level here. More than 175 couples get married here annually. When it isn't used for a wedding, the public is welcome to come gaze at the floor-to-ceiling windows that make this an architectural marvel. You can see the chapel for free (provided there is not an event) without paying the garden admission fee. While you'd never know it when you are inside, the chapel is a short walk from the parking lot.

MID-AMERICA SCIENCE MUSEUM

With a stunning woodland setting, and exhibits that go above and beyond the standard kid-friendly interactive displays, **Mid-America Science Museum** (500 Mid America Blvd., 501/767-3461, www.midamericamuseum.org, 9am-5pm Tues.-Sat., 1pm-5pm Sun., adults $10, children and seniors $8) is the kind of place that entertains both adults and kids. Highlights include a skywalk through the woods, dinosaurs hidden among the grounds, and a replica of a contraption from the movie *Chitty Chitty Bang Bang*. The gift shop is chock-full of treasures for kids. The museum is about six miles west of downtown Hot Springs.

HOT SPRINGS HISTORIC BASEBALL TRAIL

Spring training got started in Hot Springs in 1886 when Cap Anson brought the Chicago White Stockings south to practice. The **Hot Springs Historic Baseball Trail** (134 Convention Blvd., 800/772-2489, www.hotspringsbaseballtrail.com) is a collection of more than 30 sites that commemorate America's pastime. Take free self-guided tours through the Hot Springs Baseball Tour mobile app or by phone.

GANGSTER MUSEUM OF AMERICA

Just as Al Capone and Bugsy Siegel kept things hidden from the public, so too does the **Gangster Museum of**

America (510 Central Ave., 501/318-1717, www.tgmoa.com, 10am-5:30pm Sun.-Thurs., 10am-6:30pm Fri.-Sat., adults $15, seniors $14, children 8-12 $6, children under 8 free when accompanied by an adult). This small storefront hides room after room of information and artifacts from the 1930s, when mobsters were lured here by the promise of illegal gambling and getaway opportunities in the Ouachita Mountains. The guided tour will give you lots of lore about Hot Springs's lurid past.

OZARK FOLK CENTER STATE PARK

Befitting its nickname, The Natural State, there are 52 parks in the Arkansas state park system, a number of them close to Hot Springs and offering prime hiking opportunities. But Ozark Folk Center State Park (1032 Park Ave., 870/269-3851, www.arkansasstateparks.com, April-November, adults $12, children $7) is something different: Its mission is to protect the culture—primarily music and crafts—of the region. Here you can enjoy live music performances, hands-on classes and multiday workshops, and browsing handicrafts—as well as long walks in the woods. At the Craft Village (10am-5pm Tues.-Sat.), more than 20 artists offer on-site demonstrations and sell their wares in the Homespun Gift Shop (10am-5:30pm Tues.-Sat.). The Music Theater (7pm-9pm Thurs.-Sat., box office opens one hour prior to showtime) is a 1,000-seat indoor theater focusing on Americana and folk music, including banjo, autoharp, and dulcimer. If you get hooked on these sounds, you can listen when you get home; they're broadcast weekly by Ozark Highland Radio. A zip line course, Loco Ropes, rounds out the fun. Cabins at Dry Creek ($90) and a lodge are available if you want to spend a night or two. While the Folk Center is seasonal (April-November), the cabins are open year-round.

RECREATION

Fifteen intersecting trails were built by the Civilian Conservation Corps on Hot Springs Mountain in the 1930s. Called North Mountain hikes, these relatively easy walks begin right in downtown Hot Springs. The best known is the Grand Promenade, the half-mile bricked route parallel to Central Avenue that is part of the Bathhouse Row National Historic Landmark District. Where it intersects with the Tufa Terrace Trail, you can see thermal springs in a waterfall on the side of the mountain.

The majority of the other hikes are relatively easy; the few steep sections are short. All but a few are less than a mile, and most less than a half mile. More strenuous ascents include Honeysuckle Trail (0.5 miles) and Dead Chief Trail (1.4 miles). The Hot Springs Mountain Trail (1.7 miles) is a loop trail that leaves from near the Hot Springs Mountain Tower. There is a shortcut connector linking the Hot Springs Mountain Trail to Dead Chief Trail; use this to get from the tower to downtown and Bathhouse Row.

The outer edge of the park on West Mountain is four miles from downtown. The hikes on West Mountain are more what you might expect from a national park, in that they are away from the sights and sounds of downtown. These five trails are still relatively short and easy. The 10-mile Sunset Trail is the park's longest and offers the most solitude amid nature. The trail goes up to Hot Springs's highest peak.

Trail maps are available from park rangers in the Fordyce Bathhouse Row Visitor Center as well as for download on the National Park Service website.

Ouachita Outdoor Outfitters (112 Blackhawk Ln., 501/767-1373, www.ouachitaoutdoors.com, 9am-6pm Mon.-Fri., 9am-5pm Sat., rentals $40-60 per day, additional $20 for pickup and delivery) is the place to rent a kayak or paddleboard to explore these mountain lakes and rivers. It is also a good place to buy gear you've forgotten to pack.

SPAS

What listening to the blues is to Memphis, soaking in thermal waters is to Hot Springs. Visitors can indulge in this pastime at indoor bathhouses. Some are in the traditional resort-style, with pools of varying temperatures in a coed space where bathing suits are required. Others are more modern, with private areas for soaking. Cold soaks and cooling areas are the norm, as well as a bath attendant to answer any questions and ensure that proper hygiene practices are being followed. Almost every bathhouse has private treatment rooms for massages, facials, and the like. There is nowhere to soak in a bubbling spring in the forest, nor does the resort have a traditional swimming pool. (One proposal to redevelop the old Majestic Hotel site would include open-air pools.) While in the past the park offered free soaks for some who could not afford to pay to use the bathhouses, that is no longer the case.

The 1924 **Arlington Resort Hotel and Spa, Thermal Water Spa** (239 Central Ave., 501/609-2515, www.arlingtonhotel.com, by appointment 7:30am-5pm Mon.-Wed., 7:30am-7pm Thurs.-Sat., 7:30am-12:30pm Sun., $40-280) has two different service areas. The modern salon and spa has private rooms for massages, facials, and body wraps. The 3rd floor includes massage, body scrubs, and hydrotherapy using the thermal waters in more historical Hot Springs-style treatment rooms. Reservations are required.

Housed in one of the original historic buildings on Bathhouse Row, **Buckstaff Bathhouse** (509 Central Ave., 501/623-2308, www.buckstaffbaths.com, hours vary by season, 8am-11:45am and 1:30pm-3:30pm Mon.-Sat., 8am-11:45am Mar.-Nov., $25-83) has coed and single-sex thermal soaking baths for $38, as well as treatments such as manicures, facials, and massages. Soaking is on a first-come, first-served basis.

Another of the eight original Bathhouse Row gems, **Quapaw Baths and Spa** (413 Central Ave., 501/609-9822, www.quapawbaths.com, 10am-6pm Wed.-Mon. $20-150) has coed thermal pools, single-sex steam caves, and services including massages, facials, and body treatments.

Quapaw Baths and Spa

Reservations are recommended for treatments, but not necessary for soaking. The **Quapaw Cafe** (10am-6pm Wed.-Mon, $2-7) has a limited menu of healthy snacks and sandwiches, so you don't have to leave the warm environment of the baths to fuel up. Bring no-skid, fabric-free flip flops to wear in the bathhouse, or buy a rubber pair for $5. The Spanish Colonial Revival building reopened to the public in 2008. The Quapaw name comes from the Native Americans who lived north of the Arkansas River.

SHOPPING

The **Mountain Valley Spring Water Museum and Visitor Center** (150 Central Ave., 501/246-8017, www. mountainvalleyspring.com, 9am-5:30pm, free admission and self-guided tours) is the flagship for the Mountain Valley Spring Water brand. The store stocks shirts, cookbooks, and souvenirs as well as bottled water (remember that you can fill up in the free springs in the park, so purchased water may not be necessary in Hot Springs unless you crave a flavored or sparkling water.) The store is housed in a renovated 1910 Classic Revival building that is listed in the National Register of Historic Places. It serves as a museum and time machine to the Hot Springs of old. Learn about the brand and this region of the country, and ask the friendly staff questions: They know a lot about the area. The museum is north of Bathhouse Row on Central Avenue.

As one might expect, many retail businesses in Hot Springs are focused on spa, bath, and body goods. **Bathhouse Soapery** (366 Central Ave., 501/525-7627, bathhousesoap. com, 9am-7pm daily) now has stores around the South, but its Hot Springs outlet is the flagship. Shop for bath bombs, lotions, and shave creams, all made in small batches, with seasonal and offbeat scents and ingredients. **Bathhouse Row Emporium** (509 Central Ave., 501/620-6740, 9am-5pm daily April-Sept., 10am-5pm weekdays and 9am-5pm weekends Oct.-March) inside the 1923 Lamar Bathhouse, one of the original eight bathhouses, is the mega-themed gift shop. In addition to souvenirs of all kinds, you can take a selfie inside a bathtub in the middle of the shop.

There are tons of souvenir shops up and down Central Avenue with kitschy T-shirts and saltwater taffy. If you want a souvenir from Arkansas that is well designed and crafted by locals, **State and Pride** (518 Central Ave., 501/627-0759, www.stateandpride. com, 10am-6pm Sun.-Thurs., 10am-9pm Fri.-Sat.) is the place to go. The shop also has a small selection of outdoor wear, with brands like Hari Mari, if you've forgotten anything you need to enjoy the mountains.

Free glassblowing demonstrations bring people into **Riley Art Glass** (710 W. Grand Ave., 501/318-6193, www. rileyartglass.com, 9am-4pm Tues.-Sat.) on a regular basis. The works of brother Charles and Michael Riley make for lovely mementos to take home.

About three miles from downtown Hot Springs is **Fox Pass Pottery** (379 Fox Pass Cutoff, 501/623-9906, www.foxpasspottery.com, 10am-5pm Tues.-Sat.), where Jim and Barbara Larkin have been hand crafting and firing pottery since 1973. Their stoneware is one of a kind, and they welcome visitors to come chat in the studio.

the World's Shortest St. Patrick's Day Parade

ENTERTAINMENT AND EVENTS

As a resort town, Hot Springs is better known for its everyday relaxation than festivals, but a handful of regular events draw crowds.

Chicago may dye the river green, but Hot Springs has a different St. Paddy's day claim to fame: The **World's Shortest St. Patrick's Day Parade** (Bridge St., March 17, www. shorteststpats.com). The parade takes about an hour to march 98 feet, with crowds clamoring to see the hullabaloo. *Karate Kid* star Ralph Macchio was the 2019 grand marshal; festivities and live music typically begin the weekend before the holiday.

A screening at the **Hot Springs Documentary Film Festival** (Arlington Hotel, 239 Central Ave., www.hsdfi.org, passes $120-400, general admission single screenings $12) qualifies films for consideration in the category of Documentary Short Subject by the Academy of Motion Picture Arts and Sciences, so it attracts serious film fans to town each October. The movies are shown at different venues around town, with lots of local after-parties and receptions. General admission passes make one-off screenings affordable. The **Hot Springs International Horror Film Festival** (1008 Central Ave., www. hotspringshorrorfilmfestival.com, festival pass $45, individual screening prices vary) is campier, and not Oscar-worthy, but no less fun. It typically takes place in September.

Illegal gambling was part of Hot Springs's early days. **Oaklawn Racing and Gaming** (2705 Central Ave., 800/OAKLAWN [800/625-5296], www.oaklawn.com, 10am-3am Sun.-Thurs., 10am-6am Fri.-Sat., free general admission, $2 parking on race days) offers the legal take on gambling, with a casino and a horse racing season that runs from January through the Kentucky Derby (first Saturday in May). A $100 million expansion will add a hotel and more gambling space.

167

Superior Bathhouse Brewery

NIGHTLIFE

In peak season, Hot Springs can be a buzzing resort town. Off-season it can seem like the sidewalks roll up at night. If you can only make it to one evening destination, go to ✪ **Superior Bathhouse Brewery** (329 Central Ave., 501/624-2337, www. superiorbathhouse.com, 11am-9pm Sun.-Thurs., 11am-11pm Fri.-Sat.), which uses Hot Springs's thermal waters in its beers. Located inside one of the former bathhouses, Superior is also the first craft brewery in a national park.

International beers, domestic craft gems, ciders, mead, and more are on the menu at the **Craft Beer Cellar** (120 Ouachita Ave., 501/881-7232, noon-10pm Mon.-Thurs., noon-11pm Fri.-Sat., 12:30pm-7pm Sun.). Owned by a Hot Springs native, Craft Beer Cellar aims to teach you about beer and help you drink it. This is a great place to grab brews for your camping trip or picnic.

Claiming to be the oldest bar in

the state of Arkansas, **The Ohio Club** (336 Central Ave., 501/627-0702, www. theohioclub.com, 11am-2am Mon.-Sat., 11am-midnight Sun., 21 and over, $10-18) has been entertaining folks in Hot Springs since 1905. While Bugsy Siegel and Al Capone once hung out here, you aren't likely to find any gangsters today. Instead you'll get live music, burgers, sandwiches, and a full cocktail list.

One of a handful of Arkansas locations, **Core Public House** (833 Central Ave., 501/701-4390, http:// coreofarkansas.com/public-houses, 3pm-10pm Mon.-Thurs., 3pm-midnight Fri., noon-midnight Sat., noon-9pm Sun., $12-20) offers beers that are brewed in the state.

FOOD

One of Hot Springs's few true fine-dining experiences, ✪ **The Avenue Restaurant** (340 Central Ave., 501/625-3850, www.thewatershs.com/ the-avenue-restaurant, 4pm-10pm Wed.-Sat., 9am-2pm Sun., $6-120) serves small plates and entrees such as rabbit potpie and lobster chowder. The restaurant, which is located inside The Waters hotel, uses local ingredients when possible. A monthly Art Dinner offers a prix fixe menu ($65) that pairs dishes with the artworks hanging on the walls.

Dough is tossed in the air and beers are tossed back at **SQZBX Brewery & Pizza Joint** (236 Ouachita Ave., 501/609-0609, http://sqzbx.com, 11am-9pm Sun.-Thurs., 11am-10pm Fri.-Sat., $14-19) a low-key place that brews its own beer and offers traditional pizzas as well as options with gluten-free crust.

Settle in for a tasty meal and a beer at **Grateful Head Pizza Oven and Beer Garden** (100 Exchange St., 501/781-3405, http://gratefulheadpizza.com, 11am-11pm daily, 10-inch personal pies $8-13). The outdoor deck will make you feel like you are dining in the woods. The indoor space is cozy and great for groups and families. It's not unusual to find live music here.

There's something about a classic diner-style pancake shop that says "vacation breakfast" to many people. Two of Hot Springs' best options are right across the street from each other: **Colonial Pancake and Waffle House** (111 Central Ave., 501/624-9273, 7am-2:30pm daily, $5-12) has signature pancakes and waffles, plus hearty Southern breakfasts, burgers, and sandwiches. **The Pancake Shop** (216 Central Ave., 501/624-5720, 6am-12:45pm daily, $3-7) is focused more on the first part of the day, with variety of large pancakes from classic buttermilk to buckwheat and apple.

Kollective Coffee + Tea (110 Central Ave.; 501/701-4000, 7am-6pm Mon.-Tues. and Thurs., 7am-9pm

Kollective Coffee + Tea

Wed., 7am-7pm Fri.-Sat., 8am-6pm Sun., $3-9) has a large menu of teas and coffees, plus a small menu of bagels, breakfast, sandwiches, and wines. There's room to sit and check your email and work on your laptop. In the evenings you may find poetry readings and other acoustic entertainment.

Best known for their appearance on the Food Network's *Cupcake Wars,* **Fat Bottomed Girls Cupcakes** (502 Central Ave., 501/318-0997, www.fbgcupcakes.com, 9am-9pm Sun.-Thurs., 9am-10pm Fri.-Sat., $3.50) sells a wide variety of flavors, such as red velvet, salted caramel, and lemon lavender. If you don't care about the cake, icing shots (that's just the frosting), candy, and other sweets are available. The exceedingly friendly staff can pack up your purchase in boxes that make sure the icing doesn't get smooshed.

You can get egg rolls and fried rice with your classic burger and milk shake at **Bailey's Dairy Treat** (510 Park Ave., 501/624-4085, 8am-8pm Mon.-Sat., $1.25-7), an old-fashioned roadside stand with an epic neon sign.

ACCOMMODATIONS

Take a step inside ✪ **The Arlington Resort Hotel & Spa** (239 Central Ave., 800/643-1502, www.

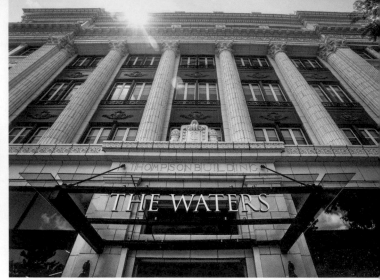
The Waters hotel

arlingtonhotel.com, $105-395) and you can imagine what Hot Springs was like in its heyday. This grand dame towers over Central Avenue and the edge of the park. The lobby has high ceilings and historical décor and wallpaper at every turn. Guest rooms are big and appointed with antique furniture, which may seem dated to some, charming to others. The Arlington has two different spas, a bar, restaurants, and hosts events such as the Hot Springs Documentary Film Festival. Even if you don't stay at the hotel it is worth walking through for the ambience.

The Waters (340 Central Ave., 501/321-0001, www.thewatershs.com, $150-240) puts you right in the middle of the Central Avenue action. The renovated rooms are modern, clean, and very large, with big windows looking out on Bathhouse Row. The hotel has a very small fitness center with limited equipment and the Avenues restaurant.

Hot Springs's plethora of Victorian homes—some of which used to be bathhouses—and its resort setting makes it a prime location for cozy bed-and-breakfasts. Many are within a two-block radius of each other, just west of Central Avenue, including **1890 Williams House Inn** (420 Quapaw Ave., 501/624-4275, www.1890williamshouse.com, $139-239); **Prospect Place B&B** (472 Prospect Ave., 501/777-3164, www.472prospectplace.com, $109-165); and **The Gables Inn** (318 Quapaw Ave., 501/623 7576, www.gablesn.com, $109-159). Slightly farther north (yet still convenient to the national park) is **1884 Wildwood B&B** (808 Park Ave., 501/624-4267, www.wildwood1884. com, $139-149).

A retro motel updated with a hip aesthetic, **Gold-Inn Hot Springs** (741 Park Ave., 501/624-9164, http://gold-inn.webflow.io, $115) is a good choice if you want to stay off of Central Avenue, and a little closer to the woods. Lovely mountain views, an in-room breakfast basket, and friendly staff make it a good vacation getaway. **The Happy Hollow** (231 Fountain St., 501/321-2230, www.happyhollowhotsprings.com, $72-94) has a similar retro motel aesthetic, with clean rooms just a few blocks from the Central Avenue activity.

If you don't mind a 40-minute drive from downtown Hot Springs, **Mountain Harbor Resort & Spa** (994 Mountain Harbor Rd., 870/867-2191, www.mountainharborresort.com, lodge area rates vary by season $85-499, Harbor North Cabins rates vary by season $199-849) is a vacation paradise. Its location on Lake Ouachita provides opportunities for swimming, paddling, and even scuba diving (yes, the water is *that* clear). Call the **Lake Ouachita Dive Shop** (501/760-1500) for details. The resort also has many hiking and walking trails and a full marina. Nearby **Lookout Point Lakeside Inn** (104 Lookout Cir., 501/525-6155, www.lookoutpointinn.com, $185-325) offers a luxury lakeside experience, but is closer to downtown Hot Springs (about a 20-minute drive), on Lake Hamilton.

To get the kind of national park experience you have elsewhere, you can sleep under the stars. The **Hot Springs National Park Gulpha Gorge Campground** (305 Gorge Rd., 501/620-6715, $15-30) is a first-come, first-served facility (no reservations). The campground is two miles from downtown Hot Springs and provides access to the Gulpha Gorge Trail for hiking. It has modern restrooms, but no showers—and of course, Hot Springs has lots of other options for bathing.

INFORMATION AND SERVICES

In a resort town, there's no shortage of places to get vacation information. Stop by the **Hot Springs Visitors Center** (629 Central Ave., 501/321-2277, www.hotsprings.org, 10am-6pm Mon.-Fri.) in Hill Wheatley Plaza for maps and seasonal details on attractions.

Park rangers at **Fordyce Bathhouse Row Visitor Center** (369 Central Ave., 501/620-6715, 9am-5pm daily, free) have maps and other information and are happy to give suggestions on hikes based on the time of year, as well as the best spots to see a sunset or a sunrise.

The **National Park Medical Center** (Hwy. 270, 501/301-1000, http://nationalparkmedical.com) is open 24 hours a day and is about two miles from downtown Hot Springs. If you have an emergency while inside the national park you can call Law Enforcement Dispatch (501/620-6739) in addition to 911.

GETTING THERE AND AROUND

No two sights are very far away from each other in this region, but allow for driving at a leisurely pace once you exit the interstate onto the mountain roads. Hot Springs is 190 miles west of Memphis on I-40. After two-and-a-half hours, take I-30 W to US 70 W. Total drive time is less than three hours.

Hot Springs Memorial Field is a small airport with commercial flights arriving from Dallas.

In general, Hot Springs is a fairly easy place to see by foot. The downtown area is compact and the national park is designed for walking and hiking. If you want to explore the area on two wheels, there are at least five bike trails in the area ranging from 10-mile beginner routes to an advanced trail clocking in at 108 miles.

If you don't bring you own bike, you can rent from **Parkside Cycle** (719 Whittington Ave., 501/623-6188, www.parksidecycle.com, 11am-6pm Tues.-Fri., 10am-4pm Sat., $25 minimum half-day rental, $45-75 per day rental, 24-hour notice with ID and credit card required for reservation).

BACKGROUND

The Landscape

Tennessee is a wide state. Shaped roughly like a parallelogram, it is less than 500 miles (800 km) from east to west and 110 miles (175 km) from north to south. Partly due to its unusual shape, Tennessee, along with Missouri, borders more states than any other in the country. Memphis is in the southwest corner of the state, near both the Mississippi and Arkansas borders.

RIVERS

The largest river in Tennessee is the Mississippi River, which forms the western border of the state and is Memphis's primary landmark and organizing principle. Memphis's nickname is the Bluff City because of its position on the bluffs of the Mississippi. The Hatchie River is among the smaller tributaries that drain West Tennessee and flow into the Mississippi. The 90-mile-long Wolf River flows northwest from the state of Mississippi into the Mississippi River and provides drinking water for much of the city.

CLIMATE

Memphis has a mild climate. The average temperature in January is 50°F (10°C); summer temperatures can hover around 92° (33°C). Summer days feel very hot and humid, but that doesn't stop Memphians from enjoying the outdoors (or from enjoying the air-conditioning inside).

Memphis receives an average of 56 inches (142 cm) of rain per year, and just 3 inches (7 cm) of snow.

TORNADOES

The mid-South, including western and central Tennessee, is prone to tornadoes, although few ever hit the city proper. The tornado season runs November-April but can continue into the summer. The danger of tornadoes is compounded because they may strike after dark and, in many areas of the state, visibility is limited by hills and trees. The best way to avoid injury in a tornado is to monitor a weather radio and move quickly to a cellar, basement, or windowless interior room if a tornado is on the way.

FLOODS

In April and May 2011, the Mississippi River threatened to cover parts of Memphis with water after some of the highest rainfall totals the city had seen in a century. More minor flooding, particularly on the greenbelt along the Mississippi, isn't uncommon in periods of heavy rainfall. Attractions on Mud Island may close as a result.

History

THE FIRST TENNESSEANS

The first humans settled in what is now Tennessee 12,000-15,000 years ago. Descended from people who crossed into North America during the last ice age, these Paleo-Indians were nomads who hunted large game, including mammoth, mastodon, and caribou. Remains of these extinct mammals have been found in West Tennessee, and the Indians' arrowheads and spearpoints have been found all over the state.

About 10,000 years ago, the climate and vegetation of the region changed. The deciduous forest that still covers large parts of the state replaced the evergreen forest of the fading ice age. Large game animals disappeared, and deer and elk arrived, attracted by the forests of hickory, chestnut, and beech. Descendants of the Paleo-Indians gradually abandoned the nomadic

Memphis-Arkansas Bridge over the Mississippi River

lifestyle of their ancestors and established settlements, often near rivers. They hunted deer, bear, and turkey; gathered nuts and wild fruit; and harvested freshwater fish and mussels. They also took a few tentative steps toward cultivation by growing squash and gourds.

This Archaic period was replaced by the Woodland period about 3,000 years ago. The Woodland Indians adopted the bow and arrow for hunting and—at the end of their predominance—began cultivating maize and beans as staple crops. Ceramic pottery appeared, and ritualism took on a greater importance in the society. The Pinson Mounds, burial mounds near Jackson in West Tennessee, date from this period.

The development of a more complex culture continued, and at about AD 900 the Woodland culture gave way to the Mississippian period, an era marked by population growth, an increase in trade and warfare, the rise of the chieftain, and cultural accomplishments. The Mississippian era is best known for the impressive large pyramid mounds that were left behind in Tennessee and Mississippi. Mississippian Indians also created beautiful ornaments and symbolic objects, including combs, pipes, and jewelry.

EUROPEANS ARRIVE

Having conquered Peru, the Spanish nobleman Hernando de Soto embarked on a search for gold in the American southeast in 1539. De Soto's band wandered through Florida, Georgia, and the Carolinas before crossing into what is now Tennessee, probably in June 1540. The popular myth that he camped on the Chickasaw Bluff—the site of Memphis today—in 1541 remains unproven, although you can visit the apocryphal spot.

It was more than 100 years until another European was reported in the Tennessee wilderness, although life for the natives was already changing.

De Soto and his men brought fire-arms and disease, and there was news of other whites living to the east. Disease and warfare led to a decline in population for Tennessee's Indians during the presettlement period. As a result, Indian communities formed new tribes with each other: The Creek Confederacy and Choctaws were among the tribes that were formed. In Tennessee, the Shawnee moved south into the Cumberland River country, land previously claimed as hunting ground by the Chickasaw Nation. Also at this time, a new tribe came over the Smoky Mountains from North Carolina, possibly to escape encroachment of European settlers, to form what would become the most important Indian group in modern Tennessee: the Overhill Cherokee.

In 1673, European scouts entered Tennessee at its eastern and western ends. Englishmen James Needham and Gabriel Arthur, along with eight hired Indian guides, were the first Europeans to enter East Tennessee. Needham did not last long; he was killed by his Indian guides early in the outing. Arthur won over his traveling companions and joined them on war trips and hunts before returning to Virginia in 1674. Meanwhile, on the western end of the state, French explorers Father Jacques Marquette and trader Louis Joliet came down the Mississippi River and claimed the surrounding valley for the French.

Nine years later, Robert Cavelier de La Salle paused at the Chickasaw Bluff near present-day Memphis and built Fort Prudhomme as a temporary base. The fort was short-lived, but the site would be used by the French in years to come in their war against the Chickasaws and later in the French and Indian War.

THE FRENCH AND INDIAN WAR

In 1754, the contest between the French and the British for control of the New World boiled over into war. Indian alliances were seen as critical to success, and so the British set out to win the support of the Cherokee. They did this by agreeing to build a fort in the land over the mountain from North Carolina—territory that came to be known as the Overhill country. The Cherokee wanted the fort to protect their women and children from French or hostile-Indian attack while the men were away. The fort was begun in 1756 near the fork of the Little Tennessee and Tellico Rivers, and it was named Fort Loudoun after the commander of British forces in America. Twelve cannons were transported over the rough mountain terrain by horse to defend the fort from enemy attack.

The construction of Fort Loudoun would not be the glue that held the Cherokee and British together. In fact, it was not long before relations deteriorated to the point where the Cherokee chief Standing Turkey directed an attack on the fort. A siege ensued. Reinforcements were called for and dispatched, but the British colonel and 1,300 men turned back before reaching the fort. The English inside the fort were weakened by lack of food and surrendered. On August 9, 1760, 180 men, 60 women, and a few children marched out of Fort Loudoun, the first steps of a 140-mile (225-km) journey to the nearest British fort. The group had been promised to be allowed to retreat peacefully, but on the first night of the journey the group was ambushed: killed were 3 officers, 23 privates, and 3 women. The rest were taken prisoner. The Indians said they were inspired to violence upon finding that the British had failed to surrender all of their firepower as promised.

The action was soon avenged. A year later, Col. James Grant led a party into the Lower Cherokee territory, where they destroyed villages, burnt homes, and cut down fields of corn.

The French and Indian War ended in 1763, and in the Treaty of Paris the French withdrew any claims to lands east of the Mississippi. This result emboldened European settlers and land speculators who were drawn to the land of the Overhill country. The fact that the land still belonged to the Indians did not stop the movement west.

EARLY SETTLEMENTS

With the issue of French possession resolved, settlers began to filter into the Overhill country. Early settlers included William Bean, on the Holston River; Evan Shelby, at Sapling Grove (later Bristol); John Carter, in the Carter Valley; and Jacob Brown, on the Nolichucky River. By 1771, the settlers at Watauga and Nolichucky won a lease from the Cherokee, and the next year, they formed the Watauga Association, a quasi government and the first such in Tennessee territory.

The settlers' success in obtaining land concessions from the Indians was eclipsed in 1775 when the Transylvania Company, led by Richard Henderson of North Carolina, traded £10,000 of goods for 20 million acres (81,000 sq km) of land in Kentucky and Tennessee. The agreement, negotiated at a treaty conference at Sycamore Shoals, was opposed by the Cherokee chief Dragging Canoe, who warned that the Cherokee were paving the way for their own extinction. Despite his warning, the treaty was signed.

Dragging Canoe remained the leader of the Cherokee resistance to European settlement. In 1776, he orchestrated assaults on the white settlements of Watauga, Nolichucky, Long Island, and Carter's Valley. The offensive, called by some the Cherokee War, had limited success at first, but it ended in defeat for the natives. In 1777, the Cherokee signed a peace treaty with the settlers that ceded more land to the Europeans.

Dragging Canoe and others did not accept the treaty and left the Cherokee as a result. He and his followers moved south, near Chickamauga Creek, where they became known as the Chickamauga tribe. Over time, this tribe attracted other Indians whose common purpose was opposition to white settlement.

The Indians could not, however, overpower the increasing tide of European settlers, who brought superior firepower and greater numbers. Pressure on political leaders to free up more and more land for settlement made relations with the Indians and land agreements with them one of the most important features of political life on the frontier.

In the end, these leaders delivered. Europeans obtained Indian land in Tennessee through a series of treaties and purchases, beginning with the Sycamore Shoals purchase in 1775 and continuing until 1818, when the Chickasaw ceded all control to land west of the Mississippi. Negotiating on behalf of the settlers were leaders including William Blount, the territorial governor, and Andrew Jackson, the first U.S. president from Tennessee.

THE TRAIL OF TEARS

Contact with Europeans had a significant impact on the Cherokee way of life. Christian missionaries introduced education, and in the 1820s, Sequoyah developed a Cherokee alphabet, allowing the Indians to read and write in their own language. The Cherokee adopted some of the Europeans' farming practices, as well as some of their social practices, including slavery. Adoption of the European lifestyle was most common among the significant number of mixed-race Cherokee. In 1827, the Cherokee Nation was established, complete with a constitutional system of government and a capital in New Echota, Georgia. From 1828 until 1832, its newspaper, the *Cherokee Phoenix,* was published in both English and Cherokee.

The census of 1828 counted 15,000 Cherokee remaining in Tennessee. They owned 1,000 slaves, 22,400 head of cattle, 7,600 horses, 1,800 spinning wheels, 700 looms, 12 sawmills, 55 blacksmith shops, and 6 cotton gins.

Despite these beginnings of assimilation, or because of them, the Cherokee were not welcome to remain in the new territory. Settlers pushed for a strong policy that would lead to the removal of the Cherokee, and they looked over the border to Georgia to see that it could be done. There, in 1832, authorities surveyed lands owned by Cherokee and disposed of them by lottery. Laws were passed to prohibit Indian assemblies and bar Indians from bringing suit in the state. The majority of Tennessee settlers, as well as Georgia officials, pushed for similar measures to be adopted in Tennessee.

The Cherokee were divided in their response: Some felt that moving west represented the best future for their tribe, while others wanted to stay and fight for their land and the Cherokee Nation. In the end, the Cherokee

leaders lost hope of remaining, and on December 29, 1835, they signed the removal treaty. Under the agreement, the Cherokee were paid $5 million for all their lands east of the Mississippi, and they were required to move west within two years. When that time expired in 1838 and only a small number of the Cherokee had moved, the U.S. Army evicted the rest by force.

Thousands of Cherokee died along the ensuing Trail of Tears, which followed four different routes through Tennessee and eventually into Oklahoma: A southern route extended from Chattanooga to Memphis, two northern routes headed into Kentucky and Missouri before turning southward into Oklahoma, and the fourth was a water route along the Tennessee and Mississippi Rivers. Harsh weather, food shortages, and the brutality of the journey cost thousands of Cherokee lives. In the end, out of the estimated 14,000 Cherokee who began the journey, more than 4,000 are believed to have died along the way.

STATEHOOD

Almost as soon as settlers began living on the Tennessee frontier there were movements to form a government. Dissatisfied with the protection offered by North Carolina's distant government, settlers drew up their own governments as early as the 1780s. The Watauga Association and Cumberland Compact were early forms of government. In 1785, settlers in northeastern Tennessee seceded from North Carolina and established the State of Franklin. The experiment was short-lived but foretold that in the future the lands west of the Smoky Mountains would be their own state.

Before Tennessee could become a state, however, it was a territory of the

United States. In 1789, North Carolina ratified its own constitution and in doing so ceded its western lands, the Tennessee country, to the U.S. government. These lands eventually became known as the Southwest Territory, and in 1790, President George Washington appointed William Blount its territorial governor. Blount was a 41-year-old land speculator and businessman who had campaigned actively for the position. A veteran of the American Revolution, Blount knew Washington and was one of the signers of the U.S. Constitution in 1787.

At the time of its establishment, the Southwest Territory comprised 43,000 square miles (111,500 sq km). The population of 35,000 was centered in two main areas: the northeastern corner and the Cumberland settlements near present-day Nashville.

Governor Blount moved quickly to form a territorial government. In October 1790, he arrived in Washington County and established the state's first capital. The territory's first election was held in 1793, and the resulting council met a year later. They established the town of Knoxville and created a tax rate. They also ordered a census in 1795, which showed a population of more than 77,000 people and support for statehood.

The territory had met the federal requirements for statehood, and so Blount and other territorial leaders set out to make Tennessee a state. They called a constitutional convention, and delegates spent three weeks writing Tennessee's first constitution. The first statewide poll elected John Sevier governor of the new state. Meanwhile, Tennessee's request to become a state was being debated in Washington, where finally, on June 1, 1796, President Washington signed the statehood bill and Tennessee became the 16th state in the Union.

FRONTIER LIFE

The new state of Tennessee attracted settlers who were drawn by cheap land and the opportunity it represented. Between 1790 and 1800, the state's population tripled, and by 1810, Tennessee's population had grown to 250,000. The expansion caused a shift in power as the middle and western parts of the state became more populated. The capital moved from Knoxville to Nashville in 1812.

Life during the early 19th century in Tennessee was largely rural. For the subsistence farmers who made up the majority of the state's population, life was a relentless cycle of hard work. Many families lived in one- or two-room cabins and spent their days growing food and the fibers needed to make their own clothes; raising animals that supplied farm power, meat, and hides; building or repairing buildings and tools; and cutting firewood in prodigious quantities. Small-hold farmers rarely owned slaves. Those who did owned only one or two and worked alongside them.

Children provided valuable labor on the Tennessee farm. Boys often plowed their first furrow at age nine, and girls of that age were expected to mind younger children, help cook, and learn the skills of midwifery, sewing, and gardening. While women's time was often consumed with child rearing, cooking, and sewing, the housewife worked in the field alongside her husband when she was needed.

There were no public schools on the frontier, and the few private schools that existed were not accessible to the farming class. Religious missionaries were often the only people who could read and write in a community, and the first schools were established by churches. Presbyterian, Methodist, and Baptist ministers were the first to reach many settlements in Tennessee.

Settlements were spread out, and few had established churches. As a result, the camp meeting became entrenched in Tennessee culture. The homegrown spirituality of the camp meeting appealed to Tennesseans' independent spirit, which looked suspiciously at official religion and embraced the informal and deeply personal religion of the camp meeting.

Camp services were passionate and emotional, reaching a feverish pitch as men and women were overtaken by the spirit. Many camp meetings attracted both black and white participants.

THE WAR OF 1812

Tennesseans were among the war hawks in Congress who advocated for war with Great Britain in 1812. The conflict was seen by many as an opportunity to rid the state's borders of Indians once and for all. The government asked for 2,800 volunteers, and 30,000 Tennesseans offered to enlist. This is when Tennessee's nickname as the Volunteer State was born.

Nashville lawyer, politician, and businessman Andrew Jackson was chosen as the leader of the Tennessee volunteers. Despite their shortage of supplies and lack of support from the War Department, Jackson's militia prevailed in a series of lopsided victories. Given command of the southern military district, Andrew Jackson led U.S. forces at the Battle of New Orleans on January 8, 1815. The ragtag group inflicted a crushing defeat on the British, and despite having occurred after the signing of the peace treaty with Great Britain, the battle

was a victory that launched Jackson onto the road to the presidency.

GROWTH OF SLAVERY

The state's first settlers planted the seed of slavery in Tennessee, and the state's westward expansion cemented the institution. In 1791, black people made up about 10 percent of the population in Tennessee. By 1810, black people were more than 20 percent of Tennessee's people. The invention of the cotton gin and subsequent rise of King Cotton after the turn of the 19th century also caused a rapid expansion of slavery.

Slavery was most important in West Tennessee; eastern Tennessee, with its mountainous landscape and small farms, had the fewest slaves. In Middle Tennessee the slave population was concentrated in the central basin, in the counties of Davidson, Maury, Rutherford, and Williamson. By 1860, 40 percent of the state's slave population was in West Tennessee, with the greatest concentration in Shelby, Fayette, and Haywood Counties, where cotton was grown on plantations somewhat similar to those of the Deep South. As slavery grew, slave markets were established in Nashville and Memphis. The federal ban on the interstate sale of slaves was virtually ignored.

From 1790, when the state was founded, until 1831, Tennessee's slave code was relatively lenient. The law recognized a slave as both a chattel and a person, and slaves were entitled to expect protection against the elements and other people. Owners could free their slaves for any reason, and many did, causing growth in Tennessee's free black population in the first half of the 1800s. These free black individuals concentrated in eastern and

Middle Tennessee, and particularly the cities of Nashville, Memphis, and Knoxville, where they worked as laborers and artisans.

There were vocal opponents to slavery in Tennessee, particularly in the eastern part of the state. The first newspaper in the United States devoted to emancipation was established in 1819 in Jonesborough by Elihu Embree. Charles Osborne, a Quaker minister, preached against slavery shortly after the turn of the 19th century in Tennessee. Emancipationists formed societies in counties that included Washington, Sullivan, Blount, Grainger, and Cocke. Many of these early abolitionists opposed slavery on religious grounds, arguing that it was incompatible with the spirit of Christianity. These abolitionists often argued for the gradual end of slavery and sometimes advocated for the removal of freed slaves to Africa.

Memphis was founded in 1819 by Andrew Jackson, John Overton, and James Winchester, and was incorporated in 1826. The name Memphis comes from the ancient city in Egypt. It's the Greek form of the word, meaning "enduring and beautiful." Though the city initially saw slow growth, its location along the Mississippi River set it up as a thriving transportation center, and the surrounding fertile river delta was conducive to growing the city's major commodity—"white gold," or cotton. By the mid-1800s, Memphis held the title of the "Biggest Inland Cotton Market in the World" and was one of America's fastest-growing cities.

THE CIVIL WAR

In the 1830s, Tennessee's position on slavery hardened. The Virginia slave uprising led by Nat Turner frightened slave owners, who instituted patrols to search for runaway slaves and tightened codes on slave conduct. In 1834, the state constitution was amended to bar free black people from voting, a sign of whites' increasing fear of the black people living in their midst. The division between East and West Tennessee widened as many in the east were sympathetic with the antislavery forces that were growing in northern states. In the west, the support for slavery was unrelenting.

Despite the efforts of several strident secessionists, including Tennessee governor Isham Harris, Tennessee remained uncertain about secession. In February 1861, the state voted against a convention on secession. But with the attack on Fort Sumter two months later, followed by President Abraham Lincoln's call for volunteers to coerce the seceded states back to the Union, public opinion shifted. On June 8, 1861, Tennesseans voted 105,000 to 47,000 to secede.

In 1862, as the Civil War crossed into its second year, the 90-minute Battle of Memphis took place on the waters of the Mississippi, with the Union navy claiming victory as citizens watched from the city's bluff; later that day, the mayor offered Memphis's official surrender, and the Union flag was raised over the courthouse; the occupation would last the remaining three years of the war.

As the Civil War ended and the country looked toward reconstruction, Memphis's economic growth was met with roadblocks: Multiple epidemics of yellow fever swept through the city during the 1870s, killing thousands and causing many more to flee the city, leaving behind a stalled economy. Once-thriving Memphis was forced into bankruptcy.

WARTIME OCCUPATION

Some 454 battles and skirmishes were fought in Tennessee during the war. Most were small, but several key battles took place on Tennessee soil. Battles were only part of the wartime experience in Tennessee. The Civil War caused hardship for ordinary residents on a scale that many had never before seen. There was famine and poverty. Schools and churches were closed. Harassment and recrimination plagued the state, and fear was widespread.

Memphis fell to the Union on June 6, 1862, and it was occupied for the remainder of the war. Those who could fled the city. Many of those who remained stopped doing business (some of these because they refused to pledge allegiance to the Union and were not permitted to re-open). Northern traders entered the city and took over many industries, while black people who abandoned nearby plantations flooded into the city. In February 1863, one observer described the population of Memphis as "11,000 original whites, 5,000 slaves, and 19,000 newcomers of all kinds, including traders, fugitives, hangers-on, and negroes."

While the military focused on punishing Confederate sympathizers, conditions in Memphis deteriorated. Crime and disorder abounded, and guerrilla bands developed to fight the Union occupation. The Federal commander responsible for the city, Maj Gen. William T. Sherman, adopted a policy of collective responsibility, which held civilians responsible for guerrilla attacks in their neighborhoods. Sherman destroyed hundreds of homes, farms, and towns in the enforcement of this policy. The wartime occupation reversed decades of growth and left a city that would struggle for years.

The war was equally damaging in other parts of Tennessee. In Middle Tennessee, retreating Confederate soldiers after the fall of Fort Donelson demolished railroads and burned bridges so as not to leave them for Union use. Union troops also destroyed and appropriated the region's resources. Federals took horses, pigs, cows, corn, hay, cotton, fence rails, firearms, and tools. Sometimes this was carried out through official requisitions, but at other times it amounted to little more than pillaging. Criminals took advantage of the loss of public order, and bands of thieves and bandits began roaming the countryside.

THE EFFECTS OF THE WAR

Tennessee lost most of a generation of young men to the Civil War. Infrastructure was destroyed, and thousands of farms, homes, and other properties were razed. The state's reputation on the national stage had been tarnished, and it would be decades until Tennessee had the political power that it enjoyed during the Age of Jackson. But while the war caused tremendous hardships for the state, it also led to the freeing of 275,000 black Tennesseans from slavery.

RECONSTRUCTION

Tennessee was no less divided during the years following the Civil War than it was during the conflict. The end to the war ushered in a period where former Unionists—now allied with the Radical Republicans in Congress—disenfranchised and otherwise marginalized former Confederates and others who had been sympathetic to the Southern cause. They also pushed through laws that extended voting and other rights to the newly freed black population, changes that led to a powerful backlash and the establishment of such shadowy groups as the Ku Klux Klan (KKK).

William G. "Parson" Brownlow of Knoxville, a vocal Unionist, was elected governor of Tennessee in 1865. During the same year, the state's voters approved a constitutional amendment abolishing slavery, making Tennessee the only seceded state to abolish slavery by its own act. Brownlow and his supporters bent laws and manipulated loyalties in order to secure ratification of the 14th and 15th Amendments to the Constitution, paving the way for Tennessee to be readmitted to the Union, the first Southern state to be readmitted following the war. Brownlow's success ensured that Tennessee would not experience the congressionally mandated Reconstruction that other former Confederate states did.

Recognizing that the unpopularity of his positions among Tennessee's numerous former Confederates placed his political future in jeopardy, Brownlow and his supporters extended the right to vote to thousands of freedmen in February 1867. During the statewide vote a few months later, Brownlow and his followers were swept to victory, largely due to the support of black voters.

The quick rise to power of former enemies and the social changes caused by the end of slavery led some former Confederates to bitterness and frustration. In the summer of 1867, the Ku Klux Klan emerged as a political and terrorist movement aimed at keeping freedmen in their traditional place. Klan members initially concerned themselves principally with supporting former Confederates and their families, but they were soon known more for their attacks on black men and women. The KKK was strongest in Middle and West Tennessee, except for a small pocket near Bristol in East Tennessee.

Governor Brownlow responded strongly to the KKK's activities, and in 1869, he declared martial law in nine counties where the organization was most active. But when Brownlow left Tennessee shortly thereafter to fill a seat in the U.S. Senate, the KKK's grand wizard, former Confederate general Nathan Bedford Forrest, declared the group's mission accomplished and encouraged members to burn their robes. The KKK's influence quickly faded, only to reemerge 50 years later at Stone Mountain, Georgia. Brownlow was replaced by Senate Speaker Dewitt C. Senter, who quickly struck a more moderate position than his predecessor by setting aside the law that had barred Confederate veterans from voting.

The greatest legacy of the Civil War was the emancipation of Tennessee's slaves. Following the war, many freed black people left the countryside and moved to cities, including Memphis, Nashville, Chattanooga, and Knoxville, where they worked as skilled laborers, domestics, and more. Other black individuals remained in the countryside, working as wage laborers on farms or sharecropping in exchange for occupancy on part of a former large-scale plantation.

The Freedmen's Bureau worked in Tennessee for a short period after the end of the war, and it succeeded in establishing schools for the black population. During this period the state's first black colleges were inaugurated: Fisk, Tennessee Central, LeMoyne, Roger Williams, Lane, and Knoxville.

As in other states, the black population in Tennessee enjoyed short-lived political power during Reconstruction. The right to vote and the concentration of black people in certain urban areas paved the way for black individuals to be elected to the Tennessee House of Representatives, beginning with Sampson Keeble of Nashville in 1872. In all, 13 black individuals were elected as representatives between 1872 and 1887, including James C. Napier, Edward Shaw, and William Yardley, who also ran for governor.

Initially, these pioneers met mild acceptance from whites, but as time progressed whites became uncomfortable sharing political power with black people. By the 1890s, racist Jim Crow policies of segregation, poll taxes, secret ballots, literacy tests, and intimidation prevented black people from holding elective office—and in many cases, voting—in Tennessee again until after the civil rights movement of the 1960s.

The Republican Party saw the end of its influence with the end of the Brownlow governorship. Democrats rejected the divisive policies of the Radical Republicans, sought to protect the racial order that set black people at a disadvantage to whites, and were less concerned about the state's mounting debt than the Republicans.

ECONOMIC RECOVERY

The social and political upheaval caused by the Civil War was matched or exceeded by the economic catastrophe that it represented for the state. Farms and industries were damaged or destroyed, public infrastructure was razed, schools were closed, and the system of slavery that underpinned most of the state's economy was gone.

The economic setback was seen as an opportunity by proponents of the "New South," who advocated for an industrial and economic revival that would catapult the South to prosperity impossible under the agrarian and slavery-based antebellum economy. The New South movement was personified by carpetbagging northern capitalists who moved to Tennessee and set up industries that would benefit from cheap labor and abundant natural resources. Many Tennesseans welcomed these newcomers and advocated for their fellow Tennesseans to put aside regional differences and embrace the northern investors.

The result was an array of industries that were chartered during the years following the Civil War. Mining, foundries, machine shops, sawmills, gristmills, furniture factories, and textile and other manufacturing industries were established. Knoxville and Chattanooga improved quickly. Over the 10-year period from 1860 to 1870, Chattanooga's industrial works grew from employing 214 men to more than 2,000. Memphis and Nashville also worked to attract industries. Memphis was on the cusp of a commercial and industrial boom in 1873 when yellow fever hit the city; the epidemic caused widespread mortality and hurt Memphis's economic recovery.

Industry also settled in the small towns and countryside. The coal-rich region of the Cumberland Mountains was the site of major coal-mining operations. Copper mines were opened in Cleveland, flouring mills in Jackson, and textile factories in Tullahoma and other parts of the state.

AGRICULTURE

A revolution was brewing in agriculture, too. Civil War veterans returned to small farms all over the state and resumed farming with implements largely unchanged for hundreds of years. Every task was achieved by hand, with the lone help of one or two farm animals.

But farm technology was beginning to change. Thirty years after the war, new labor-saving devices began to be put to use. These included early cotton pickers, reapers, and planters. Seed cleaners, corn shellers, and improved plows were made available. In 1871 the state formed the Bureau of Agriculture, whose employees prepared soil maps and studied the state's climate, population, and the prices of land. New methods such as crop diversification, crop rotation, cover crops, and the use of commercial fertilizers were introduced, and farmers were encouraged to use them.

Meanwhile, farmers themselves established a strong grassroots movement in the state. The Patrons of Husbandry, or the Grange, was organized shortly after the war to encourage members to improve farming methods and enhance their economic influence. Government encouraged county fair associations, which organized fairs where farmers could be awarded for their crops and encouraged to use new farming methods. The Farmers' Alliance and the Agricultural Wheel, both national organizations, grew in prominence in the 1880s and advocated currency reform, empowerment of farmers, and control of communication and transportation systems. The Alliance gave low-interest loans to farmers and encouraged cooperative selling.

While the Alliance and the Wheel were not political organizations as such, they supported candidates who adopted their views on agricultural matters. In 1890, the Alliance supported Democrat John P. Buchanan for governor, and he was successful. For their part, political elites did not take the farming movement or its leaders very seriously, ridiculing them as "hayseeds," "clodhoppers," and "wool-hat boys." In other places, rural and small-town residents resisted the Wheel and the Alliance, in part because they feared challenge of the status quo. As the Alliance became more radical in its views, the support in Tennessee dwindled, and by 1892 it had faded in many parts of the state.

While some black people remained on farms as wage laborers or sharecroppers, many left for the cities, causing a labor shortage. Attempts to attract foreign or northern immigrants to the state were unsuccessful. Tennessee's poor whites filled this labor shortage, now able to own or rent land for the first time.

EDUCATION

Despite popular attempts and pleas by some politicians for a sound education system, Tennessee lagged in public education during the postwar years. In 1873, the legislature passed a school law that set up a basic framework of school administration, but the state's debt and financial problems crippled the new system. Private funds stepped in—the Peabody Fund contributed to Tennessee's schools, including the old University of Nashville, renamed Peabody after its benefactor. Meanwhile, teachers' institutes were established during the 1880s in order to raise the level of instruction at Tennessee's public schools.

Today Memphis continues to struggle with segregation in its public schools. The area is home to six nonspecialized colleges and universities:

University of Memphis; Northwest Mississippi Community College; Southwest Tennessee Community College; Christian Brothers University; Rhodes College; and LeMoyne-Owen College. Community college is free to Tennessee residents.

PROHIBITION

Prohibition was the first major issue Tennesseans faced in the new century. An 1877 law that forbade the sale of alcohol within 4 miles (6.4 km) of a rural school had been used to great effect by Prohibitionists to restrict the sale and traffic of alcohol in towns all over the countryside. As the century turned, pressure mounted to extend the law, and public opinion in support of temperance grew, although it was never without contest from the powerful distillery industry. Finally, in 1909, the legislature passed the Manufacturer's Bill, which would halt the production of intoxicants in the state and overrode Governor Malcolm Patterson's veto. By the time the United States followed suit with the 18th Amendment in 1920, Prohibition was old news in Tennessee.

WORLD WAR I

True to its nickname, Tennessee sent a large number of volunteer troops to fight in World War I. Most became part of the 30th "Old Hickory" Division, which entered the war on August 17, 1918. The most famous Tennessee veteran of World War I was Alvin C. York, a farm boy from the Cumberland Mountains who staged a one-man offensive against German troops after becoming separated from his own detachment. Reports say that York killed 20 German soldiers and persuaded 131 more to surrender.

THE 1920S: WOMEN'S SUFFRAGE

The movement for women's suffrage had been established in Tennessee prior to the turn of the 20th century, and it gained influence as the century progressed. The Southern Woman Suffrage Conference was held in Memphis in 1906, and a statewide suffrage organization was established. State bills to give women the right to vote failed in 1913 and 1917, but support was gradually growing. In the summer of 1920, the 19th Amendment had been ratified by 35 states, and one more ratification was needed to make it law. Tennessee was one of five states yet to vote on the measure, and on August 9, Democratic governor Albert H. Roberts called a special sitting of the legislature to consider the amendment.

Furious campaigning and public debate led up to the special sitting. The Senate easily ratified the amendment 25 to 4, but in the House of Representatives the vote was much closer: 49 to 47. Governor Roberts certified the result and notified the secretary of state: Tennessee had cast the deciding vote for women's suffrage.

The 1920s were years of growth and development in Tennessee, thanks in part to the capable leadership of Austin Peay, elected governor in 1922. He reformed the state government, cut waste, and set out to improve the state's roads and schools. The improvements won Peay support from the state's rural residents, who benefited from better transportation and education. Spending on schools doubled during Peay's three terms as governor, and the school term increased from 127 to 155 days per year.

Peay also saw the importance of establishing parks: Reelfoot Lake

State Park was established during his third term, finally ending fears of development in the area. Peay also supported establishment of Great Smoky Mountains National Park, and he raised $1.5 million in a bond issue as the state's part toward the purchase of the land. Peay was dead by the time the park was opened in 1940, but it is largely to his credit that it was created.

THE CRUMP MACHINE

The 1930s in Tennessee was the age of Ed Crump, Memphis's longtime mayor and political boss. The son of a former Confederate, Crump was born in Mississippi in 1874 and moved to Memphis when he was 17 years old. First elected in 1909 as a city councilman, Crump was a genius of human nature and organization. Able to ensure statewide candidates the support of influential Shelby County, Crump's power extended beyond Memphis. His political power often required corruption, patronage, and the loss of individual freedoms. To get ahead, you had to pay homage to Boss Crump. He was particularly popular during the Depression, when constituents and others looked to Crump for much-needed relief.

Crump manipulated the votes in his home Shelby County by paying the $2 poll tax for cooperative voters. He allied with black leaders such as Robert Church Jr. to win support in the black community of Memphis.

WORLD WAR II

Tennessee, like the rest of the country, was changed by World War II. The war effort transformed the state's economy and led to a migration to the cities unprecedented in Tennessee's

history. The tiny mountain town of Oak Ridge became the state's fifth-largest city almost overnight thanks to the establishment of the Oak Ridge National Laboratory, and it is synonymous with the atomic bomb that was dropped on Hiroshima, Japan, at the final stage of the war.

More than 300,000 Tennesseans served in World War II and just under 6,000 died. During the war, the state's Camps Forrest, Campbell, and Tyson served as prisoner-of-war camps. Several hundred war refugees settled in Tennessee, many in the Nashville area.

The war also sped up Tennessee's industrialization. Industrial centers in Memphis, Chattanooga, and Knoxville converted to war production, while new industries were established in smaller cities such as Kingsport. Agriculture was no longer Tennessee's most important economic activity. The industrial growth was a catalyst for urbanization. Nashville's population grew by 25 percent during the war, and Shelby County's by 35 percent. The war also finally saw the end of the Great Depression.

Tennesseans served with distinction during the war. Cordell Hull, a native of Pickett County, was U.S. secretary of state for 12 years and is known as the Father of the United Nations for his role in drawing up the foundation of that institution. Tennesseans supported the war on the home front as well. Families planted victory gardens, invested in war bonds, and aided soldiers. The war also brought women into the workplace in numbers that were then unprecedented; approximately one-third of the state's workers by the end of the war were female.

POSTWAR TENNESSEE

Tennessee's industrialization continued after the war. By 1960, there were more city dwellers than rural dwellers in the state, and Tennessee was ranked the 16th most industrialized state in the United States. Industry that had developed during the war transitioned to peacetime operation.

Ex-servicemen were not content with the political machines that had controlled Tennessee politics for decades. In 1948 congressman Estes Kefauver won a U.S. Senate seat, defeating the candidate chosen by Memphis mayor Ed Crump. The defeat signaled an end to Crump's substantial influence in statewide elections. In 1953, Tennessee repealed the state poll tax, again limiting politicians' ability to manipulate the vote. The tide of change also swept in Senator Albert Gore Sr. and Governor Frank Clement in 1952. Kefauver, Gore, and Clement were moderate Democrats of the New South.

CIVIL RIGHTS

The early gains for black people during Reconstruction were lost during the decades that followed. Segregation, the threat of violence, poll taxes, and literacy tests discriminated against black people in all spheres of life: economic, social, political, and educational. The fight to right these wrongs was waged by many brave Tennesseans.

Early civil rights victories in Tennessee included the successful 1905 boycott of Nashville's segregated streetcars and the creation of a competing black-owned streetcar company. In the 1920s in Chattanooga, the black population successfully defeated the Ku Klux Klan at the polls. Black institutions of learning persevered in educating young African

Banners herald the National Civil Rights Museum.

Americans and developing a generation of leaders.

Following World War II, there was newfound energy in the fight for civil rights. Returning black servicemen who had fought for their country demanded greater equality, and the opportunities of the age raised the stakes of economic equality. In 1946, racially based violence targeted at a returned black serviceman in Columbia brought national attention to violence against black citizens and raised awareness of the need to protect their civil rights.

The Highlander Folk School, founded in Grundy County and later moved to Cocke County, was an important training center for community activists and civil rights leaders in the 1950s. Founder Miles Horton believed in popular education and sought to bring black and white activists together to share experiences. Many leaders in the national civil rights movement, including Rev. Martin Luther King Jr. and Rosa Parks, attended the folk school.

In the 1950s, the first steps toward

public school desegregation took place in Tennessee. Following a lawsuit filed by black parents, Clinton desegregated its schools in 1956 on order of a federal judge. The integration began peacefully, but outside agitators arrived to organize resistance, and in the end Governor Frank Clement was forced to call in 600 National Guardsmen to defuse the situation. But the first black students were allowed to stay, and in May 1957, Bobby Cain became the first African American to graduate from an integrated public high school in the South.

In the fall of 1957, Nashville's public schools were desegregated. As many as half of the white students stayed home in protest, and one integrated school, Hattie Cotton School, was dynamited and partially destroyed. Other Tennessee cities desegregated at a slower pace, and by 1960, only 169 of Tennessee's almost 150,000 black children of school age attended integrated schools.

The Nashville lunch counter sit-ins of 1960 were an important milestone in both the local and national civil rights movements. Led by students from the city's black universities, the sit-ins eventually forced an end to racial segregation of the city's public services. Over two months hundreds of black students were arrested for sitting at white-only downtown lunch counters. Black consumers' boycott of downtown stores put additional pressure on the business community. On April 19, thousands of protesters marched in silence to the courthouse to confront city officials, and the next day Rev. Martin Luther King Jr. addressed Fisk University. On May 10, 1960, several downtown stores integrated their lunch counters, and Nashville became the first major city

in the South to begin desegregating its public facilities.

As the civil rights movement continued, Tennesseans played an important part. Tennesseans were involved with organizing the Student Nonviolent Coordinating Committee and participated in the Freedom Rides, which sought to integrate buses across the South.

Memphis played a history-shifting role in the civil rights movement. In 1965, A. W. Willis Jr. of Memphis became the first African American representative elected to the state's General Assembly in more than 60 years. In 1968 the sanitation workers' strike called for the city to provide decent wages and safe working conditions to its sanitation employees. The protest lasted for three months, shifting into a greater fight for civil rights and grabbing the attention of the nation as Dr. Martin Luther King Jr. offered his support for the movement. On March 28, as King joined the strikers for a peaceful march downtown, violence erupted when a few individuals smashed windows and looted stores. Police took this as an opportunity to control the crowd with force, arresting and injuring hundreds and killing a 16-year-old boy. Martial law was declared and 4,000 National Guardsmen were brought in. Unwavering, more than 200 strikers showed up to march to city hall the next day with signs that read, "I AM A MAN."

King returned to Memphis on April 3, 1968, giving his now-famous "I've Been to the Mountaintop" speech—what would be his last—at the Mason Temple, telling the congregation, "Something is happening in Memphis; something is happening in our world." The following day he was assassinated on the balcony of his hotel at the Lorraine Motel. Two days later, strike negotiations with the city began; on April 16, a settlement was agreed upon, with the union's demands being met—a win for the strikers. In 1991, the Lorraine Motel became the site of the National Civil Rights Museum.

MODERN TENNESSEE

The industrialization that began during World War II has continued in modern-day Tennessee. In 1980, Nissan built what was then the largest truck assembly plant in the world at Smyrna, Tennessee. In 1987, Saturn Corporation chose Spring Hill as the site for its $2.1 billion automobile plant. At the same time, however, the state's older industries—including textiles and manufacturing—have suffered losses over the past three decades, due in part to the movement of industry outside of the United States.

During the 1950s and beyond, Tennessee developed a reputation as a hotbed of musical talent. Memphis's Elvis Presley may have invented rock 'n' roll, and his Graceland mansion remains one of the state's most enduring tourist attractions.

Racial politics continue to be an issue in Tennessee, just like in much of the country. The removal of Confederate statues, flags, and other iconography is an ongoing debate. In 2018, the City of Memphis sold several parks to a nonprofit so that it could legally have Confederate statues removed without interference from the state legislature. Black Lives Matter and other organizations are active in working toward building power in communities to reduce violence and increase opportunity.

Government and Economy

GOVERNMENT

Tennessee is governed by its constitution, unchanged since 1870, when it was revised in light of emancipation, the Civil War, and Reconstruction. Tennessee has a governor who is elected to four-year terms, a legislature, and a court system. The lieutenant governor is not elected statewide; he or she is chosen by the Senate and also serves as its Speaker. The executive branch consists of 22 cabinet-level departments, which employ 39,000 state workers. Departments are led by a commissioner who is appointed by the governor and serves as a member of his cabinet. The legislature, or General Assembly, is made up of the 99-member House of Representatives and the 33-member Senate.

Tennessee has 95 counties; the largest (size-wise, not population) is Shelby County, which contains Memphis. The smallest county by size is Trousdale, with 113 square miles (293 sq km); the smallest population is in Pickett County.

The state has 11 Electoral College votes in U.S. presidential elections.

MODERN POLITICS

Like other Southern states, Tennessee has seen a gradual shift to the political right since the 1960s. The shift began in 1966 with Howard Baker's election to the U.S. Senate, and it continued with Tennessee's support for Republican presidential candidate Richard Nixon in 1968 and 1972. Despite a few exceptions, the shift has continued into the 21st century, although Nashville, Memphis, and other parts of Middle and West Tennessee remain Democratic territory.

East Tennessee holds a distinction as one of a handful of Southern territories that have consistently supported the Republican Party since the Civil War. Today, Republicans outpoll Democrats in this region by as much as three to one.

The statewide trend toward the Republican Party continued in 2008, with Tennessee being one of only a handful of states in which Democrat Barack Obama received a lesser proportion of votes than did Democratic senator John Kerry four years earlier. State Republicans also succeeded in gaining control of both houses of the state legislature. The general shift to the right has continued in the governor's office. Previous governor Phil Bredesen is a Democrat, but he was succeeded by Republican Bill Haslam. In 2018, Republican businessman Bill Lee was elected governor. This was the first time since 1967 that a party has been able to keep the governor's seat for two terms.

Andrew Jackson may still be the most prominent Tennessean in American political history, but Tennessee politicians continue to play a role on the national stage. Albert Gore Jr., elected to the U.S. House of Representatives in 1976, served as vice president under Bill Clinton from 1992 until 2000, and he lost the hotly contested 2000 presidential contest to George W. Bush. Gore famously lost his home state to Bush, further evidence of Tennessee's move to the right.

Gore went on to champion global climate change and win the Nobel Peace Prize, and he is often seen around Nashville.

Lamar Alexander, a former governor of Tennessee, was appointed secretary of education by President George H. W. Bush in 1990. Alexander—famous for his flannel shirts—ran unsuccessfully for president and was later elected senator from Tennessee. Republican Bill Frist, a doctor, was rose to be Senate majority leader during the presidency of George W. Bush, before quitting politics for medical philanthropy.

One of the most persistent political issues for Tennesseans in modern times has been the state's tax structure. The state first established a 2 percent sales tax in 1947, and it was increased incrementally over the years, eventually reaching 7 percent today. With local options, it is one of the highest sales tax rates in the country. (The state sales tax on food is 5.5 percent.) In 2014 the legislature passed a constitutional amendment to prohibit a state income tax.

Today Memphis's county, Shelby County, remains an island of liberal-leaning voters amid a sea of majority-red Tennessee counties. Shelby County has voted primarily Democrat in the recent presidential elections, with a 62.3 percent Democratic vote in the 2016 presidential election.

ECONOMY

Tennessee has the 13th-largest economy in the United States. Important industries include health care, education, farming, electrical power, and tourism. In the past few years, most job growth has been recorded in the areas of leisure, hospitality, education, and health care. Manufacturing, mining, and construction jobs have declined.

Tennessee's unemployment rate fluctuates but generally sits a half point above the national average. In 2018, the jobless rate was about 3.8 percent.

About 13.7 percent of Tennessee families live in poverty, ranking the state 38th out of 50. The median household income in 2016 was $48,547, ranking it 45th.

All of Tennessee's cities have poverty rates higher than the state or national average. The percentage of Memphis families living below the poverty level is the state's highest: 26.9 percent of Memphis families are poor. The U.S. Census Bureau calls Memphis one of the poorest cities in the nation.

People and Culture

DEMOGRAPHICS

Tennessee is home to 6.7 million people. Almost one-quarter of these are 18 years and younger; about 13 percent are older than 65. Tennessee is 78 percent white and 17 percent black.

Memphis counts 652,236 residents and is the state's second-largest city, having been recently passed by Nashville. More than 63 percent of Memphians are African American, a greater proportion than is found in any other American city. At 33.8 years, Memphis has the youngest average age of the four major Tennessee cities. The greater Memphis metropolitan area has a population of 1.35 million. The area's population is increasing at a rate of 1.77 percent annually.

RELIGION

Tennessee is unquestionably part of the U.S. Bible Belt, and the conservative Christian faith is both prevalent and prominent all over the state: 81 percent of Tennesseans call themselves Christians, and 33 percent of these identify as Baptist. The second-largest Christian denomination is Methodist. Nashville is the headquarters of the Southern Baptist Convention, the National Baptist Convention, and the United Methodist Church. Memphis is the headquarters of the mostly African American Church of God in Christ. However, the state's major cities do have growing populations that practice Judaism and Islam.

While Tennessee's urban centers are the home of church headquarters, religious fervor is strongest in the rural communities. Pentecostal churches have been known for rites such as speaking in tongues and snake handling, although these activities are not as widespread as they once were.

Non-Christians will feel most comfortable in urban areas, where numbers of religious minorities have grown in recent years and where the influence of the local churches is not as great.

One practical effect of Tennessee's Christian bent is that many counties and even some cities are totally dry, and most bar the sale of packaged alcohol on Sunday (you can still order a drink in a restaurant).

LANGUAGE

Tennesseans speak English, of a kind. The Tennessee drawl varies from the language of the upper South, spoken in East Tennessee and closely associated with the region's Scots-Irish roots, and the language of West Tennessee, more akin to that of Mississippi and the lower South.

Little in Tennesseans' speech is distinct to the state itself. Speech patterns heard in Tennessee are also heard in other states in the region. Speech patterns that have been documented throughout the state, but that may be more prevalent in the east, include the following, outlined by Michael Montgomery of the University of South Carolina in the *Tennessee Encyclopedia of History and Culture*. Montgomery writes that Tennesseans tend to pronounce vowels in the words *pen* and *hem* as *pin* and *him;* they shift the accent to the beginning of words, so *Tennessee* becomes *TIN-i-see;* they clip or reduce the vowel in words like *ride* so it sounds more like *rad;* and vowels in other words are stretched, so that a single-syllable word like *bed* becomes *bay-ud.*

Tennessee speech patterns are not limited to word pronunciation. Tennesseans also speak with folksy and down-home language. Speakers often use colorful metaphors, and greater value is placed on the quality of expression than the perfection of grammar.

THE ARTS
CRAFTS
Many Tennessee craft traditions have their roots in the handmade housewares that rural families had to make for themselves, including things like quilts and coverlets, baskets, candles, and furniture. These items were fashioned out of materials that could be raised or harvested nearby, and colors were derived from natural dyes such as walnut hulls and indigo.

Many of the same crafts were produced by African Americans, who developed their own craft traditions, often with even fewer raw materials than their white counterparts. For example, African American quilts often used patterns and colors reflective of African culture. Blacksmiths were often African American, and these skilled artisans developed both practical and decorative pieces for white and black households.

Today, artists from around the United States have settled in Tennessee to practice modern forms of traditional crafts of quilting, weaving, pottery, furniture making, and basket making, among others. While market forces have promoted a certain false folksiness among some artists, a great many of today's practicing artisans remain true to the mountain heritage that gave birth to the craft tradition in the first place.

MUSIC
Tennessee may be more famous for its music than for anything else. Rock 'n' roll traces its roots to Elvis Presley, Carl Perkins, Jerry Lee Lewis, and the city of Memphis. Blues music was born on Beale Street; the Grand Ole Opry popularized old-time mountain music; and the Fisk Jubilee Singers of Nashville introduced African American spirituals to the world.

The blues became popular in cities from New Orleans to St. Louis at the turn of the 20th century. But thanks in large part to composer and performer W. C. Handy, the musical form will be forever associated with Memphis and Beale Street. Early blues greats like Walter "Furry" Lewis, Booker T. Washington "Bukka" White, "Little Laura" Dukes, and Ma Rainey started in Memphis.

Sun Studio recorded some of the first commercial blues records in the 1950s, but the label is most famous for discovering Elvis Presley. Stax Records created a new sound, soul, in the late 1950s and early 1960s.

Country music was born in Bristol, Tennessee, where the earliest recordings of Jimmie Rodgers and the Carter Family were made in the 1920s. In the decades that followed, Nashville became the capital of country music thanks to radio station WSM and the dozens of rural musicians who trekked to town to play on the radio. America was hungry for a type of music to call its own, and country music was it. First called "hillbilly music," country was popularized by barn-dance radio shows, including the Grand Ole Opry. Over the years, country music mellowed out, adopting the Nashville sound that softened its edges and made it palatable to a wider audience. The economic impact of the music industry on Nashville approached $9.7 billion in 2015, according to the Chamber of Commerce.

The Bureau of Labor Statistics ranked Tennessee number one in the country for its concentration of musician jobs.

DANCE

Clogging, or buck dancing, is a style of folk dance that originated with the Scots-Irish settlers in the eastern mountains of Tennessee. Characterized by an erect upper body and a fast-paced toe-heel movement with the feet, traditional clogging is improvisational. Performers move at a very fast pace to the music of string bands.

Clogging was popularized during the 1940s and 1950s on television and radio shows that showcased country music. Modern clogging is often choreographed and performed with a partner.

Clogging can trace influences from Native American and African American styles of dance as well as the traditional dance of the British Isles.

LITERATURE

The first literature inspired by Tennessee is not well known. *The Tennessean; A Novel, Founded on Facts* is a melodramatic novel written by Anne Newport Royall and published in 1827. Its plot brings readers along on a three-day journey from Nashville to Knoxville, and it is the first novel set in Tennessee. The first novel written by a Tennessean was *Woodville; or, The Anchoret Reclaimed. A Descriptive Tale,* written by Charles W. Todd and published in Knoxville in 1832.

Another award-winning Tennessee writer is **Peter Taylor,** who studied at Rhodes College and Vanderbilt University before moving to North Carolina and writing the Pulitzer Prize-winning *A Summons to Memphis* in 1986 and *In Tennessee Country* in 1994.

Few people knew Memphis-born writer and historian **Shelby Foote** until Ken Burns's landmark *Civil War* documentary. In addition to his seminal trilogy on the war, Foote wrote the novel *Shiloh* in 1952.

No Tennessee writer is better known or more widely acclaimed than **Alex Haley,** whose *Roots* won the Pulitzer Prize and inspired a landmark film and television series. Haley's other works include *Queen,* which is based on the story of his grandmother, who worked and lived in Savannah, Tennessee, on the

Tennessee River, about an hour from Memphis.

ENTERTAINMENT

Other famous Memphians include musician Justin Timberlake; actress Kathy Bates; singer Aretha Franklin; actor Morgan Freeman; singer Isaac Hayes; *Saturday Night Live* comedian Leslie Jones; actor Chris Parnell; actor Michael Jeter; Elvis's daughter and wife, Lisa Marie Presley and Priscilla Presley, respectively; and musician Booker T. Jones.

ESSENTIALS

Transportation

Most visitors to West Tennessee arrive by plane or car. The highways are good, distances are manageable, and many destinations in the region are not accessible by public transportation, although both Memphis and Little Rock have some transit options.

If you're coming to Memphis for a weekend getaway or a conference, you likely can manage

without a car. But if your trip is longer, or you plan on taking any of the excursions in this book, including those to Hot Springs, Little Rock, Tupelo, and Oxford, you will need your own wheels to get around.

GETTING THERE
AIR

Most visitors coming for a Memphis getaway will arrive via **Memphis International Airport (MEM)**. It is located 13 miles south of downtown. There are two popular routes to Memphis from the airport: I-240 north goes to midtown, while downtown is accessed by taking I-55 north and exiting at Riverside Drive. The drive takes 20-30 minutes.

The airport's main international travel insurance and business services center (901/922-8090) is located in ticket lobby B and is open daily. Here you can exchange foreign currency, buy travel insurance, conduct money transfers, send faxes and make photocopies, and buy money orders and travelers checks. A smaller kiosk near the international arrivals and departures area at gate B-36 is open daily and offers foreign currency exchange and travel insurance.

There is free wireless Internet service in the airport.

RAIL

Amtrak (800/872-7245, www.amtrak. com) runs the City of New Orleans train daily between Chicago and New Orleans, stopping in Memphis on the way. The southbound train arrives daily at Memphis's Central Station at 6:27am, leaving about half an hour later. The northbound train arrives at 10pm every day. It is an 11-hour ride overnight between Memphis and Chicago, and about 8 hours between Memphis and New Orleans.

The **Amtrak station** (901/526-0052) is located in Central Station at 545 South Main Street in the South Main district of downtown. Ticket and baggage service is available at the station daily 5:45am-11:15pm. Central Station is conveniently located downtown, where most major rental car companies have offices.

BUS

Greyhound (800/231-2222, www. greyhound.com) runs daily bus service to Memphis from around the country. Direct service is available to Memphis from a number of surrounding cities, including Jackson and Nashville, Tennessee; Tupelo and Jackson, Mississippi; Little Rock and Jonesboro, Arkansas; and St. Louis. The **Greyhound station** (3033 Airways Blvd., 901/395-8770) is open 24 hours a day.

Budget-friendly **Megabus** (http:// us.megabus.com) also serves Memphis from six cities (Atlanta, Birmingham, Chicago, Dallas, Little Rock, and St. Louis), although from a different area near the airport (3921 American Way). Megabus boasts free Wi-Fi on board and, perhaps because of that, attracts a younger clientele.

CAR

Tennessee recognizes other states' driver's licenses and learner's permits. New residents are required to obtain a Tennessee license within 30 days of establishing residency, however.

Speed limits vary. On interstates limits range 55-75 miles per hour (89-121 kph). Limits on primary and secondary routes vary based on local conditions. Travelers should pay special attention to slow zones around schools; speeding tickets in these areas often attract high penalties.

It is required by law that all drivers and passengers in a moving vehicle wear **seatbelts.** Infants less than one year old must be restrained in a rear-facing **car seat;** children 1-3 years must be restrained in a front-facing car seat. A child of 4-8 years who is less than 4 feet, 9 inches (145 cm) tall must have a booster seat.

Drunk driving is dangerous and against the law. It is illegal to drive in Tennessee with a blood alcohol concentration of 0.08 percent or more.

Traffic congestion peaks at rush hours and is worst in the eastern parts of the city and along the interstates. For current **traffic and road reports,** including weather-related closures, construction closures, and traffic jams, dial 511 from any mobile or landline phone. You can also log on to www.tn511.com.

Downtown, **parking** is plentiful if you are prepared to pay; an all-day pass in one of the many downtown parking garages costs about $12.

Car Rentals

The greatest concentrations of **car rental** agencies are found at the airport, but there are also downtown and neighborhood locations. Most rental agencies require the renter to be at least 24 years old; some have an even higher age requirement. Before renting a car, call your credit card company and primary car insurance provider to find out what kind of insurance you have on a rental. You can likely forgo the expensive insurance packages offered by rental companies. For the best rates on car rentals, book early. Most companies allow you to reserve a car in advance without paying a deposit.

Motorcycle Rentals

If you want to head out onto the Mississippi Blues Trail or Natchez Trace Parkway on **motorcycle,** Memphis is a good place to find one. **Bumpus Harley-Davidson** (2160 Whitten Rd., 901/372-1121, http://bumpushdmemphis.com, 9am-6pm Mon.-Fri., 9am-4pm Sat., 11am-3pm Sun.) rents seven different Harley models, and has storage for your car and extra belongings while you are on the road.

RV Rentals

You can rent an RV for a one-way or local trip from **Cruise America** (www.cruiseamerica.com), which has a location in Memphis (10230 U.S. 70, Lakeland, 901/867-0039). Renters should be 25 years or older. Rental rates vary depending on the size of the vehicle and other factors. They also charge for mileage, and you can buy kits that include sheets, towels, dishes, and other basic necessities.

All state park campgrounds welcome RVs and provide utilities such as water, electricity, and a dump station. For people who enjoy the outdoors but do not want to forgo the basic comforts of home, RVs provide some real advantages. RVs range from little trailers that pop up to provide space for sleeping to giant homes on wheels. Gas mileage ranges 7-13 miles per gallon, depending on the size and age of the RV.

All RVers should have mercy on other drivers and pull over from time to time so that traffic can pass, especially on mountain roads that are steep and difficult for RVs to climb.

GETTING AROUND

BUS

Buses are an option for short trips around the city. The **Memphis Area Transit Authority** (901/274-6282, www.matatransit.com) operates dozens of buses that travel through the greater Memphis area. For information on routes, call or stop by the North End Terminal on North Main Street for help planning your trip. The bus system is not used frequently by tourists. A daily pass is available for $3.50 or $16/week.

Sun Studio runs a **free shuttle bus** between Sun Studio, the Rock 'n' Soul Museum at Beale Street, and Graceland. The first run stops at the Graceland Heartbreak Hotel at 9:55am, Graceland at 10am, Sun Studio at 10:15am, and the Rock 'n' Soul Museum at 10:30am. Runs continue throughout the day on an hourly schedule. The last run picks up at Heartbreak Hotel at 5:55pm, Graceland Plaza at 6pm, and Sun Studio at 6:15pm. The shuttle is a 12-passenger black van painted with the Sun Studio logo. The ride is free, but consider tipping your driver. The published schedule is a loose approximation, so it's a good idea to get to the pickup point early in case the van is running ahead. You can call 901/521-0664 or go to http://memphisrocknsoul.org/sunstudioshuttle for more information.

TAXI AND RIDE SHARE

Memphis has a number of taxi companies, and you will usually find available cabs along Beale Street and waiting at the airport. Otherwise, you will need to call for a taxi. Some of the largest companies are **Yellow Cab** (901/577-7777, www.yellowcabofmemphis.com), **City Wide Cab** (901/722-8294, http://citywidetaxi.net), **Arrow** **Transportation Company** (901/332-7769), and **Metro Cab** (901/322-2222, http://ridememphis.com). Expect to pay $25-35 for a trip from the airport to downtown; most fares around town are under $10. Taxis accept credit cards. App-based ride-sharing services such as Uber and Lyft ($15-20 from the airport to downtown) operate in Memphis and have agreements with the local government to allow them to make stops at the airport and other destinations.

Ride-sharing services that use an app and contracted drivers in their own vehicles are becoming a popular solution in cities. **Lyft** (www.lyft.com) or **Uber** (www.uber.com) serve Memphis, Little Rock, Hot Springs, Oxford, Tupelo, and other nearby cities.

TROLLEY

Public trolleys (or hybrid bus shuttles when the trolleys are being serviced) run for about two miles along Main Street in Memphis from the Pinch District in the north to Central Station in the south, and circle up on a parallel route along Riverfront Drive. Another trolley line runs about two miles east on Madison Avenue, connecting the city's medical center with downtown. The **Main Street Trolleys** run every 10-15 minutes at most times; the Madison Avenue trolleys run every 20 minutes until 6pm on weekdays only.

Fares are $1 per ride. You can buy an all-day pass for $3.50, a three-day pass for $9, or a monthlong pass for $25. All passes must be purchased at the North End Terminal at the northern end of the Main Street route.

The trolley system is useful, especially if your hotel is on either the northern or southern end of downtown or along Madison Avenue. Brochures with details on the routes and fares are available all over town, or you can download one at www.mata-transit.com. The trolleys are simple to understand and use; if you have a question, just ask your driver.

Who knew your designated driver would be a kangaroo? That can be the case if you **Ride the Roo** (http://ridetheroo.com, Fri.-Sat. 5pm-2am, $2 per ride, $5 for all-night pass). This sleek black minibus with a martini-wielding kangaroo on top makes 12 stops along nightlife-heavy areas in Overton Square and Cooper-Young.

Explore Bike Share in Memphis

BICYCLE

With more than 60 stations around town, **Explore Bike Share** (901/292-0707, explorebikeshare.bcycle.com) is a great way to see Memphis on two wheels. Pay $1.25 for every 15 minutes as you go, or by a $5 day pass or $10 for a weekly pass. The system is set up with an app and a credit card, but you can arrange to pay with cash by calling ahead. Stations are all over the city, but concentrated downtown and midtown.

To rent bicycles, or get parts and repairs for your existing bike, try **Peddler Bike Shop** (3548 Walker Ave., 901/327-4833, http://peddler-bikeshop.com, 9am-6pm Mon.-Fri., 9am-5pm Sat., 1pm-5pm Sun.), which has three other locations in the greater Memphis area. **Bike Plus** (9445 Poplar Ave., Germantown, 901/755-7233, http://bikesplus.net, 10am-6pm Mon.-Fri., 10am-5pm Sat.) is another full-service shop for repairs and rentals, with a second location in Bartlett (7124 Hwy.64/Stage Rd., Suite 115).

Food

Throughout Tennessee, you will find restaurants that specialize in local and regional dishes. In urban centers, there is a wide variety of dining available, from international eateries to fine-dining restaurants.

Chain restaurants, including fast-food joints, are all over the state. But travelers owe it to themselves to eat in local restaurants for a taste of something more authentic.

MEAT-AND-THREES

Meat-and-threes, also called plate-lunch diners, are found throughout Tennessee, with the greatest concentration in Memphis and Nashville. The name is used to refer to both the type of restaurant and the meal itself. These eateries serve the type of food that Tennesseans once cooked at home: main-dish meats like baked chicken, meat loaf, fried catfish, and chicken and dumplings; side dishes (also called "vegetables"), including macaroni and cheese, mashed potatoes, greens, creamed corn, squash, and fried okra; breads, including cornbread, biscuits, and yeast rolls; and desserts like peach cobbler, Jell-O, and cream pies. Hands down, these diners are the best places to become acquainted, or renew your relationship, with Southern home cooking.

Plate-lunch diners focus on the midday meal. Most offer a different menu of meats and sides daily. Large restaurants may have as many as eight different main dishes to choose from; smaller diners may offer two or three. Some are set up cafeteria-style, and others employ servers. All offer a good value for the money and generally speedy food service.

Meat-and-threes exist in rural and urban communities, although in the countryside there's less fuss attached. They are simply where people go to eat.

The food served in these restaurants is generally hearty; health-conscious eaters should be careful. Vegetarians should also note that many vegetable dishes, such as greens, are often cooked with meat.

BARBECUE

Memphis is the epicenter of Tennessee's barbecue culture. The city hosts an annual festival dedicated to barbecue, and bona fide barbecue pits burn daily. In Memphis, they'll douse anything with barbecue sauce, hence one of the city's most famous specialties: barbecue spaghetti.

Barbecue restaurants are usually humble places by appearances, with characters behind the counter and in the kitchen. Most swear by their own special barbecue recipe and guard it jealously. Nearly all good barbecue, however, requires time and patience, as the meat—usually pork—is smoked for hours and sometimes days over a fire. After the meat is cooked, it is tender and juicy and doused with barbecue sauce, which is tangy and sweet.

Pork barbecue is the most common, and it's often served pulled next to soft white bread. Barbecue chicken, turkey, ribs, bologna, and beef can also be found on many menus.

The Southern Foodways Alliance (SFA), part of the University of Mississippi's Center for the Study of Southern Culture, conducted an oral history project about Memphis and West Tennessee barbecue in the early 2000s. You can read transcripts of the interviews and see photos on the SFA website at www.southern-foodways.org.

HOT CHICKEN

Panfried "hot chicken" is one of Nashville's truly distinct culinary specialties. Breasts of spicy chicken are individually panfried in cast-iron skillets at several holes-in-the-wall around Music City and interpreted on menus at higher-end restaurants. They are traditionally served on white bread with a pickle. Don't come in a hurry—hot chicken takes time to prepare—and don't be overconfident with your tolerance for spice. Start with "mild" or "medium." The popularity of hot chicken has spread to Memphis, so you'll find it there, but it is still a Nashville thing.

CATFISH

Fried catfish is a food tradition that started along Tennessee's rivers, where river catfish are caught. Today, fried catfish served in restaurants is just as likely to come from a catfish farm.

Fried catfish (it's rarely served any way besides fried) is normally coated with a thin dusting of cornmeal, seasonings, and flour. On its own, the fish is relatively bland. Tangy tartar sauce, vinegar-based hot sauce, and traditional sides like coleslaw and baked beans enliven the flavor. Hush puppies are the traditional accompaniment.

CHEESE DIP

It is a topic of much debate, but if you ask anyone who lives in Little Rock, they'll tell you that cheese dip, served warm and with chips, was invented in the Arkansas city in 1935. Other folks believe melted queso had already

contenders at the World Cheese Dip Championship

existed in many forms in other places, but true or not, Little Rock has definitely made it its own. You can find all manner of cheese dip at area restaurants—white, orange, spicy, mild, with meat, or vegan. Each fall the **World Cheese Dip Championship** (http://cheesedip.net) aims to find the best.

FARMERS MARKETS

Farmers markets are popping up in more and more Tennessee communities. The Agricenter Farmer's Market in Memphis (www.agricenter.org/farmersmarket) is open six days a week.

There is a great deal of variety when it comes to the types of markets that exist. Some markets take place under tents, provide entertainment, and invite artisans to sell arts and crafts as well as food products. Other markets consist of little more than a bunch of farmers who have arranged the week's harvest on their tailgates. Regardless of the style, farmers markets are a great place to meet people and buy wholesome food.

Pick TN (http://picktnproducts.org) offers a listing of all registered farmers markets, including locations and contact information.

Accommodations

Accommodations in Tennessee fall into four main categories, with a little gray area in between.

HOTELS AND MOTELS

Chain motels are ubiquitous, particularly along interstates. These properties are predictable; their amenities depend on the price tag and location. Most motel chains allow you to make reservations in advance by telephone or on the Internet. Most motels require a credit card number at the time of reservation, but they don't usually charge your card until you arrive. Always ask about the cancellation policy to avoid paying for a room that you do not ultimately need or use. Many of these chains are pet friendly.

Savvy shoppers can save money on their hotel room. Shop around, and pay attention to price differentials based on location; if you're willing to be a few miles up the interstate from the city, you'll realize some

significant savings. You may also be amazed by the power of the words "That rate seems high to me. Do you have anything better?" Employed regularly, this approach will usually save you a few bucks each night, at least.

By definition, chain motels do not offer unique accommodations, and only the rarest among them is situated somewhere more charming than an asphalt parking lot. But for travelers who are looking for flexibility, familiarity, and a good deal, chain motels can fit the bill.

Independent motels and hotels range from no-brand roadside motels to upscale boutique hotels in urban centers. By their very nature, these properties are each a little different. Boutique hotels tend to be more expensive than chain hotels, but they also allow you to feel as if you are staying in a place with a history and character of its own. They may also offer personalized service that is not available at cookie-cutter motels.

BED-AND-BREAKFASTS

Bed-and-breakfasts are about as far from a chain motel as one can get. Usually located in small towns, rural areas, and quiet residential neighborhoods of major cities, bed-and-breakfasts are independent guesthouses. The quality of the offering depends entirely on the hosts, and the entire bed-and-breakfast experience often takes on the character and tone of the person in whose home you are sleeping. Good bed-and-breakfast hosts can sense the line between being welcoming and overly chatty, but some seem to struggle with this.

Bed-and-breakfasts offer a number of advantages over the typical motel. Their locations are often superior, the guest rooms have lots of character and charm, and a full and often homemade breakfast is included. Some bed-and-breakfasts are located in historic buildings, and many are furnished with antiques.

Reservations for bed-and-breakfasts are not as flexible as most motels. Many bed-and-breakfasts require a deposit, and many require payment in full before you arrive. Cancellation policies are also more stringent than most motels. All of this can make it hard for travelers who like to be flexible and leave things till the last minute. Additionally, if you're bringing children with you, be sure to check that your bed-and-breakfast allows children; some don't. If your travel plans are certain and you just can't bear another night in a bland hotel room, a bed-and-breakfast is the ideal alternative.

Bed-and-breakfast rates vary but generally range $90-150 per night based on double occupancy. **Bed and Breakfast Inns Online** (www.bbonline.com) is a national listing service that includes a number of Tennessee bed-and-breakfasts.

HOSTELS

There are youth hostels in Memphis and Little Rock. Hostels provide dormitory-style accommodations at a fraction of the cost of a standard motel room. Bathroom and kitchen facilities are usually shared, and there are common rooms with couches, televisions, and Internet access. Hostels are usually favored by young and international travelers, and they are good places to meet people.

PRIVATE RESIDENCES

Website aggregators like **Vacation Rental By Owner** (www.vrbo.com) and **Airbnb** (www.airbnb.com) have become a popular way to find a room, apartment, or house to rent. Accommodations may be less expensive than traditional lodging, and may include parking and a kitchen. You have fewer recourses if something goes wrong, however, so ask questions before you book. Permitting of short-term rentals has become a contentious issue in some Memphis neighborhoods. It is reasonable to ask if a property is permitted before making your reservation.

Travel Tips

WOMEN TRAVELING ALONE

Women traveling alone in Tennessee may encounter a few people who don't understand why, but most people will simply leave you alone. Solo women might find themselves the object of unwanted attention, especially at bars and restaurants at night. But usually a firm "I'm not interested" will do the trick.

Anyone—man or woman—traveling alone in the outdoors should take precautions. Backpackers and campers should always tell someone where they will be and when they expect to be back. Ideally, establish a check-in routine with someone back home, and beware of overly friendly strangers on the trail.

GAY AND LESBIAN TRAVELERS

Tennessee's gay, lesbian, bisexual, and transgender people face a mixed bag. On one hand, this is the Bible Belt, a state where not long ago a bill was introduced that would have banned teachers from even saying the word *gay* in the classroom. (This is often referred to as the "Don't Say Gay" bill.) On the other hand, there has been no better time to be gay in Tennessee. More and more social, civic, and political organizations are waking up to the gay community, and there are vibrant gay scenes in many Tennessee cities.

For gay travelers, this means that the experience on the road can vary tremendously. You may or may not be able to expect a warm welcome at the mom-and-pop diner out in the country, but you can find good gay nightlife and gay-friendly lodging in many cities.

The decision about how out to be on the road is entirely up to you, but be prepared for some harassment if you are open everywhere you go. The farther off the beaten track you travel, the less likely it is that the people you encounter have had many opportunities to get to know openly gay people. Some may be downright mean, but others probably won't even notice.

Several specific guidebooks and websites give helpful listings of gay-friendly hotels, restaurants, and bars. The **Damron** guides (www.damron.com) offer Tennessee listings; the International Gay and Lesbian Travel Association (IGLTA, www.iglta.org) is a trade organization with listings of gay-friendly hotels, tour operators, and much more. California-based **Now, Voyager** (www.nowvoyager.com) is a gay-owned and gay-operated travel agency that specializes in gay tours, vacation packages, and cruises.

SENIOR TRAVELERS

Road Scholar (800/454-5768, www.roadscholar.org), formerly called Elderhostel, organizes educational tours for people over 55 in Memphis and Nashville.

For discounts and help with trip planning, try the **AARP** (888/687-2277, www.aarp.org), which offers a full-service travel agency, trip insurance, a motor club, and the AARP Passport program, which provides you with senior discounts for hotels, car rentals, and other things.

Persons over 55 should always check for a senior citizen discount.

Most attractions and some hotels and restaurants have special pricing for senior citizens.

TRAVELERS WITH DISABILITIES

More people with disabilities are traveling than ever before. The Americans with Disabilities Act requires most public buildings to make provisions for disabled people, although in practice accessibility may be spotty.

When you make your hotel reservations, always check that the hotel is prepared to accommodate you. Airlines will also make special arrangements for you if you request help in advance.

Several national organizations have information and advice about traveling with disabilities. **The Society for Accessible Travel and Hospitality** (www.sath.org) has links to major airlines' accessibility policies and publishes travel tips for people with all types of disabilities, including blindness, deafness, mobility disorders, diabetes, kidney disease, and arthritis.

Avis offers **Avis Access**, a program for travelers with disabilities. Call the dedicated 24-hour toll-free number (888/879-4273) for help renting a car with features such as transfer boards, hand controls, spinner knobs, and swivel seats.

TRAVELING WITH CHILDREN

It is hard to imagine a state better suited for family vacations than Tennessee. The state parks provide numerous places to camp, hike, swim, fish, and explore, and cities have attractions like zoos, children's museums, aquariums, and trains.

Many hotels and inns offer special discounts for families, and casual restaurants almost always have a children's menu with lower-priced, kid-friendly choices.

INTERNATIONAL TRAVELERS

Tennessee attracts a fair number of foreign visitors. Elvis, the international popularity of blues and country music, and the beauty of the eastern mountains bring people to the state from all over the globe.

COMMUNICATION

Foreign travelers will find a warm welcome. Those in the tourist trade are used to dealing with all sorts of people and will be pleased that you have come from so far away to visit their home. If you are not a native English speaker, it may be difficult to understand the local accent at first. Just smile and ask the person to say it again, a bit slower. Good humor and a positive attitude will help at all times.

VISAS AND OFFICIALDOM

Most citizens of a foreign country require a visa to enter the United States. There are many types of visas, issued according to the purpose of your visit. Business and pleasure travelers apply for B-1 and B-2 visas, respectively. When you apply for your visa, you will be required to prove that the purpose of your trip is business, pleasure, or for medical treatment; that you plan to remain in the United States for a limited period; and that you have a place of residence outside the United States. Apply for your visa at the nearest U.S. embassy. For more information, contact the U.S. Citizenship and Immigration Service (www.uscis.gov).

Nationals of 38 countries may be able to use the Visa Waiver Program, operated by Customs and Border

Protection. These countries are Andorra, Australia, Austria, Belgium, Brunei, Chile, Czech Republic, Denmark (including Greenland and Faroe Islands), Estonia, Finland, France, Germany, Greece, Hungary, Iceland, Ireland, Italy, Japan, Latvia, Liechtenstein, Lithuania, Luxembourg, Malta, Monaco, the Netherlands (including Aruba, Bonaire, Curacao, Saba, and Sint Maarten), New Zealand, Norway, Portugal (including Azores and Madeira), San Marino, Singapore, Slovakia, Slovenia, South Korea, Spain, Sweden, Switzerland, Taiwan, and the United Kingdom, unless citizens are also a national of Sudan, Syria, Iraq, or Iran.

Take note that in recent years the United States has begun to require visa-waiver participants to have upgraded passports with digital photographs and machine-readable information. U.S. officials have also introduced requirements that even visa-waiver citizens register in advance before arriving in the United States. For more information about the Visa Waiver Program, contact U.S. Customs and Border Protection (www.cbp.gov).

All foreign travelers are now required to participate in U.S. Visit, a program operated by the Department of Homeland Security. Under the program, your fingerprints and photograph are taken—digitally and without ink—as you are being screened by the immigration officer.

Health and Safety

DISEASES
WEST NILE VIRUS
West Nile virus was first recorded in humans in the United States in the early 2000s, and by 2007 nearly every state, including Tennessee, had reported confirmed cases of the disease. West Nile is spread by mosquitoes.

Summer is mosquito season in Tennessee. You can prevent mosquito breeding by eliminating standing water around your property. You can prevent mosquito bites by wearing an insect repellent containing 30-50 percent DEET. An alternative to DEET, picaridin, is available in 7 and 15 percent concentrations and would need to be applied more frequently. Wearing long-sleeved pants and shirts and not being outdoors during dusk and dawn are also ways to avoid exposure to mosquitoes.

Fever, chills, weakness, drowsiness, and fatigue are some of the symptoms of West Nile virus.

LYME DISEASE
Lyme disease is a bacterial infection spread by deer ticks. The first indication you might have Lyme disease is the appearance of a red rash where you have been bitten by a tick. Following that, symptoms are flu-like. During late-stage Lyme disease, neurological effects are reported.

Ticks are external parasites that attach themselves to warm-blooded creatures such as dogs, deer, and humans. Ticks suck blood from their host.

Tick bites are unpleasant enough,

even if there is no infection of Lyme disease. After coming in from the woods, especially if you were walking off-trail, carefully inspect your body for ticks. If one has attached itself to you, remove it by carefully "unscrewing" it from your body with tweezers.

You can avoid ticks by wearing long sleeves and pants, tucking in your shirt, and wearing a hat. You can minimize your exposure to ticks by staying on trails and walking paths where you don't brush up against trees and branches.

WHITE-NOSE SYNDROME
In 2006 in upstate New York, a caver noticed a substance on the noses of hibernating bats, as well as a few dead bats. The next year, more of both were found. Now bats dying of a fungus called "white-nose syndrome" have been found as far south as Tennessee.

Researchers are still trying to find out what causes the deadly (to bats, not people) fungus. Until then, certain caves may be closed to prevent the disease from spreading. Check individual cave listings before heading out.

POISON IVY
If there is one plant that you should learn to identify, it is poison ivy. This woody vine grows in woods all around Tennessee. Touching it can leave you with a painful and terribly uncomfortable reaction.

Poison ivy is green, and the leaves grow in clusters of three. There are no thorns. Its berries are a gray-white color, and if the vine is climbing, you will notice root "hairs" on the vine. The following mnemonic might help: "Leaves of three, let it be; berries white, danger in sight."

An estimated 15-35 percent of people are not allergic to poison ivy. But after repeated exposure this protection is worn down. People who are allergic will experience more and more severe reactions with each episode of exposure.

Poison ivy is easily spread over your body by your hands, or from person to person through skin-to-skin contact. Never touch your eyes or face if you think you may have touched poison ivy, and always wash yourself with hot soapy water if you think you may have come into contact with the vine.

Treat poison ivy rashes with over-the-counter itch creams. In severe cases, you may need to go to the doctor.

VENOMOUS SNAKES
The vast majority of snakes in Tennessee are nonvenomous. Only four species of venomous snakes exist there. Copperheads (northern and southern) live throughout the state, along with the timber rattlesnake. The pygmy rattlesnake lives in the Kentucky Lake region, and the cottonmouth water moccasin is found in wet areas in the western part of the state.

Venomous snakes of Tennessee can usually by identified by their elliptical (cat-eye) pupils (not that you really want to get close enough to see that). Most also have thick bodies, blunt tails, and triangular heads.

MEDICAL SERVICES
Hospitals, medical centers, and doctor offices are located throughout the state. Walk-in medical centers may be found in the yellow pages and are the best bet for minor needs while you're on vacation. In an emergency, proceed to the closest hospital or call 911.

The single most important thing you can have if you get sick while traveling is health insurance. Before you leave, check with your insurance provider about in-network doctors and medical facilities in the area where you'll be traveling.

PRESCRIPTIONS

Always travel with your prescription drugs in their original container and with a copy of the prescription issued by your doctor. If you can, get refills before you leave. National chain drugstores exist across the state.

DRUGS

Tennessee's greatest drug problem is with methamphetamine, the highly addictive stimulant sometimes called "speed," "crank," and "ice," among other names. During the 1990s and 2000s, meth use spread quickly through rural America, including Tennessee. In 2004, Tennessee passed comprehensive legislation to combat meth. A year later, some 60 percent of Tennessee counties reported that meth remained their most serious drug problem.

The state's anti-meth strategy has been to aggressively seek out illegal meth labs, increase public education about meth use, and promote recovery programs. Despite the efforts, it is still difficult to eliminate meth use, partly because meth is relatively easy to manufacture in so-called labs, which can be built in homes, hotel rooms, trailers, and even vehicles.

Meth is a dangerous and highly addictive drug. It takes a terrible toll on the health of users, creates myriad family and social problems, and is among one of the most addictive drugs out there.

While recreational marijuana use is legal is 10 U.S. states (and counting), Tennessee is not one of them. Adhere to local laws while in the state.

CRIME

Crime is a part of life anywhere, particularly in big cities like Memphis, and travelers should take precautions to avoid being a victim of crime. Leave valuables at home and secure your hotel room and car at all times (including GPS devices, tablets, and other car-friendly technology). Always be aware of your surroundings, and don't allow yourself to be drawn into conversations with strangers in deserted, dark, or otherwise sketchy areas. Solo travelers should take care to stay in well-lit and highly populated areas, especially at night.

Information and Services

MONEY
BANKS

Dozens of local and regional banks are found throughout Tennessee, Arkansas, and Mississippi. Most banks will cash traveler's checks, exchange currency, and send wire transfers. Banks are generally open weekdays 9am-4pm, although some are open later and on Saturday. Automatic teller machines (ATMs) are ubiquitous at grocery stores, live-music venues, and elsewhere, and many are compatible with bank cards. Between fees charged by your own bank and the bank that owns the ATM you are using, expect to pay $2-5 extra to get cash from an ATM that does not belong to your own bank.

SALES TAX

Sales tax is charged on all goods, including food and groceries.

The sales tax you pay is split between the state and local governments. Tennessee's sales tax on food ranges from 4 to 7 percent, depending on the type of good. Cities and towns add an additional "local use tax" of 1.5-2.75 percent; the total sales tax in Memphis is 9.25 percent.

Sales tax in Tupelo is 7.25 percent; in Oxford it is 7 percent. In Hot Springs sales tax is 9.5 percent; in Little Rock it is 9 percent.

HOTEL TAX

Tax on hotels in Shelby County, where Memphis is located, is 14.25 percent.

COSTS

Tennessee routinely ranks favorably on cost-of-living indexes. While Nashville has priced itself out of the list of most affordable cities, Memphis can still be a bargain. Visitors can comfortably eat their fill in casual restaurants and coffee shops for $45 a day, although it is possible to spend much more if you prefer to eat in upscale restaurants.

The cost of accommodations varies widely, depending on the area you are visiting, the type of accommodations you are seeking, and when you are traveling. The most expensive hotel rooms are in urban centers. Rates go up during major events, on weekends, and during peak travel months in the summer. Cheaper accommodations will be found on the outskirts of town and along rural interstate routes. Budget travelers should consider camping.

If you are not coming in your own car, one of your most substantial expenses will be a rental car. Most rentals bottom out at $35 a day, and rates can be much higher if you don't reserve in advance or if you are renting only for a day or two.

DISCOUNTS

Most historic sites, museums, and attractions offer special discounts for senior citizens and children under 12. Some attractions also have discounts for students and members of the military. Even if you don't see any discount posted, it is worth asking if one exists.

Many chain hotels offer discounts for AAA members.

TIPPING

You should tip waiters and waitresses 15-20 percent in a sit-down restaurant. You can tip 10-15 percent in a cafeteria or restaurant where you collect your own food from the counter.

Tip a bellhop or bag handler $1 per bag, or more if they went out of their way to help you.

TOURIST INFORMATION

The **Tennessee Department of Tourism Development** (615/741-2159, www.tnvacation.com) is a source of visitor information about Tennessee. It publishes an annual guide that contains hotel and attraction listings. The website has lots of links to local attractions and chambers of commerce.

Many cities have their own tourist organizations, including Memphis, Little Rock, Hot Springs, Tupelo, and Oxford. In some rural areas, counties have teamed up to develop visitor information for the region. Other organizations, such as the National Park Service, Army Corps of Engineers, and the Tennessee State Parks, publish visitor information for certain attractions. Specific listings for visitor information are found throughout this book.

Several regional tourism organizations provide useful information and publications. In West Tennessee there is the **Southwest Tennessee Tourism Association** (www.visitswtenn.com) and the **Northwest Tennessee Tourism Association** (www.reelfoot-lakeoutdoors.com).

If all else fails, contact the chamber of commerce for the county you will be visiting. Chambers of commerce will willingly mail you a sheaf of brochures and any visitor information that may exist. If you are already in town, stop by in person. You are sure to find someone who will be glad to help you.

MAPS

Rand McNally publishes some of the best maps of Tennessee, Arkansas, and Mississippi. You can buy Rand McNally maps from bookstores and through online sales outlets like Amazon. Rand McNally also sells downloadable PDF maps that you can view on your computer or print out.

For trail maps or topographical maps of parks and other natural areas, look for National Geographic's Trails Illustrated series.

The State Department of Transportation updates its official transportation map annually. Request a free copy at www.tdot.state.tn.us or by calling 615/741-2848. The official map is also available from many Tennessee welcome centers, chambers of commerce, and other tourism-related offices. The state also creates maps of dozens of Tennessee cities and towns. All these maps are available for free download from the department of transportation website.

Hubbard Scientific (www.amep.com) produces beautiful raised-relief maps of Tennessee, Great Smoky Mountains National Park, and other regions of the state. Found on display in some visitors centers, these maps make great wall art.

Many GPS apps are now available for smartphones and other smart devices, but when you don't have cell service, a paper map can be a lifesaver.

COMMUNICATION
AREA CODES

Tennessee has seven different area codes. Memphis and vicinity use 901. Both Little Rock and Hot Springs in Arkansas use 501. Tupelo and Oxford in Mississippi use 662.

CELL PHONES

Cell phone signals are powerful and reliable in cities and along the interstates. In rural parts of the state you should not count on your cell phone

TIME ZONES

All destinations in this book—West Tennessee, Arkansas, and Mississippi—are in the central time zone. The eastern third of Tennessee lies in the eastern time zone, one hour later.

RESOURCES

Suggested Reading

HISTORY

The WPA Guide to Tennessee. Knoxville: University of Tennessee Press, 1986. The Works Progress Administration guide to Tennessee, written in 1939 and originally published by Viking Press, is a fascinating portrait of Depression-era Tennessee. Published as part of a New Deal project to employ writers and document the culture and character of the nation, the guide contains visitor information, historical sketches, and profiles of the state's literature, culture, agriculture, industry, and more. The guide, republished as part of Tennessee's "Homecoming '86," is a delightful traveling companion.

Beifuss, Joan Turner. *At the River I Stand.* Brooklyn, NY: Carlson Publishing, 1985. This account of the Memphis sanitation workers' strike of 1968 is told from the ground up. It places the assassination of Dr. Martin Luther King Jr. in its immediate, if not historical, context.

Bergeron, Paul H. *Paths of the Past. Tennessee, 1770-1970.* Knoxville: University of Tennessee Press, 1979. This is a concise, straight-up history of Tennessee with a few illustrations and maps.

Bond, Beverley G., and Janann Sherman. *Memphis: In Black and White.* Mount Pleasant, SC: Arcadia Publishing, 2003. This lively history of Memphis pays special attention to the dynamics of race and class. The slim and easy-to-read volume contains interesting anecdotes and lots of illustrations. It is an excellent introduction to the city.

Branch, Taylor. *Parting the Waters: America in the King Years 1954-63.* New York: Simon and Schuster, 1989. The most authoritative account of the civil rights movement, told through the life of Dr. Martin Luther King Jr. The first in a three-volume account of the movement, *Parting the Waters* includes descriptions of the sit-ins of 1960. The final volume, *At Canaan's Edge,* includes King's assassination in Memphis.

Coe, Alexis. *Alice + Freda Forever: A Murder in Memphis.* Minneapolis: Pulp/Zest Books, 2014. An award-winning young adult account of a real-life teenage same-sex scandal, murder, and trial that rocked 1892 Memphis.

Corlew, Robert E. *Tennessee: A Short History.* Knoxville: University of Tennessee Press, 2008. The definitive survey of Tennessee history, this text was first written in 1969 and has been updated several times by writers, including Stanley J. Folmsbee and Enoch Mitchell. This is a useful reference guide for a serious reader.

Dykeman, Wilma. *Tennessee*. New York: W. W. Norton & Company and the American Association for State and Local History, 1984. Novelist and essayist Dykeman says more about the people of Tennessee and the events that shaped the modern state in this slim and highly readable volume than you would find in the most detailed and plodding historical account. It becomes a companion and a means through which to understand the Tennessee spirit and character.

Egerton, John. *Speak Now Against the Day: The Generation Before the Civil Rights Movement in the South*. Chapel Hill: University of North Carolina Press, 1995. Nashville native Egerton tells the relatively unacknowledged story of Southerners, white and black, who stood up against segregation and racial hatred during the years before the civil rights movement.

Egerton, John. *Visions of Utopia*. Knoxville: University of Tennessee Press, 1977. An accessible and fascinating portrait of three intentional Tennessee communities: Ruskin in Middle Tennessee, Nashoba in West Tennessee, and Rugby in East Tennessee. Egerton's usual sterling prose and sensitive observations make this volume well worth reading.

Honey, Michael. *Going Down Jericho Road: The Memphis Strike, Martin Luther King's Last Campaign*. New York: W. W. Norton & Co., 2007. Labor historian Honey depicts with academic detail and novelistic drama the Memphis Sanitation Strike of 1968. He documents Memphis of the late 1960s and the quest for economic justice that brought Dr. King to the city. King's assassination and its aftermath are depicted in devastating detail.

Potter, Jerry O. *Sultana Tragedy: America's Greatest Maritime Disaster*. Gretna, LA: Pelican Publishing Company, 1992. The definitive account of America's worst maritime disaster. The end of the Civil War and the assassination of Abraham Lincoln grabbed the headlines in April 1865, so much so that the sinking of the *Sultana* and the death of more than 1,800 men in the Mississippi River near Memphis went almost unnoticed. This book tells a tale more poignant and moving than the loss of the *Titanic*.

Sides, Hampton. *Hellhound on His Trail: The Stalking of Martin Luther King, Jr. and the International Hunt for His Assassin*. New York: Doubleday, 2010. A well-written, captivating account of MLK's murder and the efforts to nab his killer. Sides provides perspective on Memphis's troubled history.

Tougas, Shelley, *Little Rock Girl 1957: How a Photograph Changed the Fight for Integration*. North Mankato, MN: Compass Point Books, 2018. A kid-friendly book about the integration of Central High School and the Little Rock Nine.

Van West, Carroll, ed. *The Tennessee Encyclopedia of History and Culture*. Nashville: Tennessee Historical Society and Rutledge Hill Press, 1998. Perhaps the most valuable tome on Tennessee, this 1,200-page encyclopedia covers the people, places, events, and movements that defined

Tennessee history and the culture of its people. Dip in frequently, and you will be all the wiser.

BIOGRAPHY

Escott, Colin. *Hank Williams: The Biography.* Boston: Back Bay Books, 2004. This detailed history of the country star Hank Williams shares his failings, downfall, and remarkable legacy.

Guralnick, Peter. *Careless Love: The Unmaking of Elvis Presley.* Boston: Little, Brown and Company, 1999. Volume two of Guralnick's definitive biography of Elvis Presley. Guralnick writes in the introduction that he "knows of no sadder story" than Presley's life from 1958 until his death in 1977. The book unflinchingly examines the gradual unraveling of America's greatest rock star.

Guralnick, Peter. *Last Train to Memphis: The Rise of Elvis Presley.* Boston: Little, Brown and Company, 1994. Quite possibly the definitive biography of the King. In volume one, Guralnick re-creates Presley's first 24 years, including his childhood in Mississippi and Tennessee, his remarkable rise to fame, and the pivotal events of 1958, when he was drafted into the army and buried his beloved mother.

James, Marquis. *The Raven: A Biography of Sam Houston.* Indianapolis: The Bobbs-Merrill Company, 1929. Possibly the most remarkable Tennessean in history, Sam Houston was raised by the Cherokee, memorized Homer's *Iliad,* and was twice elected governor of Tennessee before he headed west to the new American frontier to become president of the Texas Republic.

Moore, Carman. *Somebody's Angel Child: The Story of Bessie Smith.* New York: Thomas Cromwell Company, 1969. The illustrated story of Chattanooga native Bessie Smith's remarkable rise to, then fall from, the top of the music world.

Pattillo Beals, Melba, *Warriors Don't Cry: A Searing Memoir of the Battle to Integrate Little Rock's Central High.* New York: Simon Pulse, 2007. Pattillo Beals was one of the nine African American students who integrated Little Rock's public high school. This is her story.

Twain, Mark. *Life on the Mississippi.* 1883. The tale of Twain's experiences as a steamboat worker on the Mississippi River. In true Twain fashion, these stories may be a mix of fact and fiction, but do give a glimpse of life in Memphis before the Civil War.

Walls Lanier, Carlotta, *A Mighty Long Way: My Journey to Justice at Little Rock Central High.* North Mankato, MN: Compass Point Books, 2010. Walls Lanier was 14 years old when she joined eight other students in their effort to integrate Little Rock's—and the nation's—public schools.

MUSIC

Carlin, Richard. *Country Music.* New York: Black Dog and Leventhal Publishers, 2006. This is a highly illustrated, well-written, and useful reference for fans of country music.

It profiles the people, places, and events that contributed to country's evolution. With lots of graphic elements and photographs, it is a good book to dip into.

Gordon, Robert. *It Came from Memphis*. Boston: Faber and Faber, 1995. Memphis resident Gordon takes the back roads to tell the remarkable musical story that emerged from Memphis during the 1950s and 1960s. He paints a textured picture of the milieu from which rock 'n' roll eventually rose.

Handy, W. C. *Father of the Blues*. New York: The Macmillan Company, 1941. This memoir by Memphis's most famous bluesman depicts the city during the first quarter of the 20th century. It is an entertaining and endearing read.

Kingsbury, Paul, ed. *Will the Circle Be Unbroken: Country Music in America*. London: DK Adult, 2006. An illustrated collection of articles by 43 writers, including several performing artists, this book is a useful reference on the genre's development from 1920 until the present.

Raichelson, Richard M. *Beale Street Talks: A Walking Tour Down the Home of the Blues*. Memphis: Arcadia Records, 1999. A slim, well-written book that describes Beale Street as it was and Beale Street as it is. This is a handy companion for exploring the street.

Sharp, Tim. *Memphis Music: Before the Blues*. Mount Pleasant, SC: Arcadia Publishing, 2007. Part of the Images of America series, this work includes rare and evocative photographs of Memphis people. The result is a painting of the backdrop on which the Memphis blues were born in the early 20th century.

Wolfe, Charles K. *Tennessee Strings*. Knoxville: University of Tennessee Press, 1977. The definitive survey of Tennessee musical history. This slim volume is easy to read.

Zimmerman, Peter Coats. *Tennessee Music: Its People and Places*. San Francisco: Miller Freeman Books, 1998. Tries, and succeeds, to do the impossible: tell the varied stories of Tennessee music all the way from Bristol to Memphis. Nicely illustrated.

FICTION

Bausch, Richard. *Before, During, After*. New York: Knopf, 2014. An emotional tale of a couple who move to Memphis after 9/11.

Benz, Chanelle, *The Gone Dead*. Ecco, 2019. Benz is a professor at Rhodes College in Memphis. Her first novel, a mystery, takes place in the Mississippi Delta. She writes powerfully about family, race, and justice.

Burton, Linda, ed. *Stories from Tennessee*. Knoxville: University of Tennessee Press, 1983. An anthology of Tennessee literature, the volume begins with a story by David Crockett on hunting in Tennessee and concludes with works by 20th-century authors such as Shelby Foote, Cormac McCarthy, and Robert Drake.

Grisham, John. *The Firm*. Boston: G. K. Hall, 1991. Probably the most celebrated Memphis-set novel in recent years, especially following the success of the eponymous film. Mitchell McDeere takes on corrupt and criminal mob lawyers. It includes references to many city landmarks.

Miller Santo, Courtney. *Three Story House: A Novel.* New York: William Morris, 2014. Miller Santo, a Memphis university professor, tells the tale of three cousins renovating a family home on the banks of the Mississippi.

Taylor, Peter. *Summons to Memphis.* New York: Knopf Publishing Group, 1986. Celebrated and award-winning Tennessee writer Taylor won the Pulitzer Prize for fiction for this novel. Phillip Carver returns home to Tennessee at the request of his three older sisters to talk his father out of remarrying. In so doing, he is forced to confront a troubling family history. This is a classic of American literature, set in a South that is fading away.

Wright, Richard. *Black Boy.* New York: Chelsea House, 2006. The 1945 memoir of African American writer Wright recounts several years of residency in Memphis. His portrayal of segregation and racism in Memphis and Mississippi is still powerful today.

FOOD

Lewis, Edna, and Scott Peacock. *The Gift of Southern Cooking: Recipes and Revelations from Two Great American Cooks.* New York: Knopf Publishing Group, 2003. Grande dame of Southern food Lewis and son-of-the-soil chef Peacock joined forces on this seminal text of Southern cuisine. It demystifies, documents, and inspires. Ideal for those who really care about Southern foodways.

Lundy, Ronni, ed. *Cornbread Nation 7.* Chapel Hill: University of North Carolina Press, 2006. The seventh in a series on Southern food and cooking. Published in collaboration with the Southern Foodways Alliance, which is dedicated to preserving and celebrating Southern food traditions, the Cornbread Nation collection is an ode to food traditions large and small. Topics include pawpaws, corn, and pork.

Puckett, Susan. Eat Drink Delta: A Hungry Traveler's Journey through the Soul of the South. University of Georgia Press, 2013. From barbecue in Memphis, Tennessee, to okra in Cleveland, Mississippi, this guide surveys the South's regional specialties and must-visit restaurants, city by city.

Internet and Digital Resources

TOURIST INFORMATION

Hot Springs National Park
www.nps.gov/hosp
The official National Park Service website offers details on hiking, camping, wildlife, and thermal waters at this unique national park site.

Little Rock Convention and Visitors Bureau
www.littlerock.com
Find out what to do and where to stay on this official tourism website for the Arkansas city.

Memphis Tourism
www.memphistravel.com
The official travel website for Memphis has listings of hotels, attractions, and events. You can also download coupons, request a visitors guide, or book hotels. The bureau also offers a free smartphone app called **Memphis Travel.**

Mississippi Blues Trail
http://msbluestrail.org
There are nearly 200 landmarks along this trail. Use this website to plot a trip or just immerse yourself in armchair travel.

Tennessee Department of Tourism Development
www.tnvacation.com
On Tennessee's official tourism website you can request a visitors guide, search for upcoming events, or look up details about hundreds of attractions, hotels, and restaurants. This is a great resource for suggested scenic drives.

US Civil Rights Trail
www.civilrightstrail.com/destination/memphis
An interactive resource detailing Memphis's rich, complicated, and powerful role in the U.S. civil rights movement. Read historical accounts and use the map to track your routes.

Visit Oxford, Mississippi
http://visitoxfordms.com
Explore the culture of this literary gem from the comfort of your phone at this mobile website.

Visit Tupelo
www.tupelo.net
The online guide to the Mississippi city that birthed Elvis.

NEWS AND CULTURE

The Memphis Flyer
www.memphisflyer.com
Memphis's alternative weekly newspaper publishes entertainment listings and article archives on its website.

Memphis Magazine
www.memphismagazine.com
Good restaurant reviews and useful event listings. Subscriptions available online ($15 annually).

MLK50: Justice Through Journalism
https://mlk50.com
Exploring issues of economic justice in Memphis.

HISTORY

Tennessee Encyclopedia of History and Culture

www.tennesseeencyclopedia.net

The online edition of an excellent reference book, this website is a great starting point on all topics Tennessee. Articles about people, places, and events are written by hundreds of experts. Online entries are updated regularly.

Index

A

B

List of Maps

Photo Credits

More Guides for Urban Adventure

 ASHEVILLE & THE GREAT SMOKY MOUNTAINS

 BOSTON

 BUENOS AIRES

 CHICAGO

 CHARLESTON

 CLEVELAND

 LOS ANGELES

 MEXICO CITY

 MONTRÉAL

 NASHVILLE

 NEW YORK CITY

 OSLO

 PORTLAND

 QUÉBEC CITY

 REYKJAVÍK

 SAN DIEGO

 SAVANNAH

 SEATTLE

 VANCOUVER

 WASHINGTON DC

MAP SYMBOLS

■	Sights	◉	National Capital	▲	Mountain	▬▬▬	Major Hwy
■	Restaurants	◉	State Capital	✦	Natural Feature	▬▬	Road/Hwy
■	Nightlife	○	City/Town	🌿	Waterfall	▬▬	Pedestrian Friendly
■	Arts and Culture	★	Point of Interest	♠	Park	- - - - -	Trail
■	Sports and Activities	●	Accommodation	▲	Archaeological Site	▭▭▭▭	Stairs
■	Shops	▼	Restaurant/Bar	🎫	Trailhead	···········	Ferry
■	Hotels	●	Other Location	🅿	Parking Area	▬▬▬▬	Railroad

CONVERSION TABLES

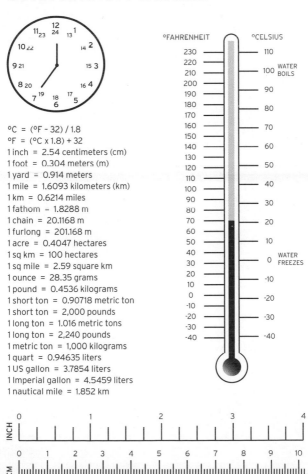

$$°C = (°F - 32) / 1.8$$
$$°F = (°C \times 1.8) + 32$$

1 inch = 2.54 centimeters (cm)
1 foot = 0.304 meters (m)
1 yard = 0.914 meters
1 mile = 1.6093 kilometers (km)
1 km = 0.6214 miles
1 fathom – 1.8288 m
1 chain = 20.1168 m
1 furlong = 201.168 m
1 acre = 0.4047 hectares
1 sq km = 100 hectares
1 sq mile = 2.59 square km
1 ounce = 28.35 grams
1 pound = 0.4536 kilograms
1 short ton = 0.90718 metric ton
1 short ton = 2,000 pounds
1 long ton = 1.016 metric tons
1 long ton = 2,240 pounds
1 metric ton = 1,000 kilograms
1 quart = 0.94635 liters
1 US gallon = 3.7854 liters
1 Imperial gallon = 4.5459 liters
1 nautical mile = 1.852 km

MOON MEMPHIS
Avalon Travel
Hachette Book Group
1700 Fourth Street
Berkeley, CA 94710, USA
www.moon.com

Editor: Kevin McLain
Acquiring Editor: Grace Fujimoto
Copy Editor: Brett Keener
Graphics and Production Coordinators: Scott Kimball and Suzanne Albertson
Cover Design: Faceout Studios, Charles Brock
Interior Design: Megan Jones Design
Moon Logo: Tim McGrath
Map Editor: Albert Angulo
Cartographers: Andrew Dolan, John Culp, and Albert Angulo
Indexer: Rachel Kuhn

ISBN-13: 978-1-64049-129-8

Printing History
1st Edition — 2016
2nd Edition — January 2020

5 4 3 2 1

Front cover photo: Beale Street at dusk © Greg Elms / GettyImages
Back cover photo: Sun Studios in Memphis © F11photo | Dreamstime.com

Printed in China by RR Donnelley.